Elephant
Songs

Michelle Frost

I would like to thank the real people portrayed in this book for
allowing me to use my memories of events to write my story. I
realise there will be portions where their memories do not
match my own. This book is not intended to hurt, harm or
offend anyone. Some names and details have been altered in
order to respect the privacy of others.

"One of the intriguing facts about elephants is that some of their vocalizations are infrasonic, and thus are inaudible to humans. The prominance of very low frequencies in the vocalizations is a defining characteristic of all three species of elephants. Sounds are generally considered to be infrasonic if their frequency is less than 20 Hz (the lower limit of human hearing). Low frequency sounds travel farther than high frequency ones, which make them ideal for long distance communication."

The Elephant Listening Project

http://www.birds.cornell.edu/brp/elephant/index.html

PROLOGUE

This book started as a series of emails to an internet friend. In the first email I sent, I wrote:

> About two years ago, my mother said, "You should write a book about your experiences." After several months of sitting staring at an empty word doc while secretly playing mah-jong, I had to admit the book wasn't exactly going anywhere.
>
> The biggest problem is freezing up. The next biggest is the "is this boring?" worry. Let's not even go near the "OMG, I'm exposing myself in public" terror. lol And where do you start? So this is a test as to whether this is interesting or just painful.
>
> _If_ this works and ever becomes a best seller, I'm thinking of calling it "Strange Letters to a Cheerful Sceptic".
>
> hahaha

I also considered calling it, "Will the Elephant in my Head Please Sit Down", but I eventually decided on a title that was less wordy and more fitting. You see, for a long time humans had no idea elephants were talkative since they came across as a very quiet animal, bar a few rumbles and trumpeting when upset.

But just because we couldn't hear them did not mean they weren't talking. Now, thanks to better technology, we know that elephants are actually incredibly chatty. We never knew because they use such a deep frequency that our human ears cannot hear them. The elephant in my head seemed unable to speak as well, but you'll need to read my story to find out how wrong I was about him.

Yes, everything in here is the truth, except for a few names and details altered to protect the privacy of others. Yes, I am sane. In fact, at one stage in my life I did actually go and check on that, just to be certain. I'm a bit of a sceptic myself, which has made my improbable life impossibly stressful at times. In my early thirties, I went and sat some tests and I was declared sane by a professional. Always good to double check. She said I was highly intuitive and even suggested I might be psychic, but it still took me another ten years to accept my psychic self and the things I have experienced.

I probably would have left that acceptance in the wardrobe in a box on the top shelf if it hadn't been for an internet friend asking for a chakra reading. I had asked for volunteers, preferably people I didn't know well. I still like to double-check my abilities. One of those volunteers was my cheerful sceptic, Richard Eldredge. His reading results led him to ask questions that ended up in me explaining my improbable life. The first email led to another, and another as he kept asking me for more information and stories. By the tenth email, Richard began to suggest it could be made into a book. By the time we were done, it had become a set of 42 emails and I had gathered several extra email readers who all said the same thing, "This should be a book."

Bearing in mind that 42 is the answer to the Universe and everything I thought, "Well, why not a book?"

And here it is.

1

The first time I proved to be different was actually a very ordinary memory as far as I was concerned. How old was I? Old enough to remember some things vividly, but young enough to be carried in my grandmother's arms. She was standing by a bedroom window in our house, talking to me and pointing out the trees and flowers in the garden. I remember being happy and feeling loved, not just by my grandmother, but also by the lady in the garden who was my friend.

The lady was there in the garden that day, looking up at us. I waved to her and she smiled and waved back. As an adult looking back, I'd guess she was in her late twenties or early thirties. Even as a toddler I remember thinking she was pretty. I think she had dark brown hair, but it was hard to tell as she was wearing a most strange and ugly hat. It looked like a baby bonnet, except it was a dull brown colour.

I wondered why a grown-up was wearing a baby bonnet as a hat and why her clothes were brown. Long skirt and a long sleeved top with buttons down the front and all of it in shades of brown. That must have been exceptionally hot and unpleasant to be wearing in an African garden. Our home was in Bulawayo in what was then (1960s) still Rhodesia.

Bulawayo is literally high and dry, situated at a fairly high altitude and only having about 50 rainy days a year. Grass was a luxury item you fought to keep alive and the temperature outside could soar to deadly levels. October, the hottest month of mid-spring dry season, was known as "suicide month" since some people could not cope with the extreme heat.

That garden outside the window was quite a different world to the gardens in my British children's picture books. The grass my father tended never grew to cover the entire area, but stayed in rows of dull green, making the lawn look like a large piece of rolled out khaki corduroy. Beyond the lawn, against the glossy dark green foliage of a tall hibiscus hedge, were my mother's treasured flower beds. They were tidy squares of arid soil and struggling flowers, edged with large stones dug up out of the ground that my father was trying to transform into a lawn.

The lady in the garden was standing in the flower bed. She waved at me and I waved back. When my gran asked me why I was waving, I pointed and said, "Nice lady", which led to my grandmother having a small freak-out fit because there was no one in the garden. Or at least, there was no one as far as she and my mother could see.

I vaguely remember being surprised that no one else could see the lady. I liked her and thought of her as a friend, so clearly I'd seen her more than once, but that memory is blurry now. All I have is a strong clear picture of her looking up at me in the window, smiling and waving, and a sense of being in the garden with this sweet, gentle female watching me play.

Winter in Bulawayo. Me by the flower beds.

It became one of my gran's favourite family stories; the time her baby granddaughter waved to the ghost woman in the garden. You'd think such a promising start would have led to a childhood like the Sixth Sense movie, with me whispering "I see dead people" while trips to school were strewn with dismembered, restless dead standing sadly at road accident spots. Nope, not the case. No dead people… just a dead dog.

His name was Teddy and before he became my "dead ghost dog", he was my grandmother's darling. The whole family's darling, really. Teddy was a charmer. He was a Maltese, a fluffy white rogue who knew all the tricks needed to get his favourite treat: peas! Fresh peas right out the pod were Teddy's idea of heaven.

I can see him in my gran's kitchen. She had a little square table in the middle of the room. She'd be standing there, shelling the peas, and Teddy would be up on his hind legs. He'd bounce about, waving his little front paws like crazy. I loved visiting my grandmother's house. It was the centre of the wheel for our entire family – aunts, uncles, cousins and friends. Everyone met at my grandmother's house.

If I close my eyes now, I am there at the gate; hot African sun scorching down on white picket fences and trellises heavy with honeysuckle, golden shower and coral creeper. A riot of plants and flowers dripping bees. Below them, along the concrete path to the door, there were sweet peas staked up against the freshly painted picket fence.

The creepers and several huge pine trees made a canopy of cool resin-scented green to the front door. Inside the house, it was always shady and shadowy at any time of day. The trees and the deep, covered front veranda kept the house away from direct sunlight, which in the scorching African summer was a good thing. Around the front, there was a swimming pool my grandfather built, two aviaries of birds and fruit trees.

My mom, holding Teddy at Grandma's house.

Down the side of the house there was a dry, sandy strip marked with little wooden crosses, for all the many departed pets. Dogs, birds, cats, rabbits, and even a monkey had their sacred space there. Gran would go there to pull the weeds from around the crosses, dropping a few tears and flowers on the "special" ones. Once we were back indoors, she'd let me have some peas or other treat to offer Teddy so I could watch him dance.

I'd sit in the chair by the telephone table, small legs dangling, laughing as Teddy pulled every charming turn he knew to get me to give him his treats. The telephone table was one of my favourite things because it had the only ornaments my gran would let me touch and play with: a brass sphinx, two pyramids and a Buddha. The sphinx was once a cigarette lighter and the head was hinged to open up the lighter. This would leave indelible scars on my understanding of ancient Egyptian history. For years to come, I thought the sphinx's head lifted off.

I'd sit on the floor and play with the sphinx and pyramids while my grandfather talked about his time spent in Egypt. He would take out the old tin boxes full of war photos, fill his pipe and sit by the window, puffing soft smoke and telling me the stories behind the photos. Grandpa was an aircraft mechanic during the war. Stationed in Egypt, he went to every ancient monument and museum he could reach. I knew about Mussolini and the war in North Africa, the pyramids and mummification before I was seven. If I got bored with the stories, there was a box of old toys at the top of his wardrobe: paper dolls from the 1950s and marionette puppets.

Going to grandma's house was always a magical adventure. But one day when we got there, everything felt different and strange. My gran and my aunt were by the front door and they were crying. Teddy was lying on a blanket in the cool shade of the pine trees, perfectly still. No dancing, no spinning and bouncing. My mom explained he had tick fever and… he was going away. She did a pretty good job of explaining death, but it had no meaning to a small child. It was just another confusing grown-up word. The next time we went to visit, Teddy was gone.

Sometime after that, I really can't say how long, I was at home playing indoors on the couch in the living room. Not sure why as the couch wasn't the most pleasant place to sit. It was made of some kind of brown, woven material, like tweed, that was VERY prickly-scratchy. Most times I'd rather sit on the carpet, even to watch TV. The couch was up against a wall opposite a large brick fireplace that we only used in winter. It could get cold enough in Bulawayo for a fire, but only for a short time in mid-winter.

From the couch, if I turned right, I could just see my mom in the kitchen making dinner. If I turned left, I was looking at the French doors that opened up onto a veranda. During the main portion of the day, the heavy curtains would be closed across the windows to keep the heat out. It was only in the early morning and the late afternoon that you opened the doors and windows. The doors were open, so it must have been about 5:00pm or later.

A movement caught my eye. I looked to my left and there in the open doorway was a little, white, fluffy dog. My first thought was that a stray dog had come into our yard, but then I realised it looked familiar. I knew this dog; it was Teddy. He stood in the doorway, his little tail wagging madly.

I remember feeling surprised because our house was in a different suburb. How had he managed to get from my gran's house all the way to ours? But mostly I just felt so smug. All the grown-ups had told me Teddy was dead and that meant going away forever, but there he was. Ha! What do grown-ups know? Teddy was back. As I sat there, he came running into the room, across the carpet and jumped up on the couch.

He sat down on the couch, SMILING up at me. If you're a dog person you'll know what I mean. Some dogs are smilers. Teddy was a smiler.

I was so happy to see him. I reached out to pat him... and my hand went through him. He was still there looking up at me, tail beating fast on the couch cushion, but my hand was inside his body. No feeling. Not cold or weird. Nothing.

I understood enough to know this was very much not normal. I panicked and ran for the safety of my mom. I remember looking back only when I was right up against her. Teddy was gone. For the rest of the day I was a limpet, sticking with my mom wherever she went. I remember she commented on it, but didn't tell her why. In fact, I never told anyone about that day for several years. I was too confused by what I had seen and experienced. I had no words to explain that to an adult.

I never found any answers as to why I saw Teddy that day, but I did find more information to explain some things about the lady in the garden. When I was a bit older, my dad gave me his children's encyclopedia. It was a chunky, blue-covered book full of amazing things about nature, history and science. On one of the pages, I found the answer to her ugly, giant, baby-bonnet hat – an illustration of women in Victorian clothing wearing the exact same style headgear.

In high school, I discovered pictures of the early settlers who travelled up North through South Africa in ox wagons. The women were dressed exactly like my lady friend. Was she a settler who died in that area? It's not impossible.

2

That sums up my exceptionally unexceptional psychic childhood. My grandmother retelling the story of the lady in the garden became an embarrassment over time since people either expected it to be the first of my many incredible experiences (nope) or saw it as proof of my ongoing weirdness. I did use the "I see dead people" line (hey, a dog is a person!) sometimes, but only to shut up the worst types of people. By that I mean those people who saw my being different as something that needed fixing or converting.

I was different in that I had severe allergies that led to high fevers, asthma and bronchitis. I had my first bout of pneumonia when I was four. As a result, I approached the world with caution, aware that at any time some random thing I touched, ate or breathed could have me sick in bed for a week or more. Books were my escape and I became an information junkie, gobbling up encyclopaedias and dictionaries as well as story books. I was a rather serious little nerd girl; Wednesday Addams was my soul mate.

My parents moved to South Africa when I was ten. My memories of moving to South Africa are a mixed lot. We never wanted to leave, but the Rhodesian Bush War was escalating and my father felt that the safety of his family came first. And plus the doctors felt that taking me to live by the sea might help my asthma and allergies. Moving to live by the sea was exciting, but nothing prepares you for the shock of leaving behind your home, family, friends and culture.

Rhodesia had been a British colony and the culture was typically British – they see personal questions as invasive and rude. As long as you used the proper cutlery most British Colonials would not comment on your choice of religion or anything else for that matter. By comparison, South Africans cared deeply what church you went to and judged you accordingly. Since my parents didn't belong to a church, we were battered regularly by converter types.

It was within my first year in South Africa that I found out how different things were. Unlike Rhodesia where religion was not a part of schooling, South Africa had Religious Vocation as a mandatory subject all the way through junior and high school. At my new South African junior school, our teacher asked the class how they saw God. I waved my hand, happy to finally have a religious question I could answer. Even though I'd never been to church, I'd always known God existed. I felt this strong sense of love everywhere. He was my best friend.

I told the teacher that I felt God's presence in everything around me, especially in trees, animals and nature. Instead of smiling and nodding, her face moved from shock to cold disapproval. In a horrified voice like she was informing me I was about to die, she said, "You do realise you are in danger of being a Pantheist?"

I shut up and... froze. I stood in complete silence as the whole room STARED at me. I sat down. I had to wait until I was home to look the word up in my dad's Oxford dictionary. When I read the description of Pantheism I felt such RELIEF because she was right – I was a Pantheist. Then came the confusion: If this was a legitimate word in the dictionary, then why did she think it was dangerous to be one? Or did she mean I was the danger?

It was the first time I had ever felt spiritually judged and it was an unpleasant feeling. By the time I entered high school, I'd learned to either hide or dodge the awkward moments with humour. And for those annoying few who refused to give up trying to convert me, I found saying I saw dead people was a very satisfying way to end the conversation.

I was in my early twenties when the "odd stuff" returned. This has been the pattern of my life ever since. I have long dormant patches of nothing happening followed by a sudden leap in my psychic abilities and experiences. No gentle trundle towards enlightenment for me; it's all or nothing. The leap in my twenties started with a dream.

It was just before Christmas in 1989, so I was 26. I dreamed a big cat had escaped from the zoo. Not a particularly strange dream, but something about it was so vivid that it stuck in my mind. Later that day, my mom and I went shopping. Half way up the road we started to see all these police cars. At the shops everyone was talking; a circus had arrived that morning and whilst setting up camp, two young tigers had escaped. They were still trying to catch them. Sadly, I think they eventually shot one.

I went home a bit rattled. At the time I'd been sleeping and dreaming, the tigers would have still been safely locked up in a travelling vehicle. There was no way I had heard about it before it happened and my dream was about a zoo, not a circus. Just a strange coincidence….

Barely a month later, I dreamt that a bear escaped from the zoo. I laughed at how my brain was still running with the idea of escaped animals, but the next morning the newspaper headline on the lower part of the front page was: BEAR ESCAPES FROM ZOO. My first thought was that the bear must have escaped the day before and my dad must have heard about it and told me. I still lived at home at the time. My dad used to get up at 4:30am in order to make a long commute to work in another town. He'd often bring me a cup of coffee and chat about the news (radio or newspaper) before heading off to work.

Sometimes I'd fall back to sleep once he was gone since my actual rising time was normally about 6:30am. I figured he must have told me about the bear and then I'd fallen asleep, dreamed about it and forgotten we'd talked. Made good sense, right? I thought so too, except when I double checked, the bear had escaped the day *after* my dream, not before. It was about the 5th time I had a dream come true that I started to really wonder what was going on. I decided to keep a dream journal in order to cross reference what I did (watch TV, listen to radio news, talk to people) against what I dreamed.

I'm good at lists and deduction. I get that from my dad who is a logic-loving problem solver. As a child I sometimes wondered if he was a Vulcan, like Spock in Star Trek. My dad brought me up to check details, ask questions and form a conclusion based on what I knew. My mother is the exact opposite. My mother's world revolves around instinct, feelings and emotions. It made for an interesting childhood. The first time I heard the old science saying about the irresistible force versus the immovable object I thought, *Oh gosh, that's my parents!*

My parents on a beach in South Africa, 1970s.

When I started my dream journal, did I secretly hope I'd prove I was psychic? Sure, of course I did. Who doesn't secretly wish they had some awesome, amazing ability or power? But I wasn't expecting it. So I kept my journal, expecting to fail, and ended up with a record of about thirty dreams that came true.

There was no particular pattern, nothing I ate or did beforehand that stood out as significant. But they did have one thing in common: they were either literally about an animal or they had an animal in them. And they were always slightly more vivid than your average dream. Some were bland stuff, like knowing what would be on TV a few days beforehand, but a few were more striking.

One particularly striking dream I actually wrote off as just a nightmare at first. It was about little white dogs being killed by bigger dogs. It was vivid with lots of blood. Really nasty. At the end, someone picked the little dogs up and threw them into trash bins. The image of their little bodies lying crumpled and bloody in the bins was horrible.

The next morning, I went through the newspaper. Nothing. I braced myself for hysterical phone calls from anyone owning a little white dog… nothing. After a few days passed with not one single dead dog anywhere, I began to relax. I was so relieved that I'd made a mistake. This dream was clearly not predictive.

It was about week later when my dad mentioned that someone he knew at work had seen a dog being killed by another dog. I can't remember how we came to talk about it, but I do remember how my stomach flipped a few times. I asked my dad if he knew what kind of dog had died. He said it had been a Maltese… a little white dog. When I told my dad about my latest dream, he was shocked.

My dad had been betting on my dreams turning out to be subconscious memories of media news or conversations, not precognition. But this time, he knew he hadn't said anything to influence me because he hadn't shared the story. Knowing how much I loved animals, he'd thought it too horrible and upsetting. We calculated that the actual dog was savaged to death four days after my dream. I had finally proven to my father that my precognitive dreams were genuine.

I was soon to discover that the smugness of realising you actually have an ability comes with a dark side. Two dreams changed everything. The first was on the 17th of October 1992. I dreamed that a religious group had moved into our town, buying land to start a type of commune. This commune was holding an open day and my family decided to go take a look. In the dream, there was a large house on the property overlooking a river. It was a bright sunny day and the house and yard were full of curious town-folk eating free food and talking to the commune members.

My parents went into the house, but I wandered off into the back yard where I began flirting with a rather cute commune member. I did notice that the commune seemed to be mostly young men, with a few drab women serving food, but that seemed more of a perk at the time. The leader of the commune came out to meet everyone. He was an extremely striking man, with a distinctive beard and long, braided, dark hair. I watched him, but didn't go over to talk. Something about the man gave me the creeps.

Even though everyone seemed so cheerful and happy, the mood started to feel oppressive. When I tried to leave, the handsome young man I'd been chatting up started to become more forceful in trying to make me stay and join their commune. I began to feel scared, but tried to act casual. I told him I didn't need to join because I already was a Christian. I pulled out a cross on a chain around my neck to show him. I actually did wear a little gold cross when I was younger. It was from my late (paternal) grandfather.

The cute guy laughed and said, "That doesn't mean anything. We crucified the last Christian on a metal cross and the water serpent ate her heart."

I suddenly realised this commune worshipped a sea snake monster thing. That was why the land was beside a coastal river. I had to get away. I tried to act normal, asking for directions to the bathroom where I climbed out the window and managed to flag down a car. I woke up while we were driving away.

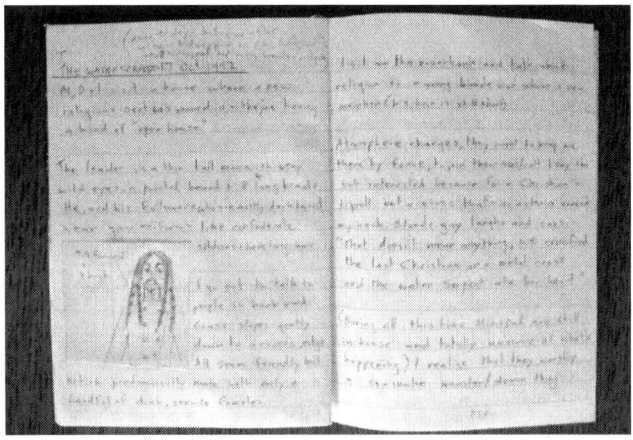

Sketch of the commune leader in my dream journal.

There was nothing in the news the next day and I wasn't expecting anything. Water serpents and human sacrifices? That was totally over-the-top nightmare spectacular! I did write the dream down and I drew the commune leader. His face had been so intensely vivid.

Two days later, I open up the newspaper and... you're wondering now aren't you? What on Earth could the real story be? There, on page two, was a sketch of a man the police were searching for.

I knew it instantly; he matched my commune leader's face almost exactly. Same cheekbones, same beard and eyes. Only the hair was different. The man in the newspaper sketch had long flowing hair, while my man had worn his long hair in multiple braids. I felt sick as I read the story that went with the picture. He was in the paper because it was believed that he was the leader of a Satanic cult.

This man, with a woman and another man, had befriended a man at a bar and gotten him drunk before taking him to a house to kill. The victim woke up while they were busy nailing him to a cross. The newspaper was a bit vague as to what happened next, but apparently the victim had managed to tear himself off the cross and escape. He had been found by a motorist as he staggered down the centre of the road, naked, bleeding and doped up with more than just alcohol.

This was one dream I didn't want to be true. I didn't know what to do with this. The police wanted witnesses, but what could I offer them? The fact I'd dreamed of this man a day prior to the event? I remember feeling sick and a little scared. I never phoned the police and I have no idea if they ever solved the case. I kept writing down my dreams, but it just wasn't fun any more.

One final dream made me stop my dream journal forever. I dreamed I was standing in front of a fireman and he was on fire. He stood there, flames everywhere, looking into my eyes and SCREAMING. I woke up with my heart pounding. I felt sick again. I checked the newspaper. That night there had been a fire. A young fireman had burnt to death.

I remember sitting there crying as I read about his death. The horror of knowing that I'd seen it, that I'd looked into his eyes and seen his terror and pain, was unbearable. I didn't want this any more. I put the journal away and started to deliberately block thinking or remembering my dreams. And I kept that up right until I met a most interesting man on an internet forum.

3

I stopped writing there to go cook dinner and realised, nope, the dreams did not stop. Not exactly anyway. There were ones that had made it through my stubborn refusal to remember, but something did change. I started seeing someone in my dreams; not often, but he had a kind of impact that made him memorable. I never saw his face. It was always as if he were standing with the sun or a bright light behind him so that he was nothing but a silhouette. I called him Shadowman.

Shadowman would loom over me in my dreams and say some one-liner thing before vanishing again. I wasn't writing down or saving my dreams to journal at that time, but I was aware that a lot of what he said came true or turned out to be good advice. I only saved one dream of him from the time I was refusing to remember. It was on the 30th of August 1997, a Saturday night.

I dreamt that I was on a rooftop. I turned around and there was Shadowman, standing on the apex of the roof. He beckoned me closer with one hand. When I reached him, I realised there was a cardboard box by his feet on the far side of the roof. He turned it over. Underneath were four little black rabbits. They were all bloody and injured. I was horrified. I asked him if they could be saved. He bent down, picked one up and handed it to me. He said, "This one will survive."

I woke up feeling really odd, just off and depressed. About ten minutes later I heard the news on the radio: Princess Diana had died in a car accident. The news said that there had been four people in the car and I instantly knew that only one would survive. And only one did survive; her body guard.

It was this dream that made me realise I couldn't simply make the dreams stop by refusing to accept them. They existed, they were there, and I had to find a better way to deal with this. I had been acting like a stubborn child, thinking that keeping my hands over my eyes would make the world change to suit me. Nope, it does not work that way.

But now came the bigger problem: what do you do when you finally accept the fact that you do have a genuine ability of some kind? That you seem to be able to receive messages from… somewhere? Someone? Who do you turn to for help and advice? I was living in a conservative religious country where many of the churches considered these abilities Satanic and the indigenous population still stoned and burnt witches to death. Was it even a safe thing to talk about?

For about twenty years, I chose not to talk about myself to most people. I told my parents, but that was it. My parents were fine with me being who I was and they still are. That has been the greatest blessing of my life. Every child should have parents who accept them and encourage them to be their true selves.

My parents and me, graduation day.

Interestingly, the local Xhosa people of the Eastern Cape (where we lived) seemed more aware and sometimes picked up on the fact that I was different. Four times during my twenties and thirties, I was approached by Xhosa people and asked if I was a sangoma: a witch doctor. I asked one of them why she thought I was a sangoma, but she just shrugged, stared at me, mumbled an apology and moved on.

Trivia moment – spell check keeps wanting to change sangoma to "a mango". That made me chuckle.

This is one of my biggest topics for soap-box style rants – the fact that there is very little help in the world for people like me. Regardless of whether others believe or not, when you yourself know you are different and need help, there is no one to turn to. If I'd had a decent talent anywhere else in life there would have been tutors, classes and support. Name a talent, from science to sports to the Arts, and I guarantee you'll find an evening class, a tutor or an organisation offering a degree in it. But this? This vague and nebulous ability I knew was there yet had no control of? No help whatsoever.

I've since discovered that this is the biggest rant of everyone with so-called psychic abilities – the lack of genuine help or support. This is especially vital for children who are different. We now offer all kinds of support for kids with special needs or particular talents, but try finding help if you are the kid who sees ghosts or knows things that nobody else does. I know several psychics who hid their true selves away all of their childhoods and most of their adult lives as well.

For every psychic out in public view there are a dozen people with genuine abilities hiding "in the closet", too afraid to be considered insane or freakish to speak out loud. Worst of all, the loudest public psychics are also often the fake ones. I was so lucky that my parents didn't think I was insane or a freak. My dad views everything in life as incredibly interesting. I was (still am) a constant source of fascination for him. And my mother was my role model on accepting intuition with grace.

My mother was precognitive. She would sense when a big disaster was going to happen. When I was a child she'd say, "Oh no…" and we'd turn on the radio to find out what had happened. A major plane crash, tragic mine accident, earthquake. She simply accepted that she felt things, no chewing over the why or how. And as a result, she never suggested I start therapy when I admitted my dreams came true. Now, you may have noticed I said "was precognitive." That's because my mom's abilities shut down for about 30 years, roughly during the time she was on strong medications for various health problems.

About four years ago, the doctors took her off two medications and adjusted the other and her abilities have been returning. Since three medications changed, it's hard to say which one was the culprit. My mom didn't mind the numbed-out decades. She hated knowing when people were going to die in large numbers. I've only once picked up on a major disaster, so I can understand why she feels such a lack of enthusiasm at having that kind of ability.

So after years of refusing to save my dreams to journal, I did get out my book and wrote down the Princess Diana dream. That dream became a marker for my strange life coughing and hiccuping back into gear. Time for another leap forward and it all started with a yearning for a cup of tea. It was a winter weekend in 1999. I'd gone to the museum with my parents. East London Museum, Eastern Cape, is most famous for housing the coelacanth, but for many East Londoners it was the tearoom that was the major draw. They used to do fantastic toasted cheese sandwiches and the most amazing chocolate brownies.

This particular weekend, we noticed that the museum display hall was open. Once lunch was done, I went over to have a look at the latest exhibition. But instead of display cabinets, I found the hall full of people. It was an Esoteric Fair; a gathering of all things New Age and strange. It was to become a life-changing experience.

I browsed the tables and stands, finding things I'd never heard of before. There were people selling crystals and candles, bright sparkly wind chimes and dream catchers. What the heck was a dream catcher? And why on earth would anyone buy stones and crystals? My dad's father was a prospector. I grew up with a literal barrel full of his lower grade agates, silica, amethyst and Tiger's Eye. To me these were merely pretty stones, but these people had them arranged as if they were sacred objects.

I remember seeing a Reiki practitioner for the first time as well as my first Pagans. I had no idea either thing existed in the modern world. I bought some scented candles and a spiralling wire thing that had crystals and tiny bells hanging from it. As I wandered around the place, entranced by the noisy cheerful vibe, I came across a bored-looking man sitting at a little table. His sign said: PALM AND CARD READINGS: R10 each. *Ahhh….* Now this was something I knew and loved – messing with readers.

I was 15 when I first discovered how to mess with fairground psychics. I was at a fair and my friend had gone in for a reading first. She came out and told me the rather trite things the psychic had foretold and then it was my turn. I went in and, much to my amusement, the psychic started to tell me the exact same things. Clearly, she had a generic reading for all teenage girls.

That was when I also noticed she would start a sentence and then drift off without ending it, as if waiting for me to finish it for her. I became a blank wall. I gave away nothing. I began to see the woman sweat, then stammer. Without me feeding her little yes/no confirmations, she fell apart. It was so much fun that I began searching out readers at other fairs to mess with their minds. Evil, I know, but great fun.

So my first thought on seeing this bored man at the Esoteric Fair was *oh goody, a new victim.* I wasn't going to cough up R20 for a bit of sport, so I chose the cards only and sat down, ready to be entertained. He asked me to shuffle a grubby old deck of playing cards. Then, in a dull "been there, done this too many times" voice, he asked me what I wanted to know.

I shrugged and said, "I don't mind. Whatever they want to tell me."

He sighed in this OMG-I-hate-my-life way and turned over a few more cards, listlessly suggested generic things. I smiled, but said nothing.

This went on for a while longer when he suddenly stopped and, with this sound of disgust, said, "This isn't working. Give me your hand."

I reached out across the little table. He took my

hand in both of his and… he gasped. No one had ever gasped before. Then he stared at me and loudly said something extremely personal about me; personal and unique about my physical health. He looked as shocked as I felt.

He let go of my hand instantly and apologised for blurting out a very private fact in a very public place, but I was too amazed to feel embarrassed. For the first time, I'd had a psychic reader tell me something no one else knew, beyond my doctor. The fact that an entire room full of strangers now knew as well seemed fairly inconsequential when placed against the fact that I was finally sitting opposite someone like me. Someone who knew things he had no way of knowing.

He asked permission to take my hand again. I agreed. He wasn't bored and fed-up now. He looked excited. He didn't read my palm; he just held my hand and stared at me. He told me things that day about myself that were true or have since proven to be true. At the end he said, "You are an old soul. You've been here many times and this is quite likely your last time here."

I left that fair on a high of energy. There were other people like me in this whole wonderfully messy world of New Age nonsense, whimsy and fact. I wasn't at all convinced that a specific stone would heal this or fix that, but I loved the prettiness of it all, the colours, crystals and scented candles. And best of all… I didn't feel so alone any more.

4

That year was a major turning point in many ways. I discovered that a brand new book store in the shopping mall had an esoteric section. The new South Africa was moving forward. I bought books on all sorts of things. I also decided it was time to stop dreaming about being a writer, my ambition since childhood, and start making that dream come true. Or, to use a new term I'd found in one of those esoteric books, "manifest my reality". And the reality I wanted more than anything was to be a writer.

Armed with new self-confidence, I wrote to our local newspaper and cheekily suggested they hire me for their new advice column slot. I needed something unique to offer, so I suggested an astrology advisor. I'd been doing birth charts as a fun hobby for years. It's not rocket science. If you have decent ephemera and a few good books anyone can make up a chart.

I clearly wrote a kick-ass letter because a few days later the paper phoned and, after a short interview, told me I'd be starting the following week. I was to be their new astrology advice columnist. It wasn't what I wanted for a long term writing career, but it was a foot in the door. I'll never forget how I felt when they asked me to bring in a photo of myself. Me, in the paper? Me? Wow.

I went and had a proper photo taken at a local store and then took it over to the newspaper office. Feeling Very Important, I handed it over to security at the front desk, telling them that it was needed for the next run. A few days later there I was, near the back on the lower left page. ME smiling back at me. What a rush! What a head swelling, ego-smug moment.

Hyperactive Virgos

Q I would like to know why my son is so hyperactive.

A If you think he is just overly energetic then astrology can definitely give you some insights. Some birthsigns are far more active than others.

You have given your son's birthdate and from this I can see that he probably is quite a handful!

Your son is a Virgo and he is also born in the Chinese year of the Rat. Virgos are the busy-bees of western astrology.

They hate being idle, even their hobbies are physical.

Craftwork, sport, gardening, playing a musical instrument ... anything that keeps them active.

Virgos worry a lot, being busy keeps their minds occupied and keeps them healthy.

As children they are sensitive, intelligent and completely incapable of sitting still.

Boredom makes them fretful and anxious.

Rats are bright charming, talkative and ambitious. Rats are leaders and innovators.

Just like the animal used to represent them, they tend to be fidgety, inquisitive and basically incapable of sitting still!

Not hard to see why your son is so active.

Added to that he also has Mars in Scorpio. Mars is the planet that rules physical energy levels.

Scorpio is ruled by Mars so this is a very powerful placing. People, like your son, with this placing have endless energy levels.

The best thing you can do is try to keep him busy.

Lots of fresh air and lots of mental and physical stimulation. Let him grow his own vegetables or take him hiking and bird-watching.

Virgo is an earth sign so anything to do with nature is bound to interest him.

I wanted to roll in the paper like a cat in catnip. I wanted fireworks and champagne. Reality set in somewhere between having breakfast and going to the local supermarket for some groceries. My photo was in the paper and now everyone would see me. It was a small newspaper in a small town, which meant gossip moved at light speed. It wouldn't take long before the entire town knew what I was doing and who I was. Everyone would know ME, everywhere I went, all the time....

All the time? The rush of excitement turned into a rush of terror. I felt as if the universe had placed a flashing sign above my head with a big arrow pointing at me. I felt incredibly VISIBLE and the feeling was not good. At the shops, a few people seemed to stop and look at me as I walked into the shopping centre. I could almost feel the stares burning my skin. Their unspoken thoughts of, "She looks familiar? Isn't she the one in the newspaper?" seemed to scream in my ears.

I grabbed a trolley and made a dash for the entrance, thinking furiously. *Try to keep cool. Breathe in. Breathe out. They aren't staring at you. No-one is staring... oh my GOD, they are STARING at me. I am VISIBLE! I am this new, huge, neon-glowing ME and it feels horrible! I want to be small, invisible, ordinary me just browsing the shops. Not this person with the LOOK AT ME arrow above her head.*

The supermarket had this turnstile entrance with a hole in the railings where you pushed your trolley through into the shop. I figured I'd sprint to the entrance and shove my trolley through as I zoomed through the turnstile to grab the goods and get out. Simple. I took a deep breath and focussed my thoughts. *Be cool. Be calm. You can do this.*

Damn, there's a fat old lady wedged in the turnstile moving slower than a sea turtle. DAMN! Okay, don't panic. You can get through this. You are cool. You are in control. Push the trolley through the gap, duck down and follow the trolley. Simple! You are short and the trolley gap bar isn't too low. You can do this….

That's the last coherent thought I remember. Yes, I am short. Yes, the trolley slot was doable as the bar was set at crouch height, not limbo dance low. No, I didn't duck down far enough. In my blind, animal panic to get in fast and inconspicuously, I ducked at the wrong moment of dashing forward and smashed my forehead into the metal bar, falling backwards flat on the floor while my trolley happily drifted off into the supermarket without me… and EVERYONE stared.

The pain of fame going to your head is indescribable.

It took a few weeks before I calmed down enough to cope with going out in public, but being visible does have its upside as well. At a local restaurant where I often met with friends for a meal and a chat, I became a mini celebrity. It started awkwardly. I was eating my lunch one day when I felt that edgy feeling you get when someone is watching you. For once, I was correct. The kitchen staff and waitresses were lined up behind a serving partition. All I could see was a row of eyeballs STARING at me.

It progressed from there to staring at me from the

end of the aisle of tables, to staring at me while taking down my order, to a few casual comments and extra chips or more salad special bits on my plate. One quiet afternoon, our waitress kept hovering. Finally, when her boss went off into the back, she took her chance. She sat down opposite me and quickly rattled off a dream that was bothering her.

Once again I had been mistaken for being a Sangoma. Her dream was fairly basic stuff and offering advice was easy. She left smiling and I got even more chips the next time I went there. Win win all the way. Once the fear of being known died down, I began to enjoy my new role. The astrology advice column was interesting to do. I wasn't doing horoscopes, but rather answering typical, everyday human problems from an astrological point of view. I'm bossy and a woman, so giving advice was easy.

The only irritation was length. The paper would often contact me to say, "This week we have a large advert, can you give us only a paragraph reply?" or "There's nothing this week, can you fill half a page?" After a few months of faxing all replies to the main office, the paper demanded that I get myself an internet connection and an email address in order to make the whole send/edit process faster and smoother.

It was the year 2000 and I truly had never been on the internet. In South Africa at that time, the internet was by phone connection that was billed by the second. Quite expensive! I'd never bothered to set it up and still wasn't keen, but the paper insisted. Within a month, I had the internet set up and a new email address. And within a few more months, it was all redundant.

A new editor took over the paper who did not approve of "occult topics." The astrology column was scrapped. I had hoped the paper might offer me another writing post, but no such luck. My burst of newspaper fame had only lasted seven months. During that time, I had started to work from home as an astrologer and I was at least able to keep that going. People began writing and phoning as soon as my picture was in the paper. Most wanted a chance to talk more than a birth chart.

That was quite an adventure and led to me meeting some very interesting people. My most favourite was a charming German who worked as a circus school teacher who travelled all over the world. Oh, and then there was the time a forceful-yet-friendly woman coerced me into making a speech on astrology at the women's prison. That was my first ever public speaking moment. Talk about a baptism by fire! I spent the first half of that speech standing behind the chair they put out for me, like a lion tamer ready to ward off the wild beasts. As it turned out, I had a fantastic time that day once my nerves calmed down.

I think I learnt more from the people I met than I they learned from me. I met Reiki and crystal healers, made friends with a Muslim psychic and a Wiccan priestess. My ambitions to be a writer may have been pushed off-course, but my hungering need to write had not diminished. I even wrote a poem about it.

One Day

I am a message
I am a word
I am a window
I am a bird

one day I will know the message,
one day I will know what to say,
one day I will open the window

and fly away.

And my psychic side? Well, things were changing there, too. I was having dreams again. One was so vivid that forgetting it was impossible, but this one was different. This dream was about the past, not the future.

5

That dream wasn't the only difference, there was more, but it's hard to explain. I was feeling things while awake and sometimes getting zapped with information. I stopped there because I realised I'm wrong. This did not start in 2000. It started much earlier in the 1980s. I just hadn't seen the connection until I wrote it down. This is about how and why I connect. In the late 1990s it became more intense, but it still took me till about 2008 to realise the pattern. A case of not seeing the forest for the trees!

I'm going to leap ahead to present day and explain what I finally figured out: the strongest and fastest connection is love. It's the telephone line that connects me to, well, everything. Love. It sounds so '60s hippy, but it is the truth. Love really is the purest intent energy you can send or receive. It works instantly, like flicking a switch.

Now, I need to wander back to the 1980s before I explain how my connection changed in the 1990s and beyond. It's the foundation of everything I am and everything I do. Cue that wobbly TV effect as the hero remembers the past....

It was the late 1980s and, once again, I was battling religious converters. This time, it was a lovely family friend who was also a Mormon missionary. Over the years, I had successfully dodged Baptists, Born-Agains, Catholics, Seventh-Day Adventists and a rather zealous Anglican, but Mormons are an entirely different league of pushy. A Mormon who calls your parents "my African mom and dad" and hangs out at your house with his fellow missionaries is exceptionally hard to deal with.

We met through my grandparents. My grandfather loved talking to people and often brought home strangers he'd met in random places. It was via this that I picked up an American "uncle" in Rhodesia, another lovely man who sent me cards from America pretending to be Santa Claus when I was a child. It was grandpa who brought home the first Mormon missionaries, which became a stream of missionaries as my gran felt young men needed to be fed.

The day we met Justin, he had just arrived from the USA. I remember he was sitting in my grandfather's chair, looking rather jet-lagged and dazed. He was a mountain of a young man, tall and bearish, with brilliant blue eyes. All of the family made him and his missionary friends feel welcome, but I think it was my mom who really won Justin's heart. He was so far away from everything he was familiar with and just out of high school. My mom was the symbol of home and solid ground.

He started coming around to our house, mostly hanging out in the kitchen to help mom with household chores. Justin was a darling bulldozer of a guy and once he'd decided we'd be REAL family if we all became Mormons, there was no stopping him. He was relentless, intelligent and charmingly persuasive and he had a back-up crew of other missionaries to help him. This led to me going to the library and dragging home books on theology so that I could argue each point with them.

I had already done some research into Bible history in my teens, so this wasn't new to me. I may never have been a church member anywhere, but I had read the entire Bible. I had been an ancient history enthusiast since childhood. I had read all of my mother's set of mythology encyclopedias before I was eight. Finding the facts woven into world myths always interested me and researching deeper into Christianity's roots was utterly fascinating. I learnt a lot during that time, including things like the fact the Romans persecuted the early Christians for political reasons, not religious.

The down side to all that intense arguing and debating was that Justin and his fellow missionary friends began to make us all feel stressed. As much as we had grown to love Justin as dearly as if he were real family, the constant pressure to convert was unpleasant. I'd had friends telling me I was going to hell since the age of 16. Justin was the 5th friend to try to convert me. I began to waver. I had never been to a church, never felt any need to, but was I wrong? Were they right? Was some giant, bearded old man up there ready to zap me with eternal damnation?

Oh wait: I said he was the 5th person to try to convert me, but he was actually the 6th. When I was eleven, I'd had that strong reprimand from a teacher, the one who warned me about being a Pantheist. Who the hell tells a child something like that? Ah wait, I know – someone who believes in hell! But it wasn't just the constant, eroding, religious disapproval causing me to feel uncertain. Justin came into our lives as our family fell apart.

The 1980s was a decade of urban terrorism in South Africa and we lost our Rhodesian citizenship when it became Zimbabwe. On top of that, several family members became seriously ill. The 1980s were a blur of hospital visits, ambulances and doctors, all at a time when South Africa was dealing with the worst decade of terrorist violence. There were so many deaths of friends and family in the 80s and 90s, through political violence, escalating crime and bad health. It was a very dark time.

By the time Justin started pushing us all to convert, we were all worn down. Looking back, I can see the signs of burn out in myself and my mom. No wonder Justin's well-meant persistence became stressful and overwhelming. One particular night, I was sitting on my bed thinking about Justin's request that I pray to God for an answer on whether to become a Mormon or not. It had been a really bad day and I felt shattered.

Instead of asking God about Mormonism, I found myself apologising to God for the general violence of mankind, the cruelty and senselessness of it all. I felt so saddened by humans and how they constantly found reasons to hate each other. I was tired of hate and violence, tired of sickness. I felt cursed, but I also felt this was probably my own fault. I was just another human, after all. Another upright ape, prone to survival instinct violence, pettiness and all those other deadly sins.

I finally could imagine hell and imagine a God so enraged at us all that He sent us there. I was unable to pray as I normally did, chatting to God as if to a friend. I felt too sad and ashamed. As I sat there, I sent out my regret and apologies as my prayer, straight from my heart... and God replied. Ordinary people aren't supposed to hear from God. That only happens in legends, to great men like Moses. But in an everyday bedroom in South Africa, a quite ordinary young woman had God speak to her and it changed her life forever. There were no words – just an overwhelmingly powerful event.

How can I explain how that feels? It's a bit like being a computer and having someone download the entire internet into you in a single second. I was taken over by another consciousness and it was HUGE. Literally mind-blowing, I suspect. You couldn't be connected to something that vast for long and stay mentally intact. In less than a second, I knew exactly what this Power felt. It felt EVERYTHING – every person and also every plant, animal, stone, star and planet. It was ALL and it felt all.

There was absolutely no anger or rage, but there was something infinitely worse: Agony. As this All scanned the planet and absorbed humanity it was in what I can only describe as an agony of sadness at our suffering and stupidity. It felt it all: the grief, cruelty and senseless violence and the pain of that was immense, vast and unbearable. Agony. And I knew instantly that there was no hell for us. This Being felt no anger or need for revenge. It grieved for us and with us. There was no anger.

I was doubled up by the emotional pain and guilt that we did this. We made this perfect ALL feel such pain and... zap. The connection was gone. I burst into tears. This Being, this All that some of us call God, had no desire for punishment or revenge. All it wanted was for us to thrive. It was the purest LOVE I've ever felt.

I'm sure some people would argue, "So if God feels that way, why doesn't He/She stop the suffering?" For the same reasons parents of drug addicts don't just lock them in a room for their own good. Because you cannot force someone to do what is best, no matter how much you love them. Because ultimately we are all responsible for ourselves. We have to make those choices. Love never uses force. I am so grateful that meeting Justin led me to that incredible miracle. It changed my perspective forever.

A short while after that event, I finally agreed to join Justin at his temple one Sunday. He was so thrilled. He saw it as my first step to joining, but it was really my farewell gesture. I was ready to tell him no, but wanted first to go to his place of worship to show my respect for all he believed in. My experience of ALL had made me realise that religions are both irrelevant and vitally important. Irrelevant to God, vitally important in making humans feel connected to God. It's not about any religion being the "right" one. It's about people finding ways to express their love of God to God.

At the Mormon temple gathering that Sunday, Justin was so excited and happy that I began to feel guilty. The fact there were many people I knew there, all equally happy to see me, made it all the worse. East London, oddly enough, was the oldest Mormon settlement outside of the USA. There were several South African Mormon families I knew and some of them were long-time family friends.

I felt guilty that they thought I was about to join them. I also felt a little sad that they lived such restricted lives when I knew then that God/All really didn't care what anyone ate, drank or did on Sundays. I regretted that I could never tell any of them that; they would never understand.

During the service, people began passing along trays of bread and water (no wine for Mormons). I'd watched Mass being performed by the Catholic Church. I had gone to a Catholic school for three years and been to the school chapel, but I'd never taken part. As the plate wove its slow way closer and closer to where I was sitting, I began to panic. I was here to say a firm, "No thank you. Nope. Never." Hardly the right time to have my first communion experience!

I was wedged in between family friends and

Justin... Justin who was now holding out the tray and BEAMING with joy. Feeling sick with guilt, I took the tray. I picked up a cube of bread, placed it in my dry mouth and flung it back with a shot of tepid water. In my mind I said a quick, heart-felt apology to that ALL for being a coward and a hypocrite. As I swallowed, a huge wave of love energy shot through my body.

How do you describe energy like that? Everything I write to describe it starts to sound... orgasmic. It wasn't. It was better! But seriously, there is no way you can describe being filled with that kind of energy. It is the best feeling ever. It's like having a wave of LOVE surge through you like a tsunami. Joy, love and all things wonderful distilled into the purest energy.

Love energy is positively cosmic in size and power and moves a thousand times faster than light. It would become the conduit through which I connected to everything, dead people as well as living. It became my conduit to Justin at that time, much to his dismay. That started as a seeming coincidence which eventually became so obvious that my dad noticed and commented on it. Whenever I wanted to talk to Justin he'd phone us, usually within seconds. We'd be talking about something Justin needed to know or be informed about and I'd think that I should call him and the phone would ring. Every time. Once I knew that, I could simply THINK his name and he'd phone within a minute.

When we eventually pointed it out to him, he gave me a look of horror, the kind of look dogs give you when you mention words like "vet" or "bath". It still worked after that, so clearly the fact that Justin seemed to find this a bit creepy did nothing to prevent it. In fact, I was still able to make him phone instantly even after he moved to Cape Town, which was 700 miles away. Love energy has no limitations of time or distance, which takes us back nicely to the 1990s and how my abilities began to change once again.

It was in the late 1990s and my father's mother had recently passed away. I hesitate at calling her grandmother since we were never close. During my life, I probably met her about four or five times and we struggled to communicate. My dad's mom became deaf at the age of three and since I never was around her, I never learnt sign language. At the time of her death, we had spent a holiday together and finally managed to get to know each other.

Before she died, she gave me some of her jewellery and an old hatbox full of lace, buttons and sewing bits. This particular day, I was busy sewing and needed some bias binding. I went to get her hatbox to see if there was anything suitable in it. As I searched through it, I thought about the fact that we both had loved sewing and craftwork. I felt sad that I hadn't known her better during her lifetime. I picked up a piece of lace while thinking about those lost opportunities... and a wave of love hit me.

This time, the energy was more like opening a curtain in a cold room and feeling the warm sun hit your face. It was warm, feminine and loving. Once again, this energy was like an instant download of information. There were no words or visuals. I simply knew it was her and that she was letting me know she loved me, too. I am so happy that I had that moment to connect with her and make up for the fact we were never close during her lifetime. Sadly, the hatbox was stolen when our house was burgled in 1999, but I'm happy to say that the burglars dumped out the contents before they took it. I used that exact piece of lace on my wedding dress a few years later.

6

Before I could marry my future husband, I needed to meet him. That came about thanks to two completely interwoven events in 2001. The first was a gift of books and the second was a gift via a book. Both I owe to a most remarkable woman. While I was still working at the newspaper, a woman phoned me. In this beautifully elegant Indian accent, she said that she had been informed that I was "the one" and would I please come visit her to pick up my books. *Uh… my books?*

During the course of our conversation, she explained that she had a large collection of astrology books she wanted to gift to a worthy astrologer. Unsure who to choose, she collected photos of all the South African astrologers in newspapers and magazines and dowsed them with a pendulum. The pendulum had chosen me. We made an appointment to meet.

A few days later, I made my way upstairs to the flat number she'd given me. I rang the doorbell and a tiny woman came to the door. She was tiny in stature, clearly quite elderly and decidedly NOT Indian. Her faded hair still showed traces of the pale blonde it had once been and her remarkably bright eyes were a clear, sparkling blue. I thought there must be some mistake, but the moment she started to speak, I recognised that lovely accent from the phone call.

How does a blonde, blue-eyed lady in Africa come to have an Indian accent? By living a most adventurous life. Over a cup of tea, Siromani told me how she had been born in India of Scandinavian parents. She had spent her childhood and early adulthood in India and that was where she had studied astrology and dowsing. After marriage, she had moved to Africa where she had studied engineering and worked as a building constructor and a water dowser.

Now, a month before her 90th birthday, she felt it was time to begin studying something new and more challenging. She was getting rid of all her old books and focusing on studying herbal medicine and alternative healing. How many people decide to study or take up a new career at the age of 90? Siromani truly was one-of-a-kind. I spent a magical afternoon in her flat listening to her stories of India and Africa, discussing astrology and books in general. She was one of the most vibrant and alive people I have ever met.

I eventually left with a box full of antique astrology books and Vedic ephemera, but the gifts she gave me that day went far beyond that. As I was leaving, I noticed a book on the small coffee table next to her arm chair. I recognised it; I had been given the same book the year before as a Christmas present. I commented on that fact and Siromani was thrilled to find we were reading the same book. She asked my opinion on it and I had to admit that I hadn't read it yet.

She said, "Go home and read it. Then come back and we'll discuss it together."

I never made that second appointment, mostly because I never finished reading the book. I did try, but my life was too busy for reading at the time. It was a complex viewpoint on ancient history and a bit hard going. One weekend afternoon, I had a moment of genius. I had this new thing called the Internet. Could I use that to find out more about this book? Perhaps some way to cheat so that I could go back to visit Siromani and pretend I'd read the thing?

I put the name of the book I was (not) reading into this wonderful new thing called Google and a whole page of links popped up. The top one was a link to the author's web page. That looked promising so I clicked on it, but instead of taking me to more information on his books, it took me to something even more magical. This author had a discussion forum on his web page.

This was the first time I had seen an internet forum and I was enchanted. There was a list of topics that people were adding replies to, and from what I could make out as I wandered through the site, these people were from all over the world. Wow... all over the world. For someone who had never stepped out of Africa, this was pure magic. I am a lot like my grandfather; I love talking to different people from different walks of life and cultures.

The topics on the forum ranged from ancient history and mythology to everyday news events. I was dying to add my own comments, but too shy and scared to try. I might not have replied at all except someone with an Indian name had shared a poem he'd written. It was about reincarnation, a concept I felt quite neutral about, but described in such a beautifully sublime manner that I longed to reply.

I gathered up all my courage and wrote a reply, telling him I thought the poem was lovely. He not only thanked me back, he also put up a new topic welcoming me to the forum. And other people replied! People I did not know welcomed me to this place. Their friendliness gave me the courage to stay. One small step into a vast, new world.

I stumbled onto that forum at one of the most significant times imaginable, a moment where my abilities leapt and the world crashed. It started one blustery morning in mid-September 2001. I had to go through to another town to deliver an astrology chart to a client. I was delivering it as a favour since this chart was for the close friend of a friend. My mom and I decided to make a day of it – go shopping in the morning, have lunch out and then drop off the chart.

We had a fun day planned, except I felt dreadful; dread-filled and dreadfully strange. I'd felt something like this twice before. It was a type of manic hyper-energy that felt horrible, like I'd drunk twenty energy drinks or turned into Jim Carey in The Mask. To make matters worse, the two times I'd felt like this before were both related to deaths.

The first time I'd felt this way was on Valentine's Day in 1997. I had used the hyper energy to zoom through the day's tasks, a little housework and some gardening. I was busy cutting my dad's hair that evening, still feeling hyper, when the phone rang. It was my uncle to say that his son, Frank, had just died in a snowmobile accident in Canada.

The second time was in September 1999. Once again, I woke up with this wired-tight, high energy buzz in my head. I didn't have long to wait that time. My aunt phoned barely an hour after I was up to say my gran wasn't well. We all rushed to the house, but she my gran was gone before we got there. Both times, the moment I found out who had died, the strange hyper-buzzed feeling eased off.

But this day in September 2001, the energy high was on an entirely different level. This was epic; I was at a level where I felt like the world around me was in slow-motion. I knew I was moving about like a frantic squirrel, but I had no control over it. When I spoke, it was a gabbled rush of sound. On top of that, I was feeling utterly ghastly emotionally.

I figured if the times before had signified the death of someone I loved, then this HYPER-GHASTLY could only mean I was going to die. So what did I do? I kept busy and tried not to wonder about the how, when or where. I can be stubborn and this day the stubborn in me decided I was not going to let dying ruin my day out. The day was a zoom-through blur of shopping, lunch, chuck a birth chart at a woman as I gabbled madly about astrology, then more shopping.

I remember very little of that day except for the fact that I felt hellish. We finally went home and were still busy unpacking when my dad phoned. He said, "Turn on the TV. America has just been attacked by terrorists."

My mom laughed. My dad's always been a joker and a tease. He had to repeat it three times before she told me to go turn on the TV. I called her to come through. New York was live on the news and something was seriously wrong. We both stood there watching as the second plane hit the second tower. Live on TV, we saw the events of September 11th and watched as hundreds of people died... and my hyper-ghastly energy vanished. I've never had that feeling on such an intense scale since and I very much hope I NEVER have it happen again. It's my own dark memory of a tragic day.

The forum I had just joined spent most of the next month talking about 911, but in between I began to find the odd topic that was less stressful to talk about. I was not an ancient Egypt buff, but I did love mythology and I knew enough scattered bits to enjoy the discussions. It was great fun, especially for someone who had spent all her adult life in a small village on the edge of a rather dull town. During the day, I wrote birth charts and held meetings with clients and in the evenings I talked to people all around the world. It was one of the most exciting times of my life.

I began to make new friends which led to being

invited to join other forums and e-groups where I discovered even more things I'd never heard of before, like Wicca and Mayan astrology. I'm not sure how I ended up sharing one of my dreams on the forum. I know we'd all been chatting casually and sharing funny stories. I think I said something like, "I had this really crazy dream."

Like all of my precognitive dreams, this one had been vivid and it had an animal in it. It was in March 1998. I dreamt I was dragging my sad, soggy self out of the sea and onto a cold beach. I had been shipwrecked. I was wearing breaches, a shirt, and woollen socks worn with buckle shoes. I was clearly male, but that didn't seem important at the time. I stood and looked around me. I was standing on a sandy beach that spread out in a wide arc to form a bay.

Ahead of me and out just beyond the edge of that arc was an old-fashioned sailing ship, listing heavily to one side. To my right was a row of sand dunes and I decided to walk up them to get a better view of the place. Even in a dream, I was aware that the scrubby grass growing on the dunes was nothing like the vegetation you would find on African beaches. From the top, I could see that there were several other men on the beach, survivors of the shipwreck like myself. Some were busy building a fire on the beach.

One of the men gathering driftwood started to shout and point at me. I realised he was actually pointing beyond me and I turned to look. A huge stag was standing right behind me. I thought about running, but it seemed a bit pointless. It was clearly going to run faster than me. In complete panic, I fell to my knees and curled up into a ball, hands over my head. I hoped the stag would see me as less of a threat and move on, but instead it stepped forward and stood over me.

The blood was pounded in my ears so loudly that I could barely hear the men on the beach shouting. They shouted for me to stay still, which I did for what felt like a lifetime. I could hear the stag's harsh breathing above me. Eventually, since the stag still wasn't moving, I decided to try crawling out and away. I slowly raised myself up onto my hands and knees....

I froze. I could feel my back touching the animal's belly. I felt its warmth and the way its body moved as it breathed. After another agonising lifetime of staying utterly still, I began to crawl forward as slowly and carefully as I could manage. I hoped to get away, but with each move I made, the stag moved with me. Our movements were perfectly synchronised, as if my arms and legs were attached to each of the stag's limbs. I began to crawl down the sand dune, feeling the stag move with me almost as if it were a living puppet I was controlling.

I knew the men were shouting for me to get out and run, but the only reality was me and the stag. Their voices seemed faint and far away. As I stopped being afraid, I began to melt into the stag. My arms and legs first, then my body moved up into its body until I was the stag and the stag was me. Stag-me began to run, hooves kicking up the sand and water as we ran along the sea's edge. I remember the men shouting and I remember the feeling of joy and exhilaration and then... I woke up.

I wrote the dream down at the time it happened because it had that vivid feeling all my important dreams had. I expected it would prove to be a story for a future TV show or something similar, but time passed and days became years without anything happening to make sense of that dream. Since the beach was so cold, I figured it was probably Canada and thought the stag could possibly have been an elk. I was from Africa. I can tell a kudu from an eland, but beyond Santa's reindeer, my knowledge of deer species was a bit iffy.

When I posted the dream on the forum in 2001, it was mostly because I thought my new friends would find it amusing. One of the forum people I was friendly with seemed excited about the dream. He asked me for my email address. I was intrigued and gave it to him. He emailed me to ask another question: could he share my dream with his brother-in-law?

Sure. *I mean, it was only a dream. Right?* This wasn't a dream that was going to come true like my others had. The place was in the past, not the future, and no one morphs into a deer. Except... some people do morph into deer. I just hadn't discovered that yet.

The forum friend's brother-in-law wrote to me within a few days to say that he was a medicine man. I can't remember the name of the North American people he belonged to now, just that it was something starting with a C. He said my dream held great symbolism and importance.

Both men told me that in their culture, the stag was

a doorway and way-shower – the one who travels between worlds. To them, the dream of me morphing into a stag was the same as a Catholic seeing Jesus. They told me my dream was a sacred Dream Quest and they both sent me links to Native American Indian beliefs. These were exciting things I knew nothing about, like totem animals.

I loved the nature-based simplicity of their beliefs and I liked their Great Spirit. He sounded a lot closer in character to the All-God I knew and spoke to. Their beliefs fitted me closer than anything I'd found before, but other things were happening in my life. Researching totem animals and shamanism would have to wait. I'd met someone on those forums and was beginning to fall in love.

7

Falling in love in 2001 came about at the same time I took another leap and began to see and hear. I think it is time to explain what I mean by those terms. Contrary to TV and films, a psychic looking at a crystal ball does not literally see a scene playing out like a mini movie in a snow globe. A crystal ball, or black mirror, is merely a blank space to stare at as you switch off your mind in order to let other things tune in. It's a kind of meditation state that shuts out the background noise. When your average psychic tells you they *see* and *hear* things, what they really mean is vivid things in their mind and not literal visions or sounds.

I tried to explain that on a blog once, by using a photo my father had taken in a museum. He was trying to capture an item in a display cabinet, but the camera picked up reflections in the glass as well. The two images within the cabinet and without superimposed over each other. That's how it is in my mind. My thoughts are the image with this second layer on top. It can be confusing, even scary at times, to have a double set of things going on in your mind. As a result, people with psychic abilities do make mistakes or jump to wrong conclusions since there's always this overlay issue of what is from your mind and what is not.

The reason I used italics for *seen* and *heard* was to differentiate between things experienced in the mind to things experienced in reality. In other words: as with the lady in the garden all those decades back, I have sometimes literally seen and heard.

The first time that happened to me as an adult was in 2001, around the time I was busy talking about shamanism and deer totems with my new internet friend. I woke up one morning and rolled over to check the time. I was just about to get up when this loud voice spoke from the bottom of my bed. It was a deep man's voice. In my bedroom. Even though I was scared I still remember exactly what he said. It seemed to be one word or a phrase, definitely not English and completely unknown to me. It started with a soft guttural sound, like clearing your throat.

"ch-AH-mun-KAH!"

I knew it had to be important as I had never heard anyone before. I wondered who had said it. The voice had been firm and authoritative. I did try finding the word and even asked others. Someone suggested Amun-ka, which was cool, but it didn't feel quite right. Eventually, I shelved the hunt for meanings as more interesting things were happening in my life. I had met someone on the internet forums.

We met in the strangest way, which is my normal. He and I were members of two forums I went onto at night and we shared many mutual friends, but we never met on either forum. Then, for a few brief months, one of those mutual friends started their own forum. It was a small, private place, only open by invitation. It felt cosy, a safe place to chat more freely amongst friends. So safe that on New Year's Eve, I went a little mad and posted one of my personal stories about my crazy, psychic life.

The next morning, I woke up to a new year thinking, *WHAT THE HELL HAVE I DONE?* I dashed for my computer and logged on, palms sweating. No one had replied to my post yet. As I sat there feeling utter relief, I noticed a new post had come in just an hour after mine at 1:00am. Curious, I clicked on it to have a look. It was another confession-type story written by a member I'd seen on the forum, but didn't know personally.

He was a Scotsman (Alexander aka Sandy) on the other side of the world. He had a most unique story to tell and like me, he was aware that writing it carried the risk of sounding crazy. I sat staring at his story, seeing so much of myself in it. I had to reply. I wrote that I understood how he felt and told him to please go read my own confession post. *Couldn't delete it now, damn.* I ended with, "I know you. I'm sure we were friends in some former life. Let's take the rest of this year to get to know each other again." Little did we know that a year later we'd be married in South Africa.

That New Year's day in 2002, I waited anxiously for him to reply and once he had responded, I quickly deleted my original post feeling HUGE relief. I have since learned how to fling my life out before others because it is always useful, healing and educational, but it is never easy. There's always that moment of fear and vulnerability just as I take the leap to share something about myself. Sandy is better at trust and leaps of faith, but utterly loathes being visible and takes his privacy very seriously. I'm fine with waving my naked soul at people one-on-one, but flop badly with trust and hate change. Leaps of faith give me ulcers.

Right from the start, I knew I trusted Sandy and that feeling of knowing him never went away. In fact, being in contact with him seemed to act as a catalyst. My abilities leapt once again. The most impressive instance came about one night when we were chatting online. I decided to go make myself some tea. I turned in my chair and there in the doorway was a wolf. Not a mind-image, but a real, solid animal.

She was staring right at me from barely two metres away, standing in the doorway. Pale grey, almost white, it looked to be female. It's amazing how many thoughts can zoom through your mind in seconds. I wasn't scared, but I was stunned. This was a real animal. I could see everything down to the damp shine on her nose. She flattened her ears and lowered her head slightly, doing that dog-smile thing a submissive animal does. She took two steps forward, I blinked and she was gone.

That has never happened again, which breaks my heart. I would love to see her again. She was absolutely gorgeous. I can't give you a rational reason why, but I felt without any doubts that she belonged to Sandy. My first thought as she started to walk towards me was that she was there to check me out. When I told Sandy what I had seen, he admitted that wolves were his favourite animal.

A short while after that, I *heard* my mystery man speak again. It was morning and this time I had been awake for a while. It was a weekend and I was putting off getting up. I was lying there contemplating the miracle of coffee, when the same deep voice spoke out LOUD. This time the sun was up and I was awake and able to see the end of my bed. There was no one there. The same voice said, "Don't go to Laredo," in this dry, slightly tongue-in-cheek tone.

Beyond the old cowboy movie reference, I actually knew two people who lived in Laredo at that time. Both were internet acquaintances and both had begun making tentative moves on me. I'd been dodging both for a while. Mr Laredo #1 would eventually fade into the sunset. Mr Laredo #2 was an entirely different matter. He was supposed to be teaching me html coding, but I had noticed how he tried to shift the online chat onto things more flirtatious.

Up until then I had managed to keep him in check, but the weekend following my Laredo warning, things got messy. Let's just say a drunk Laredo beats a drunk Lothario and leave it at that. I am sure my experience that weekend was only one of many things Mr Laredo

#2 deeply regrets. A warning to all cheating men: do not go into chat rooms drunk, especially if your wife/girlfriend is in the other room.

It was Sandy who rescued me from the unwanted advances of Mr Laredo #2, entering the chat room like a knight in shining armour. That quickly became as hilarious as a French farce, when Ms Laredo stormed into the chat. She was convinced "Sandy" was also female and thus thought her man was in a dirty little chat room threesome.

I never spoke to Mr Laredo #2 again after that night, but he had proven most useful. That ridiculous event made me stop and think, *This Scotsman is a really nice guy.* It wasn't long after that this nice, Scottish guy decided he had better make some moves before anyone else came along. Sandy proposed in chat and I wrote YES three times. Then we both went off to bed and had small panic attacks the next day at what we'd just done.

We returned to chat and phone calls to discuss how to meet each other. It made more sense for me to take time out to visit him than for him to come to me. Sandy had recently started a new job and could not take leave, while I had just recently lost my job on the paper. Plus, if we married I'd be moving to Scotland and I wanted to see what the country was like before making that big a decision.

It took us about two months to get things sorted. I was going to come over and stay with his family for a month. The best way to get to know someone is to meet their family. The day I went to the bank to sort out traveller's cheques (now I feel old – does anyone use them any more?), the TV in the bank lobby was showing a travel advert for Edinburgh. I walked out of the bank to the sound of one thousand pipers playing bagpipes. And the day I boarded my plane, the passenger in front of me had his phone ring. His ring tone was Scotland the Brave.

I ended up spending a fantastic 40 days in Scotland. Since Sandy couldn't get time off work, I went with him. In most cases that would have not been possible, but Sandy was sub-contracted to do building work all over Northern Scotland. He was mostly his own boss, travelling long distances to the remote corners and crannies of Northern Scotland. It couldn't have been a more perfect way to see Scotland.

Clava Cairns, near Inverness.

On the weekends, Sandy took me to the ancient ruins and more touristy "must see" sites, places like

Clava Cairns, which I still love. Seeing all those amazing places was wonderful, but I loved the work days even more. I not only visited parts of Scotland many people never get to see, but I also got to meet the people. While Sandy was working, I'd be sitting having a cuppa and a chat with the home owner.

The Northern Scots are mostly friendly and hospitable, but some stood out above the rest. On my third day in Scotland, we were off before dawn to drive up to a job at Thurso on the very northern tip of Scotland. That lovely family not only fed us a huge lunch, but invited us to stay for dinner as well. All of us crammed around their kitchen table eating roast chicken and the biggest mountain of mashed potatoes and gravy I have ever seen. To top it all, they gave us an engagement present! A beautiful, crystal bottle etched with local wildlife.

A year later and newly married, we once again travelled up to Thurso and John O'Groats. This time it was for fun and Sandy took me on a more scenic drive along the northern coast. At one stage, we turned a corner and came out on a stretch of coastland. I gasped, stunned... there was my bay from the deer dream in the 1990s. I swear my mouth dropped open. I made Sandy to stop and turn back. I had to be sure. We parked at the edge and I sat there stunned. It was perfect in every detail. A cold, northern beach, but not Canada. Scotland!

I went home and looked up the details. The beach is Dunnet Bay and it is the scene of many shipwrecks. The most famous was the Spanish Armada, who tried to sneak up on England by going around Northern Scotland. Many Spanish shipwreck survivors chose to stay in Scotland and you do find Spanish surnames jostling shoulders with Scottish ones up North. My dream, beyond morphing into a deer, was all completely factual.

And the deer? The stag? He was one thing I did get to see on my holiday. Not an elk, but a Red Deer. I wrote about that experience in 2010. It won 2nd prize in the John Muir Trust Wild Writing competition. The story of the stag is in the last paragraph.

Leap of Fate by Michelle Frost

Love stories usually end with a marriage proposal, but this story started with one...

I was born in Africa and had lived all my life in Africa. I'd have probably died there too, if it wasn't for a Highlander I'd met on the internet having other ideas. In 2002 he turned my life around with once sentence on a chat room window.

"Will you marry me?" He asked...
...and I said, "Yes."

I can't explain why I was so certain. I'm not the kind for leaps of faith or impulse – I can take thirty minutes to decide between tea and coffee! All I knew was that I had no doubt I loved this man I'd never met and never seen. We did realize that arranging a meeting between a man in the North of Scotland and a woman in the South of Africa was going to take some serious effort.

Since he had recently started a new job it made more sense for me to travel to Scotland than him to Africa. So, two months after I first said that fateful "Yes", I was on a plane and on my way to spend a month in the far North. Little did I know that I'd be falling in love all over again... not once, but twice before my travels were over.

I fell in love with the idea of a man on a computer screen, but I had to travel to the far side of the world to find the real man behind the words. Since he had no chance to take leave from his new job we did the next best thing... I went along with him to work during the week. You can forget your guided tours and bus trips; I can tell you the best way to see Scotland is in a builder's Transit van. Thanks to a building contract that was mostly rural I got to see more of the countryside in my month's holiday than any package holiday provides. Admittedly I did have to shovel one ton of sand and scrape thousand year old carpet tiles off a farm floor, but in between was pure magic. What more romantic gift could a man offer than to share the country he loves with the woman of his dreams?

And that was exactly what he did. During workdays he'd take the more scenic routes and he'd stop for lunch in the places he loved the most. There is nothing more romantic than sharing a pork pie in the middle of absolute nowhere with your true love. We shared ours on the way up to Thurso on a spring morning when the air was so sharp and clear it was like breathing diamonds. Every weekend he'd be up at dawn planning where to take me and what to show me. We'd spend the whole weekend driving and walking. I wore the soles off two pairs of African shoes climbing Scottish hillsides.

I think I realized I'd fallen in love with my Highlander the second time when I didn't kill him for taking me through a bog, a stream, a field and over two gates and a barbed wire fence. How can you not love a man who makes you ruin your last pair of packed shoes, and freezes your thin African skin to the bone marrow, to show you a woodland bursting with bluebells? And how do you describe seeing a bluebell for the very first time – the amazing colour of them and how they smell? Just one would have been incredible and here he had laid out, beneath my muddy feet, an entire woodland of misted blue magic.

How do you explain the wonder of all that mud-making water to African eyes? Rivers, burns, lochs... so much water and all so beautiful, but especially the waterfalls. Rushing down hills and mountains and even tiny ones along the road sides ... they're everywhere! It was all so alien from my childhood of dry riverbeds and violent rain storms, this Northern world of soft seeping waters. I will always remember my first rain, fine as mist on my skin when we walked around Loch Ness and the surprise of richly golden peat tinted water frothing up like creamy ale over rocks and river beds.

I think, if I had to use any word to describe Scottish countryside it would be "rich". Rich with water and trees and wildlife; rich in history and beauty. We'd drive all weekend and my eyes would be glutted on so much richness... forests of trees I had no names for and wild flowers I'd only ever seen as names in children's books. I never knew buttercups were so small... or chestnut trees so big! And gorse! Why doesn't anyone write about gorse? Never mind hosts of daffodils – why hasn't anyone written odes to the fire of golden gorse flowers blazing on dark hills?

I remember so many richly treasured moments during that holiday. One perfect Sunday afternoon we drove to the valley of the eagles and came across a whole herd of red deer standing in the sun-sparkling Findhorn River. The day our van was stalked by a magnificent male grouse, with outraged scarlet eyebrows, who seemed to think the rough sound of an old Transit van engine was the battle cry of some invisible rival.

Deer in the Findhorn River.

Even more magical was the night we drove to Skye to catch the morning ferry to the islands. That night we saw a fox cub dancing after moths by starlight, his baby fur as woolly as a lamb's. Later, on the ferry, we watched puffins that flew past like frantic flapping feathered bullets. Twilight was an adventure in itself; the sun does not linger in African skies. The glow of Scottish gloaming over wild empty places has got to be one of the most enchanted things anyone could ever experience.

How do you describe falling in love? Does it lie in an unexpected touch or the moment your eyes meet? Is it an instant knowing or a slowly growing realisation? For me it was all of those things.

Near the end of my holiday we were returning from a job on the West Coast. It was early evening twilight when we came around a corner... and there in the road was a red deer stag. He leapt up the bank beside the road and then paused, looking back over his shoulder as we passed. Like a scene in a dream I watched him as he watched me. He was so close... so still and so beautiful.

There was an instant of knowing that my heart was as trapped in this beautiful wildness as my eyes were caught in his calm curious gaze. It was a slowly growing realisation that I had fallen in love a third time... with this lovely, cold strange world of water and stone, sharp light and deep shadows.

And I would never be the same again.

8

Scotland is magical. There is an energy here that is quite different from anywhere else I've been. I've had four friends from different countries come here and comment on that as well. This country makes an impact, but there are specific places here that have hit me hard, one way or another. Before I tell those stories, I must confess that when I met Sandy in 2002 I knew practically nothing about Scottish history. Embarrassing to admit that now, especially when taking into account the fact my mother has Scottish ancestry. I didn't even know that Macbeth had been a real king of Scotland, or that the witches in Shakespeare's story were based on historical fact. When I thought of Scotland, I saw men in kilts, bagpipes and the Loch Ness monster.

When I arrived on holiday in May 2002, Sandy took me to see many beautiful places, but two stood out in my mind because of the experiences I had at those places. The first place I remember was the day Sandy took me into the forest where he had played as a child. It was one of his favourite places and I was expecting to love it, but... nope. The forest felt cold, even on that warm, sunny day. We stopped at one spot for a rest and he asked me what I thought. I surprised myself by blurting, "It tastes like cold blood." *Yeah, Michelle, really cool to tell your fiancé that about his childhood playground!*

But Sandy nodded and said, "That makes sense. This is Culloden Forest. Part of the battle of Culloden took place here. A lot of men died in this forest."

Now, in fairness to my sceptical side, there could be another reason for Culloden forest tasting like cold blood. There is a clootie well at its centre – a sacred well of mineral-rich water. It is possible that the blood taste I noticed was from the iron-rich water running through the ground, but the oppressive vibe was not. I love forests, just not Culloden. As for clootie wells: I had no idea such things existed, so it is probable you might not know either. A cloot is a cloth in Scotland. You will find clootie dumpling on Scottish menus. It's a steam pudding wrapped in a cloth. A clootie well is a sacred spring where people leave prayers in the form of strips of cloth tied to nearby trees. I've seen everything from very old faded ribbons to socks and even a whole shirt tied on trees at clootie wells.

In ancient times, these natural springs were the homes of goddesses, but ownership was transferred to the Virgin Mary after Christianity arrived. The belief is that you dip your cloth in the sacred water and then tie it to a tree as a prayer for healing. As the cloth decays your illness fades, so it is advisable to leave an item that is biodegradable. A polyester sock may have you waiting for an answered prayer for a VERY long time.

We took an American friend to see the Black Isle Clootie well in 2014. As we were getting ready to start up the hill, a burly young man with two children stopped and told us to watch out for fairies. I think our friend thought he was joking, but the man was quite sincere. He told us how his mother had seen fairies at the well and how the waters had saved his life. He now carried on the family tradition of regularly visiting and taking his children there. This is typical of Scotland, full of surprises and unexpected magic.

I love clootie wells, but the one in Culloden made me cry the day I was there in 2002. It was in a bad state through vandalism and it all felt desperately sad. While Sandy was busy taking photos, I went about touching the trees and apologising to them. I could feel their slow, deep anger. Oh, me and trees. I forgot! We can't go further into my adventures in Scotland without explaining that the first time I felt a tree was back in Africa.

I've always loved trees. In Rhodesia, I used to climb our peach tree, wishing it was big enough for a tree house. When we moved to South Africa, the house my parents bought had two big Coral trees in the front yard. In Rhodesia we called them Lucky Bean trees, as the bright orange flowers turned into bean pods full of hard, bright red beans. Lucky Beans were popular for beadwork and crafts made by the local people.

The room I chose for my new bedroom in South Africa was actually a portion built onto the main house as a holiday flat-let/guest room. Due to the sloping site the house was built on, my bedroom was as high as an upper story building. My window gave me the perfect view right into the tree tops. In my teens, on weekends and holidays I'd climb onto the window ledge and sit with my feet dangling out the window. I'd sit there for hours, drawing, writing or just watching the birds.

This one lovely morning in 1979, I was sitting in the window listening to the breeze rustle in the leaves and the sounds of birds. I started to drift, daydreaming as I stared at the tree. Something shifted and suddenly, I was the tree staring at me.

And.... Time.... Slowed.... Down.

I felt and heard my bark creak as the wind bent my branches. I could feel the sunlight soaking in everywhere and this sensation of my roots in the cool damp earth and the sense of life energy flowing up and down through me. I had this sense of ageless, patient slowness, of sun, wind, water and earth. It was wonderful, but only lasted a moment. It was over far too quickly.

The trees of Scotland are on a completely different

level, especially the north west trees. The first time I went out to the West Coast of Scotland was during my holiday in 2002. I felt that the trees wanted me to stop, as if they were calling to me. The urge to stop was really intense, but it felt too silly to say to Sandy, "Stop. The trees are calling me."

In 2004, an English friend came up to visit us. He had never been to Scotland, so he took the scenic route from Glasgow up along the coast and then across Northern Scotland to our house. We were chatting about his trip when he, most sheepishly, admitted he'd had this crazy feeling that the trees were calling him. Since it was quiet, he stopped the car, went for a walk and hugged a tree.

He was half amused, half embarrassed at his own confession. He joked that the trees "made him do it". I asked him where this had happened. I had a hunch. He showed me on a map and it was in the same area where I'd felt the trees calling me. He obviously felt a bit idiotic, so I told him my story. It was a relief to realise we'd both felt the same thing in almost the exact same place.

The next time I was out that way was about a year later. Sandy had to give a quote for a job and I'd gone along for the drive. We were travelling through an area of fully grown pine forest and I was watching the trees zoom by when I started to hear a most peculiar sound. It was a bit like when you have ringing in your ears, but much deeper in tone. It sounded like thousands of voices singing an OHM sound, like the Tibetan monks chant. It was mesmerising.

As we moved from the forest into an open area, the sound faded away. We moved on through a forestry area of seedlings and young trees and a new sound started up. Here the note was a much higher pitch, like an "aaaah" sung by a choir of schoolboys. It was really lovely, but over so fast. We came home by a different route, so I wasn't able to see if they were willing to give a repeat performance. When we got home, I went online and found the exact pitch/sound. The seedling forest was like a flute playing in the key of A.

We don't go out to the West Coast often. It was years later in May 2009, that we returned. We took my parents on a day trip to Skye. For the route home, we decided to travel north along the coast before coming back via Loch Ness. We reached a portion of wooded coastline and there it was again; the feeling that the trees were aware and calling to me. Once again we couldn't stop, but this time because we were on a narrow and winding road with nowhere to pull over. It is most frustrating that Scotland's road department never thought of tourists wanting to stop to take photos or admire the views.

On this section of coastline, the trees aren't pine. I'm not quite sure what they are, but I think most probably beech. I was half dozing in the car, tired from our long day out, when I felt this feeling on my face, like the lightest fingertip tapping. I knew it was the trees showing me how the wind felt on leaves and branches. It felt nice.

Further on, there were pine trees and I tried to tune in to them to see what wind in pine trees felt like. No result. I felt nothing. I was about to give up when we turned a corner and up ahead was a huge old Scots pine. I tried to focus completely on that tree and it worked. My mind filled with this image of birds on branches and it was tickly! Big, annoying, irritating TICKLY. I could sense that this tree felt prickly-itchy-scratchy irritable. This tree, if it had the chance, would shake off birds like a dog shakes off water. It was so funny to meet an irritable tree that doesn't like bird feet that I burst out laughing.

Why are the West Coast trees so different? I have no idea. Sandy pointed out that the West Coast is unusual in being warmed by the Gulf Stream. There are semi-tropical plants growing in gardens out west. Could this affect the energy of the plants in some way? Or is it the other way around? Does the West Coast energy allow me to tune in to what is around us all the time? Maybe all trees are aware and it's us who are the ones not paying attention. Maybe all trees could do with a hug now and then.

There's another place in Scotland that calls me, but in this case I'm not sure if it is the trees or something else. I've been there twice and both times were equally intense, no difference in my reaction. It had a similarly intense effect on a friend we took there. The name of this place is Rosslyn.

I had heard of Rosslyn long before all the Da Vinci Code hype. I'd seen the chapel discussed on internet forums and looked at online photos. The photos of the stonework were stunning and the stories about the Holy Grail were intriguing, but I can't say I felt anything significant looking at the photos. I did wish I could see it in real life someday. I even joked on the forums that as someone living in Africa that was NEVER going to happen. Never say never!

In our first year of marriage, my husband's sister needed someone to drive her to a big business meeting in Stirling and Sandy volunteered to take her. She normally went down with colleagues, but no one else was going. It takes several hours to drive south from Inverness and the road through the mountains is a killer. We regularly have bad accidents along that road. It's out-dated, too narrow and tired, foreign tourists regularly wander off onto the wrong side of the road. Stunning scenery, but it's a stressful road to travel.

We drove down early, dropped her off for a full day's meeting, and then went off to do some exploring.

Back then, Rosslyn was a low-key interest spot, nothing big on the tourist map. We arrived at the little village of Roslin, went down what looked like a farm lane and stopped outside this big, old, stone wall. There was a tiny booth where you paid your entrance fee before going out and through a small gate in the wall.

We stepped through and there it was, a perfect Gothic chapel on a hilltop. At that stage in 2003, it was almost completely encapsulated by roofed scaffolding as renovations were under way. I couldn't move. I felt winded by the blast of energy. Sandy stood staring at me as the tears ran down my face. I have never, anywhere else, felt such a punch of warmth and love. It felt like heaven.

Rosslyn Chapel, 2010.

That first time I thought it was the building, but when we returned in 2010 I was hit again by intense LOVE energy as I looked over the back wall into the wooded valley below the chapel. There is something strange and magical at Rosslyn, but I'm still not sure what it is or where it is coming from. The first trip in 2003 led to a unique problem: I suffered withdrawal pains. For about five years after that visit, I'd have moments where the longing to return to Rosslyn would be so strong it was literally painful.

Even looking at photos of the place would have me instantly in tears. I have no idea why. It was like the worst level of homesickness mixed in with a big dose of being parted from a loved-one. It eased off after the second visit, but even now when I looked at a satellite map to get the correct spelling, I felt a soft tug at my heart as I looked at the valley itself. I hope I make it back again someday.

9

I said that there were two places Sandy took me on my holiday in 2002 that had an impact. The second place was a completely different experience from Culloden forest. This was Tomnahurich, a strange hill in Inverness also known as the Hill of the Fae. It's shaped exactly as if someone flipped a ship over and left the hull sticking up out of the ground, which suggests that it is probably an esker. Eskers are deposits of sand and gravel left by glaciers as they moved and then melted. Scotland is full of hills that are eskers since most of Scotland was under ice during the last Ice Age.

Nowadays, Tomnahurich is an Inverness cemetery, but go back a few centuries and this was supposed to be a portal into fairyland. As a mythology and folk legend lover, it was the fairy hill legends that had me excited to be there. The most famous legend tells of two men staggering into a local church in Inverness and asking the priest what day it was. They told him they were fiddlers hired to play at a banquet inside the hill. They'd played all night, but on returning home found everything changed. The priest told them the day and year and the men cried out in horror; a hundred years had passed in their one night within the hill. Before the priest could ask more, both men collapsed into heaps of dust. There are variations to this story and I've heard other fairy hill stories on the same line from other places.

The day we went up Tomnahurich hill, it was beautiful and sunny. It's a lovely part of Inverness on the far side of the Ness river near the sport's fields, Bught park and flower nurseries. We walked up the hill that first time. I love graveyards and this one is probably the nicest I've ever been to. The sides of the hill are covered in trees and bushes with a winding, gravel track leading up to the top. All the way up, there were flowering plants and a loud, spring birdsong.

There are glorious views over the city and the countryside from up there. I highly recommend visiting Tomnahurich if you ever go to Inverness. The top of the hill is flat and mostly covered in graves from the late 1800s and early 1900s. There is a path down the centre and a place to park in the centre and at one end. We started at one end and walked towards the centre. The centre is slightly lower with steps down to this circular space. I'd guess it was created as a turning place for a hearse. I had just reached the steps when I walked through something that I can only describe as invisible, electric jelly.

I experienced this most odd feeling all over my body of gooey, wobbly static. If I had to create an image for the feeling, I'd go with the TV show Star Trek's force-field barriers – sparkly-zingy, wibbly-wobbly energy. I spun around instantly and walked back over the same spot. Nothing.

I've been back several times since then and never had that happen again. I've thought about that a lot over the years, especially the legends of the hill being a doorway to fairy lands.

What if there was an explanation to it all, something mind-boggling and yet not impossible? Science says there could be any number of other dimensions around us. I suspect there are times when energy fluctuations create connections between those dimensions. Then the legend of Tomnahurich might not be about a doorway into fairyland, but rather a portal into another dimensional reality. If energy and light can create a hologram, why can't fluctuations in energy or light sometimes make other dimensions, or even other times, visible? Wouldn't that be a more feasible reason why some people claim to have seen the Loch Ness monster than believing there really is a family of plesiosaurs in Loch Ness?

Another strange experience Sandy and I had in 2003 helped me come to this conclusion. On the surface this event was not supernatural, but the more I looked into it the stranger it became. It was a morning in September and we were on our way to Inverness for a business meeting. Sandy was driving and I was enjoying the scenery of late summer. The fields were full of hay bales and golden grains ready for harvest.

Just before Aldearn, Sandy said, "Black cat in the field." I looked right and noticed a black cat walking in the field just beyond a farm fence. As we passed, the animal was at an angle facing away, so all I could see was its straight back and a long tail held in a dipped curve the way all cats do.

I looked away and as I did so my brain said *that was a BIG cat!* I had mentally calculated the height of the cat in comparison to the fence posts it was walking behind. The cat was half the height of those poles, so roughly the size of a collie dog. I looked back thinking I must have made a mistake; it must have been a dog. I watched as the creature turned slightly and I could see it most definitely was not a dog. It walked in typical cat fashion with head held low. The neck was longer than most cats and the head was small and flat-muzzled with large, pointed ears.

I was still thinking I must be wrong with the size when Sandy turned to me and said, "Wow. That was a BIG cat. A very big cat!" Unfortunately, the road had no place to stop and by then we were losing sight of the field. Plus, we had a business meeting to attend to. I told Sandy not to say anything to me about that cat until we got home. I wanted to try something first, without my opinion influencing him in any way.

This animal was like no big cat I had ever seen before. To put that statement into perspective: I'm not an expert, but I am an information junkie and an animal lover. My gran used to sit with me on her lap when I was little and we'd go through the encyclopaedia of animals together. I know a Caracal from a Lynx. Growing up in Africa, I had been lucky enough to hold a lion cub and meet a tame cheetah.

My dad with two cubs.

The black cat we saw looked like a black cheetah, except its ears were pointy, like a Serval. To add to the mystery, you don't get black cheetahs. Melanism in cheetahs creates a distinctly different pattern of spots and stripes and they are called King Cheetahs. When our meeting was over, we went home and I went online to look up cat species. I took a photo of a cheetah and altered the shape and colouring to make it look like the animal I had seen.

I then found pictures of leopard panthers, melanistic pumas and jaguars. I put all the pictures up on my computer and asked Sandy to pick which one closest resembled the cat we had seen. He picked my altered cheetah photo, an animal that did not exist. What had we seen? Sandy reported it to the authorities and we were interviewed by a man doing research at that time. His theory was that we saw a Kellas cat, which is a hybrid of a domestic cat and Scottish wild cat. Kellas cats do exist, are often darker in colour and are usually twice the size of normal domestic cats. But I have seen a dead Kellas cat in the Elgin museum and it is a heavy set chunky animal, like a pet cat on steroids. Our black cat was slender and tall.

I was curious. I went online and looked for more information about big cat sightings. Most people think these big cats are discarded pets, but what we saw matched no known species. It made for interesting reading. Many did turn out to be unwanted pets, like the puma found in Inverness in the 1980s, but in all those cases the animals were fairly tame and tended to be drawn to houses and people, looking for food. The sightings of big black cats were different. These tended to be in rural or wild settings and the animals were far wilder in their behaviour.

I stumbled onto something completely different when I tried a search for black cats with large ears. I found the legend of Big Ears, the demon cat of Scotland. That in turn led me to finding that Scotland had legends about elfin cats called the Cait Sith (cat shee) who were the size of dogs and very ferocious. So black cat sightings are nothing new in Scotland. Either Scotland has a species of big cat that has managed to evade detection for centuries or there's something very odd going on.

If portals do exist, could these big black cats be visitors from elsewhere? But then that just heaps up a whole bunch of new questions and problems. Like, why just big, black cats? If we can connect to another dimension, wouldn't it be possible for other species to stumble through as well? And if they did, how come no one has ever captured one? My dad suggested a third possibility; that these cats exist in a between-state dimension and are only visible to people with psychic abilities. As technology improves, perhaps we might one day have the answer.

10

Speaking of searching for answers, back in 2003 I was still on the trail of the dream quest. Oh yes, I never forgot that medicine man saying my dream stag was part of a dream quest, but it was only after I married and moved to Scotland in 2003 that I was able to look into that more seriously. Even though I had fallen in love with Scotland on my holiday a year earlier, moving countries permanently is an entirely different thing. I had left behind my business as an astrologer, my family and friends, but I was discovering all the things you forget about, like my doctor and dentist.

Even shopping for groceries was surprisingly stressful since I had no idea which prices were cheap or expensive and no idea which brand names were better quality or junk. On top of that, I was struggling to find a job. I had worked as a part-time librarian and newspaper columnist. Beyond that, I had always been self-employed as an artist and astrologer. Not many jobs for any of those! Eventually, I found a small paying job doing reviews online for a German company. The pay was rubbish, but it was writing for money and I did eventually land a better work-from-home job through it.

It only took a few hours a day to do the reviews and then I was left bored and lonely. I finally had enough time to research Native American ideas about dream quests. I'd been given some good links on totem animals by that medicine-man in 2001, but where did I go from there? Searching one day, I stumbled onto a forum that said it was for teaching all things shamanic. It was based in New Zealand and was run by a slightly over-zealous woman who scared the bejeebers out of me. I read a lot, but replied very little for fear of committing some shamanic faux pas.

One of the first things this forum owner wanted to know was what my totem animal was. *Umm…?* I hadn't a clue, which led to her next question: Had I met my spirit guide? *Uh, spirit guide?* I'd heard the term in the 1990s, but thought it sounded exceptionally creepy. It was bad enough having the strange ShadowMan appear in my dreams. The last thing I wanted was to have to deal with someone in my mind while I was awake. The memory of that loud voice in my bedroom returned. Was he my spirit guide? Was his name Hamunkah or my name Hamunkah? *Did I care?*

Quite honestly, I really was not enthused about the idea of letting some unknown person/entity into my mind space so that they could tell me how to live my life. Reluctantly, I agreed to try a meditation to meet my spirit guide. Not surprisingly, it was a complete flop. I was supposed to meditate and imagine I was sitting by the tree of life. I was to then imagine that I travelled down the roots into the caverns of the underworld to meet my spirit guide. But when I tried to imagine a tree, I saw an elephant.

An elephant? Well, I was from Africa and had always loved elephants. I loved all animals really. I had wanted to be a vet as a child, until the logic of being a vet seriously allergic to fur and feathers hit me in high school. Clearly, my mind preferred animals to people, so I decided to focus on finding my totem animal. I could cope with that. I trust animals way more than I trust humans, even ancient, enlightened, dead ones.

The forum suggested I learn more about journeying and gave me a totem meditation to try. Now, before I go into that story, I need to tackle the issue of online forums that teach shamanism. Being clueless and completely green, I honestly thought I was learning the real thing at first, but over the years I realised that most of these online places deal with neo-shamanism. I'm sure a few purists will gasp at my using that term, but that is what it is: neo-shamanism. A mishmash of the ancient with New Age. I have no problem with patchwork, just don't try to sell it to me as a pure, ancient, uncut cloth.

If you go looking for shamanic lessons online, be aware that unless you are dealing with genuine tribal shamans from some part of the world, what you will really be learning about is New Age neo-shamanism. There still are real shamans, sangomas and medicine men out there, so be respectful of their beliefs and ways. This is not something you take on for "fun", any more than you would join the Catholic Church because you think lighting candles and saying mass is pretty.

Now, back to that meditation and journeying. Journeying, from what I could understand back in 2003, was a type of meditation where a shaman would travel between worlds in order to find answers. I've never been any good at regular meditation as my mind never shuts up, but this had potential. Journeying seemed to be more a case of settling down and letting your imagination run wild, which was what normally happened when I tried to meditate anyway.

It's been 14 years since I did that journey and I must admit I can't remember all of what I was supposed to do. I only remember that it went totally off-course for me. I think I had to meditate and imagine myself standing in a forest. Then, I was supposed to walk into the forest where my totem animal would be waiting for me in a central clearing, beside a huge tree whose roots went into the underworld and branches into the higher realms. Needless to say, what I had was NOTHING like that.

Thankfully, I had begun to keep a new dream journal on my computer and I put my meditation journeys into it as well. This is what actually happened that day: I visualised the forest fairly easily and focussed on creating a path into the undergrowth. I struggled with that. As hard as I tried, no path appeared between the tall, dark trees. Instead, the first thing that happened was that a bush baby leapt out of the trees onto my shoulder. Bush babies are tiny nocturnal animals from Africa. They look like something from a children's cartoon, half monkey and half squirrel. My dad had one as a pet when he was a boy. It used to sleep in his shirt pocket all day.

My first thought was, *Wow. I hadn't even entered the forest and I already have my totem* except another animal stepped out of the forest to greet me. A griffin, but a griffin wasn't a real animal. A mythological beast could not be a totem animal, surely? I was confused already. The griffin turned away from me and a path opened up in front of him. Okay, that was cool. I followed the griffin into the forest my mind had created, hoping it would all make sense by the time I reached that central clearing where I was supposed to find my totem. You can guess, can't you? No clearing. Instead, the centre of my forest had a castle.

I went through an arch in one wall and found myself in a cobbled courtyard. In the centre of the courtyard there was a well with a low stone wall around it. There, sitting on the wall, was an old man. The griffin took me to him. The old man is still vivid in my mind as is that courtyard. The stonework was pale grey and looked new, as if built minutes before I arrived there, which of course it was, come to think of it. The old man was wearing a long robe that reminded me of Merlin in old story books. Just like Merlin, he had a long grey beard, but unlike the picture-book Merlin, this old man was a tad chubby.

He was drawing on the low wall he was sitting on with a stick of charcoal. I went closer to see and realised he was marking out lines to play tic tac toe. He drew a cross, then handed me the charcoal, smiling widely. I always lose at this game, but it seemed rude to refuse, considering he was in my totem journey. I drew a zero and handed him back the charcoal. He drew a daisy. Confused, I took the stick again and drew my next zero. He took it back and drew a heart.

I was beginning to feel irritated. This made no sense. As if able to read my thoughts, the old man chuckled and wiped the wall clean with one hand. We started a new game. I drew a cross. He drew a butterfly. In frustration at this nonsense, I drew a star.

He burst out laughing and I finally got it. The game wasn't about winning or keeping to the rules, it was about being imaginative and having fun. Once I realised that, we played several more games, drawing all sorts of crazy doodles and laughing ourselves silly.

It took me six years to realise the bigger lesson to that experience. The game is Life. As children, we enter Life full of love, hope and joy, but everyday life can spiral downhill fast with all our "serious adult responsibilities" and we forget how to have fun. We forget our childlike wonder and we stop experimenting. Sometimes we need to be reminded that it is okay to break the rules and draw daisies for zeros and kittens for crosses. There are no rules except those limitations we create ourselves.

Back on that day in 2003, I only knew I was having a lot of fun with a charming old man, but still hadn't found my totem animal. Near the end of our time together, the old man turned away from me and I realised that several more animals had joined the griffin in the courtyard. As I watched, they lined up in front of me in a tidy line. The old man nodded and each animal in turn spoke to me in my mind. I wrote down the order as well as what each one said:

Lion said, "Be gentle."

Then wolf said, "Be wise, cautious."

Next was a huge elephant. It looked at me and said, "Be aware."

Then bush baby leapt from my shoulder shouting, "Love IS!"

And lastly, rhino said, "Be kind."

As the rhino finished speaking, the castle began to fade and I was back sitting in a flat in Inverness. It was a beautiful experience, but I still didn't have a totem animal. Or did I? The elephant reminded me of something. I had dreamed of an elephant just a few weeks before I'd joined the forum. It was one of my vivid dreams that clearly was meant to be remembered, yet made no sense.

I had dreamt that I was visiting a hospital in India where people were being miraculously healed by an elephant who was a god. On this particular day, he was due to arrive and the nurses were dashing about telling people they must keep their heads bowed and eyes closed. To look at this elephant god would bring about instant death.

I was about to leave the ward when I realised the elephant god was already in the building. I could hear him coming along the main corridor towards my area. In my panic to get out of there fast, I tripped. I was busy scrambling up to my feet when I looked up. He was standing in front of me. He was a huge, bull elephant, old and wise. He stared straight into my eyes and I waited to die. I stood in complete silence, feeling this peaceful sense of connection and understanding. Without a noise, the elephant turned and left the ward. I woke up.

Was elephant my totem animal?

11

By the time I'd started wondering about the elephant, I had made a few friends on that forum. A good thing too, because one morning I went to log on and it was gone. The owner had shut the whole place down overnight. Thankfully, one of my new friends had already recommended other forums to me, so I went to take a look. I eventually settled on a forum that was much bigger and far more friendly than the original. I was to spend the next three years there, making new friends as well as a few enemies. Being a much larger place, it was never boring. I also joined at least four other forums, discussing topics ranging from Shamanism to Paganism and New Age.

Joining these forums meant I had to have a log on name. All of them demanded a pseudonym of some kind. This was new for me. The first forum I'd belonged to in 2001 had a policy of making people use their real names. I could understand the difference. The original forums I'd been on dealt with ancient history and a lot of the members were real archaeologists and historians who preferred to use their own names so as to link to their writing and websites. The Esoteric forums were places where people often wanted to separate their everyday selves from their personal spiritual lives. A lot of them not only kept their spiritual beliefs or psychic abilities away from their working life, but also kept this secret from their own families.

This policy meant I needed a name. But what? I wanted something that sounded shamanic without it being too daft or presumptuous. I was chewing this over one afternoon in the kitchen while doing the dishes, when I noticed a crow on our back fence. We had recently moved from our first flat in Inverness into a much nicer house in a town called Forres. It had a beautiful little garden surrounded by a high picket fence covered in ivy and honeysuckle.

The crow was standing carefully on one point of the picket fence. As I watched, he began to hop along it, from point to point. He went to hop again, but tripped and fell so that his head stuck between the two pickets. For a few seconds he flapped madly, before calming down and realising he could stand on the cross bar and pull his head up and out. I was grateful he was okay, but still laughing. Falling between the pickets was just the kind of thing I would do.

I am smart, I am funny, but I am a klutz. I have a long history of falling. I have stepped off a canoe into thigh deep river mud as a teenager, trying to impress the boys by offering to tie up at the dock. I have slipped on gravel in a public parking area and shot under a car. My clumsy moments are so epic that years after I finished high school, I bumped into someone from my old school and she said, "You're the girl who managed to fall UP the stairs!"

I was just like that crow.

I went and looked up crow symbolism on the internet and I liked what I found. There were a lot of crow legends and stories. I particularly liked the fact that crow was supposed to be the keeper of the laws and the messenger between realms of reality. Crow, as a totem, was all about finding your voice and speaking out loud and clear. Those all sounded like things I aspired to be or become. I especially liked a little folk rhyme I found: "One crow for sorrow, two for joy." I decided to name myself Two Crows, hoping it would bring me joy.

Armed with a cool name, new friends and a confidence like jelly, I began to study further. First thing I needed to do, I decided, was find out if elephant really was my totem animal. As the months passed, I noticed that the more I tried to see him, the more he was there. Even more amazing was the fact he was beginning to interact with me. He was MOVING in my mind, not simply a static image popping up in my thoughts at random times.

To put this into perspective for anyone who doesn't quite understand the difference: I can easily visualise things in my mind. Ask me to think of an elephant and already I'm seeing an African elephant, ears moving slightly, standing in long dry grass. So what was the difference with this particular elephant? A lot. The first time I tried to check whether or not I was simply having elephants pop into my mind because I was thinking of them, I did exactly as I've just described. I sat and imagined an elephant. Once it was there in my mind, all nice and tidy and logically my mind's creation... a second elephant zoomed past on a skateboard wearing a pink panama hat.

Uh.... Where did THAT come from? I cleared my mind and tried again, creating a tidy image of... once again, a second elephant I was NOT trying to visualise went past. This time it was wearing a sombrero and shaking maracas. The more I tried to get rid of it, the more it was there. Clearly, I had finally made contact with my totem animal because this elephant refused to go away. I went onto the forums and formally declared that I had found my totem, but as time went by I began to notice something disturbing.

I'm not sure if it's spiritually correct to compare totems, but that was what I did and the results were embarrassing. Other people on the forums spoke about these great dreams or grand meditation journeys where their totem animals came to them with amazing and profound stuff. In all of them, these totem animals were noble wild beasts who acted accordingly. Leopards snarled, wolves howled and eagles soared in their stories. And me? Well, my ellie stood upright on his hind legs and danced past me, grinning wide, wearing a hula skirt.

Yes, you read that right. Instead of seeing some proud, wild beast in my mind, my totem had firmly morphed into a cartoon elephant. The kind of ellie you'd expect to see in a Disney movie, except... he was kinda vulgar. That was equally embarrassing. How could I tell the forums that the day I was wondering if my ellie was a he or a she, HE had come up close and waggled enormous male elephant genitals in my face? And how on earth could I ever share the fact he was fond of fart jokes?

I tentatively shared some information about him, but I could feel the unspoken vibe of "Your totem did WHAT?" in some of the replies. Like the fact he shot peanuts at me with his trunk when I wasn't paying him enough attention. Honestly, I felt like those parents who take their little darling to pre-school only to have the teacher tell them that their child is the class oddball. My elephant was neither noble nor wild, but he was amusing and I loved him all the more for that. Plus, he did have this adorable habit of blowing little, pink, heart-shaped bubbles from his trunk.

I wasn't the only one to fall for his quirky charms.

Several of my forum friends were equally delighted by his complete disregard for fitting in to the rules of totem animals. One friend suggested he might be a trickster spirit. I had to look that up and in doing so found another Native American belief I liked – Heyoka, the sacred clowns. Yeah, my ellie was certainly a clown! But was he sacred? What on earth was this twinkly-eyed, fat-bottomed grey imp who was slowly taking over my mind? Was this mad elephant really my totem animal?

A turning point in our relationship was the day he came in waving a feather in his trunk. It was a white feather. He kept waggling it at me, playfully. My first thought was Dumbo, the Flying Elephant. The crows gave him a feather and told him it was magic so that he'd believe he could fly. The humour of an elephant now waving a feather at a woman named Crow was very much his style. Was my ellie trying to tell me something? I tried mentally acknowledging the Dumbo story of trusting your abilities, but my elephant waggled the feather harder, as if frustrated. Clearly, I was missing something.

This feather was white, not black. Not a crow feather, so what was it? I tried dowsing a few questions, but the results were too vague. I had started using a pendulum for YES-NO answers in 2001 after meeting Siromani who had dowsed my photo to leave me her astrology books. My father's father was a genuine dowser, using a fresh cut stick to find water for farmers in Africa. He also used the same technique to find the stones and minerals he collected.

I had hoped I shared his talent, but hadn't shown any until I met Siromani and she showed me how she used a pendulum on a chain. I had a small crystal ball about the size of a marble which hung from a necklace. I found that I could use that more easily. Holding it so that it was free to move on its chain, I would ask for a circle for YES or a straight side-to-side movement for NO and the opposite direction for MAYBE.

A side note and warning to anyone considering trying dowsing or using a pendulum: if you are dowsing for water or minerals, you are picking up on pure energy. This was how Siromani used it. Her doctor would lay out proposed new medications so that she could see for herself which ones suited her health problems best. That type of dowsing is completely safe, but using a pendulum to connect to God or your Higher Self in order to answer questions always has some risk that you may accidentally connect to something/someone else. Always say a prayer or blessing of some kind before you use a pendulum to ask questions. You want to be certain your replies come from a reliable source!

I had used my crystal pendulum a few times in Africa and found it worked well. I decided to try using it on my clearly frustrated, feather-waving elephant. I started trying out a few basic questions about this feather. I asked if the feather was important. It swung to MAYBE and my elephant winked. *Was it related to Dumbo?* MAYBE. Ellie did a few cabaret style dance moves.

Was it about trusting myself? MAYBE. Ellie waggled

the feather again. Was it a swan feather? Seagull? My mind raced through white birds and my crystal pendulum stopped swinging. Not even a maybe. I went onto the forums and asked for help.

The replies were in-depth shamanistic suggestions and questions. What colour was the feather? Had I looked up that colour symbolism? On which side did the elephant hold the feather? Had I looked up directional symbolism? Had I read feather medicine? Had I studied the medicine wheel directions? All excellent questions, except none of it felt right and my ellie was still waving madly. The real message would come through a completely different source, thanks to a dream I'd had a day earlier. I dreamt of a whale that swam up to me and said, "Trust. Believe."

So how did a dream of a talking whale and an impish, feather-waving elephant connect? Well, that happened about a day after I asked for help on the forum. It was a friend's birthday and I went looking for a nice e-card. I was browsing cards when one caught my attention: it was a picture of a whale. I went to look at it and the website put a row of other e-cards below it. That "People who chose *that* also liked *this*" type of thing many places do to advertise. In the row of cards below the whale was a card with a big white feather floating in a blue sky.

A big white feather? I clicked on the link to go look at the feather e-card. It was an animated e-card. As I watched with my heart thumping in my ears, the white feather became a feather pen and the sky became a scroll.

The pen wrote out these words:

BELIEVE

To believe is to know in your heart
that life is happening exactly as it is meant to.

TRUST

To believe is to trust that everything
is going to be alright.

To believe is to look for hidden gifts
in every new day.

I believe in you.

As I read those words, my ellie came in and wrapped his trunk around me in a hug. He had finally found a way to send me words. He believed in me; I remember having tears in my eyes at that thought. My dream whale had said, "Trust. Believe." Both words were used on that e-card. I wonder if a chubby ellie had wedged himself into a dream whale shape in order to leave a clue to follow.

Hmmm… I think I just felt an elephant wink.

12

In Scotland, my dreams had started again, but these were more complex as well as more vivid. At this stage, I was saving them into a computer document instead of writing them into my old dream journal. I'll jump ahead here and say that I have since been told by my spirit guide that dream interpretation should be approached with open-minded caution. In the dream state, our minds are less attached to this dimensional reality and that makes it easier for others to connect and communicate with us. The dream state also sets our subconscious free, allowing us space to problem-solve and release fears, desires and old memories.

Basically, there are three types of dreams:
1. Dreams that are purely our minds sorting out our recent experiences in order to store them for future reference.

2. Dreams that are our subconscious urging us to deal with our life problems. These dreams often include deeply personal symbolism.

3. Psychic dreams where we travel elsewhere or others communicate with us.

To make things more complicated, everyone is capable of having a mix of all three types in one dream. That is why it is never a good idea to trust dream symbolism books completely as their symbolism is too generic. It's also important to understand that not everything in a dream is symbolic. Sometimes a cigar really is just a cigar.

During the early years of studying shamanism, I experienced lucid and shared dreams, which are both exceptionally cool experiences. Lucid dreams are those dreams where we are consciously aware of dreaming. These can be great fun since you get to play the role of dream director as well as actor. My most thrilling lucid dream happened in the first week after we moved from a flat to a house in 2003. It was also my second out-of-body (OOB) experience, those rare times when your consciousness separates from your physical body.

The first time I ever experienced an OOB state was sixteen years earlier in 1987. I was a student in college and I had woken up extra early, mostly due to pre-exam nerves. As I lay on my back planning the day ahead, I suddenly had this feeling of being poured out my own skin. Have you ever turn over a bottle of water and watch how the water spins and gurgles as it rushes out? That is exactly what it felt like, except I rushed out of my own navel and went UP instead of down.

I went from bewildered amazement at being up on the ceiling looking down at myself in bed to instant panic as I realised that was MY body in the bed. The moment I panicked, there was this feeling like a giant, elastic band going *TWANG* and I was back in bed in my body. Of course, the moment I was back in my body I felt immense disappointment. If only I had not panicked and shot back, what flying adventures would I have been able to have?

The OOB dream I had in 2003 was far less dramatic... at first. This dream started pleasantly with me travelling down a corridor in a fancy hotel. Everything felt so real. I could hear the muffled footsteps of staff walking past me on the hotel's thick, soft carpeting and hear them talking. I noticed the gold wallpaper and marble pillars. As people passed me, I realised that I seemed to be slightly above them, as if I were flying. That was also when I noticed that I couldn't see my feet. I had no body.

I was completely thrilled to realise that this was more than a lucid dream. I seemed to be in a real place. I was actually there out-of-body, travelling in the dream state. *Oooooh... super cool!* I floated about for a while, exploring the building. Judging by the staff, the ceiling fans and luxury, I guessed it was a hotel in India that had once been a palace or grand home.

I decided to take a look at it from outside and flew out the main front doors, over the heads of people at the reception desk and young men in crisp, white uniforms carrying their cases. I felt the sudden change from the cooler interior to harsh, hot sunlight. There was a small, formal garden between the hotel and a busy main road. It was a hot, arid place with no grass, just lines of trees with benches and flower beds set out along paved pathways.

I noticed a man sitting on one of the benches and flew over to take a look at him. Even though the hotel and street were full of people, this man stood out. He seemed brighter and clearer. He sat on the bench in the lotus position, wearing only a white loin cloth. He was thin with shoulder length hair. Unlike everyone else, he looked up at me as if he could actually see me. *Must be my imagination.*

I turned away to look around me. The street was noisy with vehicles and people. *Was I really in India?* I felt excited as I looked up at the bright blue sky showing between the branches of the trees. *Could I fly up there?* My mind thought *I could see the stars,* and I flew up like a torpedo. I was a comet, zooming through the blue and beyond into darkness. I felt drunk with elation as I flew through a billion stars. Finally, I remembered Earth and turned to look back at my world from above....

There was nothing there.

I had flown out so far that I had lost sight of the planet. I turned in a circle, suddenly aware that there was nothing but stars every way I looked. My elation became worry, then outright fear. I was completely lost with no idea where Earth was or how to get back.

There is no way to describe how that felt, how completely alone and empty space seemed at that moment. Then I heard him. A soft, monotone voice with a gentle Indian accent said, "Lady? Lady? Lady."

He kept repeating the word until I calmed down. I focussed on his voice and felt myself being pulled back, zooming faster than the speed of light. I was back in front of my Indian guru-man on the bench. This time, it was obvious he could see me and I realised he was quite young, probably in his twenties. He smiled at me and I remember he had distinctive crooked or broken front teeth. That was where the dream ended. I haven't ever again managed an OOB experience and don't particularly want to. I don't think I'm responsible enough to be left in charge of myself without a body.

The shared dreams were the most quirky I've experienced. The first one was fairly bland as far as dreams go. I dreamt that I owned a pet bird. He was a small, brightly coloured parrot, more cartoonish than real bird. He could smile and I remember how he laughed like a person when I tickled him. He was adorable... and then he died. I was sitting holding his little dead body when the dream ended.

That afternoon, I went onto the forums to browse a bit and noticed that a person I knew vaguely had left a post on the dream forum. I think it was actually titled "Bird Dream" or something similar. I was curious and went to read it. The forum member, a woman named Kim, said that she had this sweet dream about a cute little bird she owned, more cartoonish than real, brightly coloured. It laughed when she played with it, tickling it… but then it died. She wanted to know if anyone had ideas about what this dream might mean.

I'm sure my mouth was hanging open by then. Her dream was almost identical to my own, except the bird colours she saw were slightly different. I had to reply. Feeling like a bit of an ass, I went in and wrote that I'd had the same dream. I explained my version, hoping I didn't sound completely nuts. Thankfully, Kim not only believed me, she found the idea of a shared dream fascinating. We started to chat, which in turn led us to email and we have been close friends ever since.

About a year later, we shared another dream and this one was even stranger. In this dream, I was in the bathroom at night. The house we lived in at that time had an upstairs bathroom with a window set into the roof looking directly up at the sky. By then we had moved again to a bigger house, as my parents had joined us in Scotland and we needed two double bedrooms. My parents had wanted to have their own place, but due to various problems we eventually decided that it made more sense to live together.

Our plan at that stage was to rent this bigger house while we looked for land to buy. With a husband who was a builder and a father who was an electrician, we figured we could buy some decent land and build a house with a "granny flat" to suit all our needs. The new, bigger house had two double bedrooms and two bathrooms, which made life a lot easier for everyone.

In my dream, I was washing my hands when I looked up at the window and realised that the sky was full of fireballs. There was no sound, just these fiery things, like enormous comets, flying quite slowly across the night sky. You would think that would be terrifying, but I felt excited. I told Sandy, then went and woke my parents who were asleep in bed. I said to them, "It has begun," and they nodded at me, as if they were not surprised.

My parents got up and started to dress, while I took their already packed suitcases down to the car. I have no idea where we were going, but the mood was good. It felt as if we had been expecting this for quite some time. I remember that I put our luggage into the back of a blue hatch-back car. At the time, we owned a dark green hatch-back and my parents had recently bought a large blue sedan. If I look out the window today, that blue hatch-back from my dream is parked outside. We bought it in 2012 from a dealer, but we did not know the colour until it arrived. Quite a strange feeling.

Returning to 2006 and my dream: I was talking to Kim a day or so later and I spoke about my strange dream. She told me that once again we had shared dreams, but hers was a bit different this time. Kim dreamt that she was at a barbecue at an old boyfriend's house. She was outside with friends and family. When I started this book, I wrote and asked her if she remembered the dream. Here is what she replied:

> I looked up and saw meteors or stars (fireballs?) shooting across the sky from right to left, one after another. I had this feeling of awe, anticipation and excitement. I knew it was time (for what??) and said, "It's started."

Since our dreams happened in 2006, we both joked about the so-called Mayan 2012 Apocalypse at the time and whether there be giant fire balls in the sky. 2012 came and went with no end of the world, but there have been sightings of giant fireballs in the skies over the past few years. I've looked at news coverage of some of them and my friend confirms the same – they look exactly like the ones we dreamed of, except for us the sky was full of them, not just one at a time.

There has been one small update to this story. In 2016 I woke up one morning thinking, "It's started." A few hours later, Kim emailed me and said that she knew this made no sense, but she had a feeling that something had changed worldwide. I wrote back, "It has begun?" She replied, agreeing that was her feeling as well, except neither of us knows what that means. Such are the joys and frustrations of being psychic. It can leave you with more questions and riddles than answers.

But of all the dreams I had during my first years in Scotland, there is one that stands out above them all. I keep it in a separate word document along with all the research I have done as well as research friends have sent me. This dream happened in 2004 and I call it "The Last Rider." Here it is, exactly as I wrote it down that first morning:

> I'm working at a restaurant at a seaside holiday hotel. There's a young guy there who has become my friend. He's about 15 years younger than me, dark curly hair and good

looking. He works as a waiter, but he's quit as he hates the job. I get the feeling my time working there is at an end as well. We're standing in the back chatting and I ask if he's going to go down to the beach before he goes. He lives far away and won't get a chance to see the beach again. He says he never thought of that and seems pleased I suggested it.

He goes to his backpack and takes something out of it. It looks like a gold rod with knobs on each end. It's about 4 inches long. Then he grabs my hand and pulling me through the kitchen saying we're both going to go look at the sea. The chef yells at us as we dash past out the back door. I say "They can't fire you, you've resigned."

We dash out and down back metal steps, laughing like naughty kids. There's grass and bushy vegetation and a steep slope down to a rocky coastline. Kind of scrubby land, like bog/moor vegetation. I can see the coastline is shaped and the closer to the edge of the drop down we get the clearer it is to me. The coastline is shaped like a giant horse with its head flung up into the sea, its flared nostril is a shallow rock pool full of sea sand. The head was shaped like the Grecian horses you see carved out of marble. Lovely, but a bit chunky and angular, not the graceful, narrow nosed Arabian horse profile. At first it seemed huge, but as we got closer I realised the head was roughly twice the size of a life horse. So big, but not gigantic.

The stone it was made of was a dark grey coastal rock, volcanic maybe. It was quite smooth. My friend bent down by the horse's head and took sandpaper out his pocket. The ear had been slightly chipped and he started smoothing it. As he worked the horse opened its eye! The eye was real! A big, brown horse eye looking at us! I was scared my friend would hurt the eye with the sandpaper, but he put the sandpaper away and took out a tiny pot and small paintbrush instead. He started painting gold lines on the horse's head.

At first I was really angry that he was defacing this incredible creature with graffiti, but it slowly dawned on me what he was painting and I felt an incredible rush of exhilaration. I knew what he was doing and why. He was painting on a bridle and the odd gold rod he still carried in his other hand was a bridle bit. I was thrilled by my sudden understanding. I knew that he was bringing the horse to life, that my friend was the "Last Rider".

I was kneeling beside him on the rocks and as he painted, I started to say these words. Like a poem or a prayer. My voice was loud, strong and full of certainty. I felt incredibly good and exhilarated and such joy. It was time for the Last Rider to ride the dark horse.

I knew I was speaking Hebrew even though I had no idea what the words were about. Unfortunately, after I woke up I could only remember bits as I spoke too long to remember it all. It seemed to be in verses as each "portion" started with the same line of one repeated word: "Elohim, Elohim, Elohim." That word three times at the beginning of each verse, which I would say was about four or five lines long. I remember saying Shaddai and/or El Shaddai Addonai. (? unsure of spelling here, I'm spelling them as they sounded.) Also something with an "M", but that's all. It's hard to remember entire verses in a language you don't speak!

At one stage, I ran out of breath and fell forward onto my hands, gasping. I heard an old man's voice saying, "I haven't done that in a while!" and I realised I'd been channelling someone. By the sounds of the voice I'd say an old Jewish man. He sounded a nice, jolly sort. That was where I woke up.

I awoke feeling amazingly good. Reborn. This dream was too big not to share, so I put it up on a forum I trusted. I pointed out that although I did not speak Hebrew, I had recognised the word Elohim. The really interesting thing at the time was that this dream felt more Jewish than Christian. I realised part way through the dream that my young friend, the Last Rider, was Jewish. The only horses I've ever heard of were those in Revelations. I did read up on them, but it all felt wrong. The last horse in Revelations is white. This was a dark horse and it wasn't a Christian message. Don't ask me how I know that. It was just a feeling.

Another dear friend, Minna, was the first to respond. She knew a few of the words and since she was retired and had more spare time than me, she had gone and done research. All the words are Hebrew names for God and are often used in similar format for Jewish and Kabbalah invocations. I still have all her research saved, which includes that M word I couldn't remember correctly – Malachim, the Biblical name for angels who work as messengers.

At this stage I still don't completely understand this dream, but I have never forgotten it. My friend, Minna, still remembers it, too. She regularly sends me photos of rocky coasts or horses that remind her of my dream. Even now, years later, if I stop and remember that dream I still feel this wave of exhilaration. I still have no clear idea what it means, but I was to find out a lot more about the old Jewish man in the future.

13

By 2006, I had become accustomed to the goofy elephant in my head. He would pop into my mind at completely random moments. Since the feather-waving message, I was trying to take him more seriously. Not easy, since most times he seemed to stop by merely to make me laugh. My forum friends suggested I turn to him for advice, as any good shaman would do with their totem animal. I can't remember anything specific from that time, but I do remember thinking that I was finally understanding my elephant properly.

How wrong I was! The truth is that I was never good at charades and there were times when I failed badly in my attempts to translate elephant mime. One of the best examples is the day my elephant sat on a friend's boyfriend. A friend of mine came to me for help. Her boyfriend had dumped her without any notice or explanation. She was hoping I might be able to use my abilities to find out why.

I formally asked my elephant totem for help. My ellie appeared and showed me a picture of himself sitting on the man and squashing him flat. This made perfect sense to me. I knew how broken-hearted and shocked my friend was. If any man did that to me, I'd also want an elephant to squash him flat! I told my friend what I had seen and we both agreed that this was well-deserved punishment. We both had a good laugh at the idea. My friend went away, thanking me for cheering her up and I went off feeling triumphant in my new vocation of elephant whisperer. But I was totally wrong.

Months later, I bumped into the friend and asked her how she was doing. She told me she was back with her ex and everything was sorted out. In fact, he had always loved her and never wanted to let her go. I was confused. So why had he dumped her? She told me that he had been going through some personal problems and suffering badly with depression. He felt that he was a burden and decided it would be better to set her free. He told her that the depression felt like a grinding weight pushing him down.

Umm… a bit like having an elephant squash you flat?

That was my most humbling moment of getting a message utterly wrong. I had jumped to a conclusion instead of simply telling my friend what I saw. I still have moments when I do this. The urge to deduce the meaning in things is something I always have to be aware of. My personal opinions are like pesky buzzy insects I have to constantly bat out the way. I like to think I'm much better at simply sharing the messages without trying to interpret them, but I'm sure my ellie would roll his eyes in mock pain if he saw me write that. He won't because he's not here much nowadays and the reason for that is the next stage of my story.

It all changed one night in 2006 while I was watching TV. It was a show where they trace family trees for people. That week, it was a British actor who was tracing his family tree, in particular his mother's side which was Jewish. In one rather gruelling portion, he returned to the small village in Eastern Europe where his mother's family originally came from. The tiny place is deserted now; all the inhabitants were sent away to Auschwitz and other camps.

As he was walking through the long-deserted buildings, a man's voice began to wail in my head. This was different to anything I'd experienced before. This voice was LOUD. So loud that it completely wiped out my own ability to think. So loud it was almost an actual sound. I couldn't understand what he was saying, but the language sounded like Hebrew. I can only describe the tone as lamenting. I was so surprised I finally managed to send a thought back.

Who are you?

A shocked voice said, "You can hear me?" and then went silent.

I don't remember the rest of the TV show. I was sitting there in a daze. Another Jewish man. Was this person the same man who spoke Hebrew through me in the Last Rider dream? Were the two voices the same person? And if so, who was he? I honestly can't say how long it took for me to sort this mystery out, but I'd guess that it probably took at least six months. A lot of things were happening in my life at that time. I was working from home at a writing job that often kept me at the computer all day and most of the night. Watching TV was a rare treat.

I spent most of that time too busy and tired to look into who the Jewish man was, but I did notice a change in my elephant totem. He was becoming more active in trying to send me messages, using more obvious mime and sometimes even writing words onto an old-fashioned child's chalkboard. He'd hold the chalk in his trunk, write on the little blackboard and then hold it up and wave it at me. It would only be a word or a very short sentence, but that was still quite a significant breakthrough for me.

It was also rather peculiar behaviour for a totem animal. Totem animals are supposed to be the spirits of actual dead animals or the essence of real animals. Surely real animals didn't write words? I think I had always suspected my ellie was more than an elephant totem. Actual elephants do not normally wear berets, sombreros or any other type of hat, nor do they dance upright shaking maracas.

Months passed by in a blur of doing too many things, but I finally found some quiet time. I'd had my doubts about this elephant for a while now and I needed answers. I went and got my crystal pendulum necklace, which I hadn't used for several years. Armed with that and a notebook, I sat my ellie down and gave him a thorough interrogation.

Are you an animal? The pendulum swung to NO.

Are you a totem? There was a pause, then the pendulum once again answered NO.

My elephant hid his face behind a large paper fan, eyes peeping over the top like a flirtatious Japanese maiden. Cute, but I wasn't buying it any more.

Are you a spirit guide? MAYBE.

He blew me kisses with his trunk that turned into tiny, pink, heart-shaped bubbles. I took a deep breath, ignoring the bubbles floating around me. It was time to ask the big question.

Are you the man I heard speaking Hebrew? The elephant wobbled, like heat haze. YES.

My elephant became translucent, like mist or steam, and for a few moments I could see a man sitting where it had been. He was rather chubby, bearded with dark greying hair and slightly olive skin. He reminded me a lot of Obelix from my teenage-years favourite Asterix cartoon books, if Obelix had been Jewish. This unknown man had a sweet smile and the naughtiest sparkly eyes. Smile of an angel, but eyes like an imp, just like my elephant! He waved at me and blew me a kiss that turned into tiny, pink, heart-shaped bubbles.

From that day forward, I began fitting the pieces into place. A spirit-being had been using the form of an elephant to communicate with me. He'd chosen that shape because my mind found the idea of seeing a person too disturbing. A cartoon elephant in your head is quirky, maybe even a bit crazy, but still amusing enough to cope with. The idea of a person wandering around in my thoughts was simply creepy.

Through the use of my pendulum, I managed to patch together a story from this man. YES, he was Jewish. YES, he was my spirit guide. YES, he was dead and had last lived here a long time ago. We plodded back through time, pendulum swinging to NO until I had gone back over 500 years. YES, he had lived on Earth over 500 years ago. I asked for a name, reciting the alphabet until he swung the pendulum to YES when I reached S.

My mind searched for Jewish names starting with S.... *Samuel?* NO. *Solomon?* YES.

THE Solomon? Was my dear mad ellie the Biblical man of wisdom? The man in my mind turned back into an elephant and made loud fart noises with his trunk as the pendulum answered, NO.

That was a relief. I didn't want a famous person as a spirit guide. Too cliché and far too much of a burden. My elephant had a name at last. Yes, I still saw him as an elephant. Now and then I'd catch glimpses of the man smiling at me lovingly, but most times he preferred mucking about in my mind as an elephant. Much more fun being an elephant.

I went onto the shaman forums and declared that I had a spirit guide after all and his name was Sol. A few people admitted they'd had a hunch my mad ellie was more than I thought he was. Impressed at my breakthrough, people asked if I could hear him better now. Not really. I had to admit we were still using the chalkboard and mime.

Someone suggested meditating to connect deeper, perhaps even channelling his spirit and letting him talk through me. Absolutely not. I refused to try that. As fond as I was of Sol, that sounded far too invasive. I was still getting used to having my mind invaded by a Jewish, miming elephant. The last thing I wanted was for him to find his voice.

14

During the months that my elephant was becoming Sol the spirit guide, I had two profound experiences. They have nothing in common except the time period in which they happened. One of those experiences is hard to write about, but it needs to be here. It was one of the saddest yet most beautiful experiences of my life. It was also the first time that music was used as a form of communication. The other was a puzzle that is still ongoing. I'll start with that one first. This story actually started in 2002 when I first met Sandy. I dreamt of him and a distinctive house.

In the dream, Sandy, a mutual friend and I had pooled our money to buy an old house. The mutual friend in the dream was a complete stranger – no one that either Sandy or I actually knew in real life. The dream started with me standing outside looking at the house. It wasn't like any house design I knew from

Africa. It was a very large, double story with two big bay windows and a central front door at ground level with two matching, big bay windows upstairs.

It was in a bad state, with white paint peeling off and the garden overgrown. It seemed to be in the countryside because I don't remember seeing any houses around it. I went inside and it was in the same state of neglect, with old paint and faded wallpaper. There were paint pots and tools lying about, but no furniture anywhere. It seemed that the mutual friend was living/sleeping in the basement, mostly because he was a musician. I could hear the sound of someone practising on a guitar coming up from below my feet.

I don't know where Sandy was sleeping, but in the next part of my dream I was upstairs in a room that I had taken for myself. This bedroom had no curtains or furniture, just a bed in the middle of the room. Then we were all outside, in the back yard this time. The mutual friend was clearing up the garden and wanted to show us these weird oblongs of slightly raised earth out back. They looked like newly dug graves. I wrote the dream down at the time, but then forgot all about it when Sandy and I married and we started our life together in Scotland.

In 2005 we moved to a bigger house when my parents joined us. This interim, big house was a brand new property built on the edge of town. We decided to use the smallest upstairs bedroom as an office. I was too busy unpacking and reconnecting computers to take much notice of the view, but when I did finally look out the window I was stunned. From ground level, there was nothing to see. Our property was enclosed with a high, wooden fence and beyond that was a row of large old trees, but you could see over the trees from that back bedroom window.

There, beyond those trees, was an old house. It was stately, but clearly shabby… and it looked exactly like my dream house. I wondered if this "meant something." Were we going to buy this house? Or were we going to end up friends with the owner? Was the owner the unknown musician friend from my dream?

Well, we did get to meet the owner, but that was only because Sandy went over to complain. The owner was an anti-social man who kept very odd hours. He'd come screaming home in his sport's car at 3:00am and then do a bit of gardening, often burning garden refuse at the bottom of his driveway at 3:00 or 4:00 in the morning. He was obviously burning household rubbish as well because the smoke stank dreadfully.

That acrid, awful smoke was not only annoying, it was also revving up my mom's allergies and mine. When I started having asthma every night, Sandy went over to talk. The owner just laughed at Sandy and shut the door in his face. Long story short – we complained to every official we could think of and they were all useless. It was a harsh lesson in red tape idiocy. I could write quite a rant on the complete lack of common-sense of that whole fiasco.

In a strange twist of fate, we left before the issue was ever resolved. We moved to a much nicer house in the countryside, where the air was clear and the nearest neighbours were cows. Jump forward a few years and one day Sandy saw a photo of our anti-social ex-neighbour on the local TV news. He had been arrested for making and selling drugs. Our neighbour had a meth lab in his house! Heaven only knows what he was burning at 4:00am or what exactly he was burying when he gardened in the middle of the night.

Jump forward again to March 2017: Sandy called me to come take a look at something on his computer. The old house was up for sale. I was curious to see if it looked anything like my dream version inside. I went to the agent's website and clicked on the photos of the house. It was in a bad state with peeling wallpaper and bare floorboards. It looked exactly like my dream house, except dirtier. Do you remember the back yard in my dream with those raised, earth oblongs that looked like graves? I know what they are now. The back yard had raised beds for growing vegetables.

I still have no idea why I dreamed of that house in 2002 or why it still keeps popping up in our lives. One thing I am certain of though, we have no intention of buying it. It might have been a house in my dreams, but it is in no way my idea of my dream house!

Now I need to tell the second event that happened while we lived at that address. This began in early July 2005. I woke up one morning from a dream and found myself singing a song. I was actually moving my mouth and hearing the lyrics in my mind as I woke. The song was "How Deep is Your Love" by the Bee Gees. The dream had been exceptionally vivid, the way my important dreams always are, and the lyrics to this song made it all the more haunting.

The song is a love song, but it has a wistful and slightly challenging tone. The lyrics are about someone who isn't always there or who may not be there in the future. It speaks of knowing another completely and of feeling that loved-one's presence in the natural beauty of summer. That summer morning, I knew who the loved-one was. I had dreamt of her that night.

In my dream, I was sitting in a sunny room watching a little girl riding about on a tricycle. She had shoulder-length brown hair and a serious little face. I called her over to me and asked her if she'd let me make her a dress. I asked if she would wear it if I made it for her. Would she wear my gift? She stared up at me, very thoughtful for such a young child. She never smiled. She seemed uncertain, but she did nod YES before cycling away.

I knew who she was. Or at least, I knew who she could possibly become. I'd known for a while that I was pregnant. I'd felt the changes in my body within days. I wasn't surprised that this little girl soul had serious doubts. I knew what the dress meant; it was the body my biology would create for her. The outer self she would wear if she agreed to be born. I was forty-two with a history of severe endometriosis; the chances of this ending well were not great. The likelihood of children born with physical defects increases as women get older. I understood why my little girl was so serious. Would she be as elusive as the lyrics of that haunting song?

Later that morning, I told Sandy about my dream and my suspicions that I was pregnant. While I made a doctor's appointment, he dashed off to the pharmacy to buy a home pregnancy test. By that afternoon, I had confirmed what I already knew: I was pregnant. It was the 4th of July, but we waited until the doctor's official confirmation before celebrating the news with friends and family. Sandy and I were determined to be optimistic and that is exactly what we did, from beginning to end. I remember going for our first ultrasound. Sandy sat next to me as they pointed out the tiny blob that was to be our baby one day. It all feels surreal looking back.

Days became weeks as I adjusted to this new adventure happening within my own body. I was in town on a sunny, summery day, having lunch out with my mom and husband, when I realised something wasn't right. A part of me knew even before I realised I was bleeding. That feeling of life-force energy inside me had vanished.

We returned home and I phoned the doctor. It was an automated service: dial 1 for appointments, 2 for emergencies. I remember the main line was engaged with a long waiting list and it was already quite late in the afternoon, so I pressed the button for emergencies. Our local medical practice at that time was a miserable place full of equally miserable staff. The woman who answered the emergency line blasted me when I said I wanted to see a doctor.

"You are not supposed to use this line," she snapped. "This is for emergencies only!"

But she shut up and put me through when I said, "Well... I think I'm having a miscarriage."

The doctor saw me straight away and made certain I was sent directly for another ultrasound the next day. This time it was so different. Once again, I was back in the same dark room with the same nurse, but this time she quickly asked us to wait as she went to call a doctor. Two doctors came in and looked at the screen before going to talk outside. It is one of the worst memories. Even though I already knew, when the nurse came back to explain there was no heartbeat (I'd already noticed) I could not stop the tears.

No heartbeat. The nurse put us in a side room to weigh up our options. I think they offered us tea. No heartbeat. They told me that I could be put into a ward straight away for a medical abortion, or we could just wait for nature to take its course. We decided to wait. I don't remember going back to the car, but I do remember that Sandy took the back road home. It was a quiet route through farms and fields. We stopped on the side of the road and cried for a while, then went home and told all the family.

The next day, I went online and updated all my internet friends. My friends on the shaman forums were amazing, offering all sorts of help which all basically boiled down to, "You are our friend and we love you." Don't let anyone tell you internet friends are not real friends. When I have needed support of any kind, those internet friends have always been there for me. One man did long distance healing on me and another posted me a box of sage for smudging as well as several crystals. Two women tried reiki. So much love. It was amazing, but I already knew it was over.

Our little girl had decided to refuse my dress.

One morning, I woke up with a new song whirling in my mind. It was another Bee Gees song, "Run to Me." The lyrics have to be some of the most comforting ever written. If you have been torn apart, run to me. The message was very clear this time: No matter what the trouble is that you are facing, I am here for you. And there he was, an elephant in the room looming over me as I lay in bed. He was so big his head was partially through the ceiling. Once again, he had found a way to talk to me without speaking.

Later that day, I started having contractions. No one had told me that would happen. Seems crazy now, but not one medical person had actually told me what a miscarriage would entail or feel like. No one warned me that the same contractions that herald a birth can happen when your body chooses to let go of hope. I spent several hours waiting as the contractions picked up pace. It was an exceptionally long day.

That evening, I was supposed to be going into a forum chat room for a group study session. We were going to work on tarot card readings, but once they realised what was happening, they simply stayed in the chat room with me and kept my mind occupied as I waited. In all the pain and fear there were these people who loved me. A strange night of such extremes.

It was also the first (and the last!) time I ever got drunk. The contractions had put my back out, adding an old pain on top of the new and all I had at home were paracetamol tablets and they were no use at all. Sandy brought me a whisky or two or three. I flung them back without counting and by midnight I was finally feeling no pain. I remember standing in the doorway, getting ready for bed and not being able to stop giggling. I thought, *so this is why people get drunk.*

I fell asleep instantly, but woke about two hours later with a hangover slammed down on top of a body fighting loss of blood as well as hormone and electrolyte imbalances. I will never, EVER get drunk like that again. Sandy had to take me in to hospital, where they gave me medications and loads of sympathy before popping me into a bed at the furthest end of the maternity ward to ensure I wasn't more stressed by where I was.

Months passed and life returned to how it had been before. Except things never are the same as before, are they? I kept busy with my writing job and when I had the time, I would go to the forums to discuss and learn. One day, a woman from one of the forums emailed me. She said that she had a message for me, but wasn't sure how I'd react. We knew each other on the forums, but were only acquaintances. This woman told me that a little girl had contacted her. She suspected it was the baby I'd lost. I hadn't told anyone that I had known the gender of my baby, so I was impressed that this woman knew as well. I wrote back and told her it was okay to tell me.

I hadn't read that email message in years. I had to dig around in my computer to find it and the reply emails we sent to each other afterwards. There are things in them that I don't remember at all. I won't put that here, it is too long and personal, but I will say that the forum woman was 100% spot on with some things and partially correct with others.

She wrote about choices, life paths, and then said that this pregnancy had been two hearts joined. She finished by describing the little girl who came to her, but the child she saw was not my serious little dream girl on the tricycle. This woman saw a slightly older child, but an equally serious little girl. She described this girl's hair and clothes as well as the little dog standing on a chair behind her. I knew the girl and the dog because I had the photograph. It was a picture of my late grandmother, my mother's mother.

15

Talking about my grandmother and messages from the other side reminded me of something I had completely forgotten: how and why I picked my first shaman forum. It was all due to a message that was left there for me before I knew the place existed. I think I need to tackle the topic of messages before I go any further. I've had messages in dreams as well as messages given to me while awake. They can come from all kinds of sources; God, angels, spirit guides, elementals, dodgy elephants or dead people.

In many cases, the reasons for a dead person wanting to send a message are fairly obvious. A big percentage of messages are from people who die too fast and leave behind some unresolved issue. Mostly this boils down to everyone wanting a chance to say a proper goodbye and "I love you" one more time. Other common messages are warnings and words of comfort.

Anyone can be sent or receive a message. This is not an exclusive club for psychics. People with strong psychic abilities might tune in better and faster, but if God, angels, or someone you loved really wants to contact you, they will find a way. There are endless stories about people who were warned, in one way or another, away from potential death and harm. Most of us have had them happen without even realising it because messages can be subtle and complex with multiple layers of symbolism.

An example I experienced several years back was the day I went into an office on a business meeting. There, inside the office on the floor by reception, was a white feather. I'm not sure why, but I picked it up. I was going to throw it into a bin, but before I could do any such thing, the man I was there to see came out his office. He held out his hand to shake mine, and there I was, holding a feather. To my surprise, his eyes filled up with tears. Once we were in his office, he told me how someone in his family had recently passed away. His wife had read about passed loved ones sending signs that they were still there, watching from heaven. This man had decided to pray for such an answer and he asked for a specific sign – he wanted a white feather.

Messages can come to anyone and in so many ways and for so many reasons. In most cases, they are so subtle we can easily overlook them. Although psychics might be the best at receiving all types of messages, anyone can improve their own abilities. It's mostly about being aware and paying attention. As a bird-watcher, I can walk down a street and recognise several birds around me by their calls. That isn't a supernatural gift. It comes about through me loving, listening and observing birds. As I said, it's all about paying attention and trusting that what feels like the truth is the truth.

I personally don't believe that psychic abilities are spiritual or supernatural. I think some of these abilities are vestiges of some primitive ability we lost as we evolved, while others are simply human talents we don't understand and therefore have never bothered to nurture or train. Think of a normal child born into a world of deaf people. What would happen if that unique, hearing child discovered they could sing? With no one to hear, would that child be considered delusional, supernatural or even evil?

There is, from my experience, a definite connection between these extra-sensory abilities and the physical. My mother's ability to sense disasters stopped when she went onto strong medications. That is a physical connection. My abilities leaped forward twice after major surgeries. Physical.

This is also why I roll my eyes when I read about people who consider themselves spiritually superior because they are psychic. Nope. It's just another human ability, the same as singing. Some of us are going to sing opera and some of us will sound like dying frogs, but to some degree all of us understand and enjoy music. What frustrates and saddens me is the fact that the child who can sing will probably find tutors while the child who sees things may either be laughed at, told they are evil/delusional, or popped onto pills to stop them seeing things.

I once read on a forum about a psychic who had hidden their abilities for thirty years. This person told how they had spoken out as a child, but been beaten for being bad and different. Sadly, many people choose to attack and destroy anything they don't understand out of fear. To refuse to deal with something simply because we don't yet understand it seems like such a waste of a human potential. Maybe that's why we need more people like me, who are willing to talk and share instead of hiding away? Maybe....

Back to messages and in particular the kind that include actual words. For most people, if you mention those types of psychic messages they automatically think of that person on TV standing in front of an audience saying something like, "I have a Bob here. Bob? Barry? Ben?"

A lot of cynics use the TV psychic fumbling for an answer as a prime example of this all being fake. As a psychic I tend to agree. I suspect a lot of that kind of thing is faked. Not all of it, but a lot of it. It has to be because it's such a forced situation. I remember one psychic admitting to blood-cold terror at times when he'd stand in front of an audience and... nothing. Not one single dead person popped in to say hello. In his case, he was honest. He admitted he wasn't picking up anyone and a disappointed hall of people went home, but you can't exactly do that on a TV show! That tells me that TV producers must put "plants" into the audience. TV shows cost too much to have a psychic say, "I'm just not getting anything today."

In reality, receiving psychic messages is a bit like having a pet talking parrot. When you're alone, your parrot shouts, sings and talks all day, but the moment you invite your friends over to show off your amazing pet… dead silence. I have learnt that I can't force things. It either happens or it doesn't. The power isn't in my hands, I am merely the telephone wire. A bridge between worlds.

I have found that words can often be as easy to misunderstand as images. You would think that my elephant guide writing on a chalk board would be more clear and precise than him miming, but not necessarily. It took me ten years to understand why. I'll use my dear elephant as an example. Does Sol the ancient Jew speak modern English? No. And yet the words he used to write on the chalkboard were in English, so how does that work?

Think of the human mind as a computer. Your computer can upload English and tell you if you spelt something wrong, but the programming itself is written in computer code first. The human mind is similar. As babies, we experience life before we learn a language. None of us are born speaking a language. Instead, our baby minds experience the world purely through our senses. Long before we deal with grammar and syntax, our minds are absorbing things through our senses of sight, sound, touch and taste.

Now let's get back to Sol, my elephant spirit guide. Let's say he needs to communicate with me. We'll make up an imaginary thing such as a warning of danger. He could mime it or he could use symbols. The human mind loves symbols. Wouldn't it be easier to just write DANGER on his chalkboard? Yes and no. In his reality, he would be thinking of a word that meant danger, but it would be in his language. When he projects that image of himself into my mind, he is writing a word in his language, not English.

So how do I see the word as English? That is because the human mind is like a computer. What Sol projects into my mind is basically a coded command for me to see a man (or elephant) writing on a chalkboard. The command specifies that the word means danger. Since my mind is set to think in English, my brain creates an English word on the chalkboard and I see him write DANGER.

This is open to error since my mind has its own personal thesaurus. I have sometimes had a similar, but not quite right word show up. This is why psychics can struggle with details and get things almost right, but not completely correct. We are only as good as our own personal mental coding, you could say.

Now I can return to that message left for me on the first shaman forum I went onto. I admitted I was very nervous that day in 2003. I felt out of my depth. What I'd forgotten was what made me join that forum. I was browsing the various sections of this forum, reading about shamanism, when I noticed that they had a section for dream journals and messages. I went to take a look and in the list of posts was one titled: "A message from Cecil for V."

I had to read it because I knew a Cecil who had been married to a woman whose name started with V. I noticed that the post was about two weeks old and no one had replied to it. The person who had left the message said that a man named Cecil wanted to let V know he was fine now, happy and at peace. She should stop worrying and let him go.

I think I cried a bit before I answered. I said that the message made sense to me, even though I'd never known this place existed at the time this unknown psychic person wrote it. She replied back, saying that Cecil must have known I'd be passing through in the near future. Then I wrote and told her all I knew about my great uncle, Cecil.

Cecil was born in England and went out to Rhodesia as a pilot during WWII. We had an RAF base there during the war. That was where he made good friends with a man named Len Frost and eventually met and fell in love with Len's younger sister, Veronica. What can I tell you about my great uncle Cecil? I never got to see him often, but the few times I did were wonderful. He had the most wicked-funny sense of humour.

He built his own house in Rhodesia with a basement for all his handmade liqueurs. I still have his recipe for orange liqueur. Aunty Veronica was an accountant and ran her own business school with her sister. Uncle Cecil and Aunty Veronica were a kick-ass couple. Their home was in an area that was heavily attacked during the Rhodesian Bush War. They experienced some frightening things and yet it never seemed to get them down. Instead, they turned their experiences into adventure stories.

I remember Aunty Veronica telling us about the day

she fended off a group of terrorists who attacked her at home. She calmed them down by feeding them and then showed them into the wine cellar to help themselves. Once they were drunk and sleeping it off in the garden, she radioed for help. In the ensuing battle, all the terrorists were killed. Uncle Cecil showed us the bullet holes in their caravan when they came to visit us in South Africa.

That caravan was pretty much all they had when they finally fled Rhodesia. They just packed whatever they could into the caravan and left. I remember how we all laughed at Uncle Cecil when he told us how the border control had confiscated their double bed, strapped to the car roof, because they said it was too new to leave the country. At an age where most people are retiring, they got new jobs and kept laughing at life. The last time I saw Uncle Cecil was on a weekend holiday when he taught me to play pool like a hustler.

There are moments in your life that are so huge you never forget them or how you felt at that moment. I'm feeling that now and it is horrible. I feel sick, but I need to finish this story. Years passed by and then one day the phone rang. My dad took the call. I don't know how I knew it was bad news, I just remember going through to where the phone was with this feeling of terrible, heavy dread.

My dad turned around to look at me and said, "Uncle Cecil is dead. He's been murdered."

And I howled. I've been through other unexpected deaths over the years, but that was the only time I totally lost it. I fell to my knees and howled. Maybe I sensed all the horror that lay behind those few words.

It had been an ordinary morning for Uncle Cecil and Aunty Veronica. She had left early to go to work as a part-time book-keeper, but as she reached the gates of their home some young men stopped her. They said they were hungry and looking for work. She told them there was no work, but if they went to the house her husband would cook them breakfast. That's the kind of people they were.

When Aunty Veronica returned that afternoon, she found her husband tied to a chair in the bedroom. The young men had taken his toolbox and used what was in it to torture him before finally killing him. A hammer and screwdrivers. They took a charity tin full of coins when they left.

Writing this out, I feel as bad as I did the day we heard the full story. I am crying writing this. Uncle Cecil was such a funny man and a genuine gentleman, even if his humour could be risqué at times. He did not deserve to die that way. So the message on that forum, about a Cecil wanting V to know he was okay and she could let him go, made perfect sense to me.

Did I pass on the message to Aunt Veronica? No. I thought about it for a long time, but in the end I chickened out. I wasn't sure how she'd take it. After his death, she became more fragile as well as more religious. I was afraid the message might open up wounds rather than heal them. I don't know if I did the right or wrong thing. I just made a decision and hoped it was for the best.

As my abilities have changed and strengthened over

the years, I have had dead people come to me and ask for my help. I have most often refused. I suppose that sounds awful, but it's something I truly hate. You are dealing with approaching the grieving living who are often vulnerable and emotionally-wrecked. That is a huge responsibility. I only pass on those kinds of messages when I'm 100% certain the living need to hear them. Otherwise, the dead who want a messenger service can go somewhere else, please.

And what about the message I received when we lost our baby. What purpose or reason was there for that? Well, my grandmother and I were close when I was young, but over my adult life we drifted further and further apart. We were both fiery people, not good at forgiveness. By the time my grandmother died, our relationship was a mess.

Was my grandmother going to be the soul that stepped into the baby growing inside me, or had she merely used this opportunity to connect with me? Was that the reason the message spoke of two hearts joined? I'm still not sure, but that message did bring me closure and eventually healing, both to losing my never-born child and the older loss of my close relationship with my grandmother.

There is a lot more to my relationship with my grandmother, but that's another story. I'll end here with a quirky twist to lighten the mood. Aunty Veronica's brother Len, the pilot who brought home his friend to meet his family, was a psychic and a seer.

16

We moved from the big house to a country house in June 2006, leaving behind the mad neighbour who burnt things in the middle of the night and also leaving behind some unresolved mysteries. There were a few things that happened at the big house that I still have no answers for. I don't consider all of those events to be supernatural. Some of them seem more a case of proving Einstein right: that time and space are more fluid than we realise. The big house seemed to have a problem with time; sometimes it hiccuped.

The first time was one morning when Sandy left early for work. I had been unwell and stayed in bed. I was thinking about getting up, when I heard Sandy come back into the bedroom. I had my back to the door and thought that he must have forgotten something, but then I heard him sigh and the bed sagged as he sat down. I heard the thump of him taking off his shoes, one by one. Was he sick? I sat up, concerned. No one was there. It was not a ghost. I know my own husband. The sigh and the way he sat on the bed to take off his shoes were things he'd done dozens of times.

Another strange and annoying thing was the fact that house made me sing particular songs. When I was in the kitchen or working around the house, the same specific songs would be in my head or I'd find myself actually humming and singing them. It's not that strange to have songs that won't leave you alone, but these were all songs from a specific era – World War II. I grumbled about it to my husband and he, on a hunch, decided to do some research.

He looked into the history of our area. I wasn't expecting him to find anything since the big house was newly built on the edge of town. In WWII, our area was probably a farm field. Not so, as it turned out. Sandy discovered that our house was built on the edge of a defunct WWII air field. The night after Sandy found out about the airfield, I dreamt I was on this small stage, singing WWII songs. The room was full of men in uniform, listening to me sing.

I told Sandy about the dream and he decided to see if there was a connection. He discovered that dances had been held for the airmen in a local farmhouse. When he searched for the farmhouse's address, he found that it was just a quarter of a mile from us. We could see it from our bedroom window. I was singing songs that would have been played at those dances. Had I somehow heard those tunes through time?

One of the most striking events in the big house

didn't happen to me. It happened to Sandy. He woke me up one morning with an amazing story. He suffers from insomnia and regularly gets up early, as in 4:00am kind of early. Unlike me, who can drift in a semi-coma state for hours, Sandy has an on-off switch in his brain. He'll wake up and be wide awake and fully coherent instantly. Which is very annoying for a slob like me who needs at least one cup of coffee in the morning before I have a working brain.

This particular morning, Sandy woke way before dawn and noticed that I was already up, standing to look down at the bed. Then he realised the woman he was seeing couldn't possibly be me because of two most pertinent facts: one, I was still in bed sleeping next to him and two, the woman wasn't standing by the bed, she was flying above it.

Sandy doesn't scare easily ever, so he was quite fine with discovering a strange woman floating in our bedroom. He noted that she was looking down at me and realised that even though the room was in darkness, she was perfectly clear as if in bright sunlight. She was wearing an emerald green dress and had dark hair, like me. As he studied her, she became aware that she was being watched and turned to look at him. He said that she reacted as if she was startled to realise he could see her. Then she began to float up away from the bed before she vanished. I still have no idea who, or what, she was.

In this respect, Sandy and I are opposites. I don't mind not knowing. He hates it. I quite like the fact there are unsolved mysteries in life. I find that romantic, but Sandy needs to know the truth of everything. It is the fuel his fiery mind runs on. And while I tend to be fearful and prone to anxiety, constantly double-checking myself, Sandy has always had complete faith in my abilities. I know that I can tell him anything I have seen or experienced and he will believe me, but I also value the fact that his insistence on digging for the truth means that he pushes me beyond my fears and preconceptions.

That reminded me that I haven't yet spoken about the connection I have with Sandy. This first showed up when we were chatting online in 2002. We'd been discussing TV shows and books we both liked. I wanted to recommend a particular TV series I'd enjoyed, Merlin with Sam Neill, but I could not think of Sam Neill's name and Sandy didn't remember a show about Merlin. In the end, we laughed it off and went to bed. That night I dreamt of Sam Neill, but not as Merlin. It was really odd. He was in space! He was talking about planets and stars. I woke up thinking how wild that was and I still couldn't remember his blasted name.

That evening, I went onto chat and told Sandy about my funny dream. He said, "Oh, that was Sam Neill."

I recognised the name *hooray*, but why would Sandy know it from my dream? That led Sandy to telling me about a TV series he'd watched called SPACE. Sam Neill was the narrator. We never got that show in Africa, but Sandy found me some information online. I recognised two stills from the TV show instantly – they were scenes from my dream.

What we figured is this: I went to bed fretting over a TV show I wanted to tell Sandy about that had Sam Neill in it. It seems that in the dream state, I managed to access Sandy's mind and do a "file search", looking for that actor through Sandy's memories. Sandy had never watched Merlin, but he had watched SPACE, thus those were the Sam Neill memories I accessed.

It happened again on holiday in Scotland in 2002. We were going to the Outer Hebrides and I was really excited. The night before we took the ferry, I again dreamt of a TV show. This one was a comedy, set on board a quirky, little ship in Scottish seas. I forgot about the dream at first. The trip to the Outer Hebrides was too exciting. We drove through the night in order to reach the ferry at 6:00am and I saw a fox cub and heard a real live cuckoo at dawn. The novelty of that wore off during our stay on the Isle of Harris. Being woken up at 4:00am every morning to a live feathered alarm-clock loses its charm after the third day.

Harris was incredible. The landscape looked like a post-apocalyptic world, bleak, bare and rock-strewn. It was not my idea of appealing, but it was impressive and the sea made up for everything the land lacked. The beaches of the Outer Hebrides are stunning; miles of pristine, creamy sand and seas of turquoise crystal. We managed to see Callanish as well, the only henge in Britain built to follow the moon rather than the sun. As a psychic, I should have some epic tale about the magical qualities of being at my first henge circle, but I spent most of my time there throwing stones for an over-excited sheepdog who had gate-crashed the place.

The next best memory I treasure from that trip is us chasing a bank. The novelty of that still hasn't worn off. How many people ever get to chase a bank? Sandy needed to deposit a cheque and we asked someone where the nearest bank was. The woman said, "Oh, you just missed it. You should be able to catch it, if you hurry." Missed it? Oh yes, out in rural Scotland there are mobile banks that drive through the countryside, stopping when and where needed.

So off we dashed in Sandy's transit van, going a bit fast down a dirt road in order to catch up with this boxy blue van that was the bank. It was completely surreal chasing and waving down a bank. It stopped on the edge of a road where we were surrounded by nothing. No houses, no trees, not even a sheep or two. In South Africa where crime was and still is way off the scales, such a concept would be completely insane.

After we returned to mainland Scotland, I still didn't remember the dream until Sandy was at a job in Keith. He was working for a retired couple who had bought an old croft that needed fixing up. The husband looked exactly like the cartoon character Popeye and was an ex sailor. It was the sailor's wife who asked me if I'd read any Scottish books. She told me her favourites were the Para Handy books.

On the way home that evening, feeling mellow from a very nice day out, I asked Sandy if he knew the Para Handy books. He said he'd never read them, but he had watched the TV show. When we got home, he found information online and once again I was staring at pictures I had already seen in a dream. This time, I had added proof that once again I must have accessed Sandy's memories. The TV show was in colour, but my dream was in black and white. Sandy grew up with a black and white TV. He never saw the show in colour and so neither did I.

The cute-yet-annoying side to this connection we have is that I simply have to think of Sandy and if he's near, he'll turn and say, "Hmmm? What did you say?" He literally hears me say his name as if I was speaking out loud. This can become annoying as heck at times, particularly when I am silently plotting ways to manipulate him into making me coffee.

17

I am keenly aware of connecting emotionally to others (empathic), but the mental link has only been with Sandy and my "brother" Justin. Emotional connections can be upsetting because it's so hard to tell whose emotions I am feeling. Here's an example that happened over a weekend in 2012/13. I woke up one Saturday so unhappy that I couldn't get out of bed. I spent most of that weekend rolled up in a ball on the bed, crying my heart out. I had no idea why and so I lied to my family, saying I felt ill and using that as an excuse to stay in bed. Until I knew why I was feeling so bad, I had no way to explain it to anyone else.

I'd find out why on Monday. A few months earlier, a close friend's husband had died unexpectedly. At the time, she was too shocked to grieve, then too busy with the funeral arrangements. When it finally hit her, she spent that weekend in bed grieving… and so did I.

Both my friends, Em and Kim (of the fire ball dream), have similar problems with being empathic. It's extremely difficult to tell who the emotions belong to and can make you seem kind of crazy. There's nothing like bursting into tears, crashing into depression or becoming angry for no reason to freak out your spouse and/or family. Nowadays, I ask my guardian to strip back emotions that aren't mine, so I can figure out where mine begin and end. That way, I check the two states and then go email people to see who is having the bad day. Em and Kim often do the same and email me to say they know I'm having a bad day before I tell them.

Another type of connection I have experienced, although less frequently, is a connection to dogs. I've always loved animals, especially dogs. Ghost dog Teddy may have been my most spectacular experience, but I've had a few others that range from unusual to amusing. The first time I noticed this was with two dogs that used to hang out at our house every day. In South Africa, most people let their dogs roam free, which led to us regularly having furry visitors.

We always kept a bowl of water by our front door for any thirsty passers-by. As a child, I remember how many shops had water troughs for dogs out on the pavements. African heat can be brutal. My mom and I would often hear the tackity-tack of dog claws on our front steps, then the slurping as someone had a quick drink. Over the years we lived in South Africa, we had regulars who not only stopped by, but often stayed to lie on our cool, concrete front porch.

Two long-time furry friends were Snoopy and Flagtail. Snoopy looked like a border collie, but was smooth-haired and brindle in colour. He wasn't the smartest, but he was a sweetheart. Flagtail was... beyond deciphering. He was a well-built, tall dog with smooth, golden fur, floppy ears and a long tail he held upright when he walked, like a flagpole.

Flagtail was the alpha male and a most unusual dog. I can't remember hearing him bark and it wasn't until we'd known him for a year that we realised he was almost blind. Perhaps that was why he was so intuitive as his other senses compensated for his lack of vision? We eventually made friends with his owners. They were a nice family, but commuted to jobs in the Transkei, leaving their dogs bored and lonely. They were happy to have their pets spend the day with us.

We started keeping dog treats for them and that was when I noticed how different Flagtail truly was. Most times I'd give them their treat by the front door, but this one day we had an unknown stray dog hanging around and I was worried they might start a fight. I decided to call them into the back yard. As I thought about it, Flagtail stared at me and then turned around and ran down the stairs. When I went to the back gate he was already there, waiting.

I thought it was a coincidence, but started an experiment. Each time I went and got the treats, I'd think of which door I was going to feed them at. Every single time, Flagtail would be waiting at the right door or gate. Snoopy, on the other hand, would still be lying on his back snoring. After that, I did try sending thoughts to other dogs I knew and found that mentally saying "hello" always got me a tail wag, but I never again had any dog respond like Flagtail did.

I have also had it work the other way around. When we were first married, Sandy had a job building a dry-stone wall in a garden. One weekend, tired of sitting home alone, I decided to go with him to work. I noticed when we got there that the house owners had a pet Labrador. He brought me a ball and I threw it a few times before we started working.

Sandy asked me to sort through the pile of stones he was using to find particular shape pieces as he needed them. It was a bit like building a 3D stone jigsaw puzzle. I was bent over, sorting through the pile, when a puzzled voice said clearly in my mind, "Stones?" Surprised, I turned around to see the Labrador lying behind me, head tilted to one side in that way dogs do when they're puzzled or curious. For a brief second, his expression changed. I swear he looked startled, as if he'd realised I had heard what he was thinking. Then he picked up his ball and ran off.

When I told Sandy what I'd heard, he was amused and suggested I try to see if it worked on other animals. I did try mentally saying hello to a field of sheep a few weeks later. They all turned and ran off in hysteria, leaping like popcorn in a hot pan. I didn't try that again. Better to stick with dogs.

As in Africa, my thinking hello to dogs always got me a response, but I didn't have anyone speak back for several years. We had taken Sandy's mum out for a Sunday drive. It was a lovely warm day and we had driven along the edge of Loch Ness all the way down to Fort Augustus. Loch Ness is stunning, but a bit oppressive. The high cliffs and dark water aren't my thing, but Fort Augustus is a lovely spot. It has the usual tourist kitsch, including neon green toy Loch Nessie monsters wearing Tartan bonnets, but it's so pretty you can forgive it for a few tacky souvenirs. The locks that link the loch are always full of boats and even the odd, small sailing ship passing through.

We decided to have an ice cream and were sitting outside in the sunshine when a collie dog came our way. He was trying to sneak a lick off my mum-in-law's ice cream when Sandy noticed and shouted at him. The dog ran off and we continued enjoying our ice creams in peace... except a voice popped into my mind. Once again, it sounded puzzled.

The voice said, "Why hate dogs?"

I looked around, trying to figure out where the voice was coming from. It took me a while to see the collie. He was hiding behind a building. All I could see was his nose and these eyes STARING at me. This time, unlike with the Labrador, he didn't seem shocked that I was staring back. Instead, the voice became more insistent.

"Why hate dogs? Why shout at dogs? Why? Why?"

I tried sending a message back that ice creams belonged to people. You didn't just take without being offered. The collie poked its whole head around the wall then. "Why? Why?" I'm not sure if that related to why Sandy shouted or why ice creams weren't free for licking as at that moment the dog's owners called him away.

Since then I've never again heard a dog or animal, but I have had to stop saying hello in my mind. I realised that after a few embarrassing moments. I get dogs into trouble saying hello since their owners don't understand why their pet suddenly takes off to run and greet a complete stranger. How can you explain to an owner shouting at their dog that their dog was only being polite and saying hello back? I felt especially guilty when a guide dog turned around in a supermarket to greet me and his blind owner strumbled. That could have been dangerous.

18

The country house we moved to in 2006 was the complete opposite of the big house. Here we had complete peace, fresh air and a garden overflowing with flowering plants. We all loved that house and spent a lot of our time there outdoors, either gardening or having barbecues. My mom and I filled the back vegetable area with herb plants and I made jams and pies from the fruit that grew semi-wild around the property; cherries, bramble-berries and crab apples. We have a lot of happy memories from the time we spent there and at one stage hoped to buy the place.

It was also the house where my abilities changed dramatically. This was the house where I used a pendulum to interrogate an elephant until he confessed to being a fraud. Here is where I went through a physical trauma that led to me to seeing chakras and was given my own chakra reading that led me to a great battle. And in between I made a most unlikely friend from an animal I said hello to.

It started one weekend when I had another lucid dream. I dreamt I was in a forest that was inside a theatre. At the time, I thought this was typical dream fantasy, but thinking about it now... dreams are merely plays we perform in our minds, so why not have it inside a theatre! It was night in my dream and very dark. I was trying to get through the trees in the auditorium to reach the brightly lit stage at the far end.

I knew there were "things" in the forest that wanted to stop me. I did see lots of black moths walking on the trees, but I could feel there was something bigger and nastier in the dark watching and following me. I finally reached the edge of the forest where the trees started to thin out. I could see the stage. I knew that the moment I stepped up onto the stage, the dream monster hiding in the dark was going to attack.

I stopped, turned back to face the forest and shouted out. I told the invisible monster that this was stupid. I said I wasn't scared of dream creatures and I wasn't going to be stopped or harassed by one now. I demanded whatever it was step out into the light. A big, black wolf with glowing yellow eyes stepped out of the trees on my right. He was growling and snarling, showing lots of sharp, long teeth. He was an ugly wild thing, skinny with matted fur.

I stood my ground as he came closer, but I was actually beginning to feel nervous and a little scared. Then I had an idea. I told him I'd groom him and remove the burrs in his fur if in return he'd leave me alone. I "created" a dog brush and comb, making them appear on the edge of the stage. The wolf never moved, so I went over to pick up the brush and started grooming him. I even trimmed out some really tough knots. He kept growling, but the growling got quieter.

I talked to him as I brushed him. I commented that he must be a lone wolf to get that dirty; in a pack he'd have others to help him pull the burrs from his fur. He stopped growling when I said that and I began to feel sad for him. There was something different about this wolf. He felt more alive somehow. I finished by giving him a good all over brush to bring up the shine on his coat. He looked great. Still big and scary, but most impressive. I told him that he could come back to my dreams any time he needed grooming and I'd give him the full treatment. The dream ended and I woke up.

Around midday that Sunday, I was sitting by my dressing table sorting through letters and bills (I leave all sorts of junk on my dressing table) when I felt there was something behind me. I sent my mind out, trying to feel what was there... it was the black wolf. The moment I acknowledged that I could see him in my mind, he started acting like an excited puppy. A very big and slightly scary puppy. He'd come up and lick me and then run in circles, jump on the bed, off the bed, going crazy. It was a bit overwhelming. I had never expected a dream creature to follow me home.

As he bounced about the bedroom, I got a distinct message from him. It wasn't in words, I just instantly knew, as if a chunk of information was downloaded into my brain. No words, no mime or using senses or emotions – just pure, clear knowing. I knew the black wolf was happy because he wasn't alone any more. I asked him for a name to call him and a plant kept popping into my head: Myrtle.

A plant seemed a strange name for a giant, black wolf. I suggested Myrt and he seemed happy enough with that. Myrt was quite a character. He was there every morning when I woke up, full of joy and devotion, but in a slightly alarming way. The energy that came off him in waves was wild, unfettered by morality, affectionate and devoted, but slightly dark.

Myrt was, to be totally honest, a lower entity. The kind of creature some would call a demon, but on a low-grade scale. I had dealt with dark things before. Not everything out there is good. Just as with humans themselves, the beings beyond our dimension are a fairly mixed bag. In the past, brought up in a Christian culture, I'd run a mile from anything that felt demonic.

But Myrt was different. How could I look into those adoring, yellow eyes and push him away? He confused me terribly at first. All of my instincts were to make him go away, but then he'd hit me with this… love. It truly was like taking home a dog from the pound that you know is dangerous, know has a past history of attacking and killing things, and yet each time it looks at you it's like you are god/goddess and all things wonderful. For the next three years, Myrt was around me constantly. He was still a bit scary, but always friendly in his wild, exuberant way.

Myrt was also excessively protective of me. He'd come into my mind snarling and ready to attack if anyone bothered me in any way. I was genuinely worried about that. I had no idea how far his powerful presence was able to project itself. As superstitious as it may sound, some dark things can do actual harm. Not physically, but certainly mentally and emotionally. I didn't want a guard wolf that took his job so seriously that he harmed someone.

In the end, I managed a happy compromise. I asked Myrt to protect me when I used my pendulum. I'd started to use it again, mostly to communicate with my elephant spirit-guide, Sol. I also found the pendulum helpful when the odd dead person came by wanting me to pass along a message. By making Myrt focus (somewhat fanatically) on sniffing along the perimeter of my psychic space, I was left relaxed and free to use the pendulum, receive messages, ask questions and jot down answers. Myrt also took it upon himself to guard the forum I moderated. I wasn't the only one there to see or sense him. Others commented on seeing or feeling the presence of a large wolf, especially in the chat room. Myrt clearly took his job very seriously.

Some psychics I spoke to at the time felt I was mad keeping him around since he was a dark entity, but Myrt taught me so much about the power of unconditional love. More than I can ever put into words. As time went by, I grew to love Myrt dearly and he began to change. He was less manic-hyper and how he looked changed as well. Less the Big Bad Wolf from folk tales and more like a regular, wild animal.

One evening, I was looking at him and thinking how much I loved this strange creature, when he shattered in my mind. White light exploded from his eyes and body, so bright I couldn't see anything for a few moments. When it cleared, Myrt was a wolf made of pure white light, his tail dripping stardust like a sparkler. I tried to draw Myrt with photo paint at the time. Sandy looked at the picture and said, "Why is your wolf farting fairy dust?"

The white light Myrt was much quieter and calmer. I sometimes barely noticed he was there, but any time I pulled out the pendulum he'd be by my side instantly. Still protective. Life moved on, years passed and a lot of things changed. One day, Myrt came bounding in to greet me, but then he stood up on his hind legs and morphed into a man. I realised this man had large, black wings. I thought, *WOW, is Myrt actually my guardian angel?*

But I heard a clear reply, "FALLEN angel." It took a while for him to get the images clear enough for me to understand.

Myrt showed me a young man caught up in the crime and gangs of the prohibition years in America. This young man did terrible things before he died too young and quite violently. When he died, he was so terrified that there might truly be a hell that he refused to move on. So instead of moving on into God's love and finding out that there isn't a real hell, he stayed and created his own. Trapped in his self-imposed limbo, Myrt began to believe his own insane fears. He literally created the monster wolf from his own self-image. He began to believe he was a fallen creature, demonic, but clearly some part of his heart still held hope because he chose that puzzling name: Myrtle.

It was only very recently that I finally thought to look up the symbolism of the plant. Anyone as afraid of hell as Myrt must have been brought up Christian, so I searched for myrtle in the Bible. Oh my.... Why didn't I think to do this sooner? The answers were always there. Myrtle is a sacred evergreen tree, used to purify and bless.

> Instead of the thorn shall come up the fir tree, and instead of the brier shall come up the myrtle tree: and it shall be to the Lord for a name, for an everlasting sign that shall not be cut off.

> *Isaiah 55:13*

An everlasting sign that shall not be cut off.... With that name choice my scared, wild wolf had been telling me so much. Myrt never gave up hope of redemption. How was I so thick to not realise his name had meaning? And how perfect, how utterly right his name choice was. The last time I saw Myrt, he came to me as a happy, healthy, young man. He smiled at me, then threw his hands upwards and all these white doves appeared flying about him. For me, Myrt is proof of Grace, that subtle, elusive thing so many religions speak about. The Grace of God is a Love that really can work miracles.

19

It was in the country house that my health began to fall apart. I had been battling with endometriosis for two decades by that time. This often misunderstood illness can cause a lot of pain and damage. Basically, endometrial tissue goes a bit insane and decides to float off inside a woman's body and wherever it ends up, it creates internal scarring and damage. It causes infertility and heartache as well as physical pain.

In my case, my internal organs are so scarred that they have become completely fused together. Basically, everything in my tummy is glued together and that is glued to the muscles of my back. This sometimes causes me to get back pain and sciatica. I also cannot wear tight-waisted clothing any more, as that triggers an ache like a toothache in my tummy and back that grows and GROWS.

In the 1990s, the endometriosis caused my right

ovary to rupture. I was sent in for emergency surgery and nearly died due to internal bleeding and complications during surgery. It was probably the main reason why I had a miscarriage in 2005. When we moved to the country house, I started having more extreme tummy and back pain.

I had been working from home for quite a few years by then, but at that time I began to struggle with keeping to deadlines. In the end, I had to admit I wasn't coping and, after some consideration, I quit my job. At that stage, both Sandy and my dad were in well-paying jobs, so money wasn't a problem. I decided to focus on myself for a while.

The pain was most severe if I lay down. I could only sleep for an hour at a time. I'd be so exhausted I'd fall asleep instantly, but as the pain increased it would eventually wake me up. Then I'd have to either stand or kneel for about three hours until the pain eased off before trying for another hour of sleep. Yes, I did say kneel. Once the pain was that bad, sitting was equally unbearable. Being up most of the night was depressing and boring. I needed some way to keep busy, so eventually I started a blog.

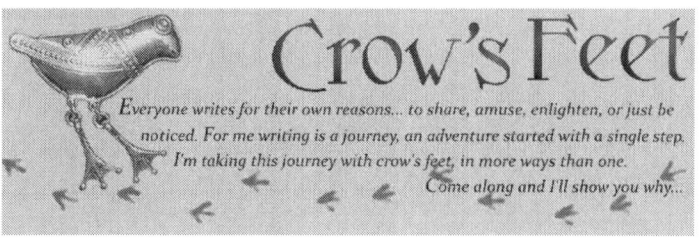

Crow's Feet

Everyone writes for their own reasons... to share, amuse, enlighten, or just be noticed. For me writing is a journey, an adventure started with a single step. I'm taking this journey with crow's feet, in more ways than one. Come along and I'll show you why...

I named my blog Crow's Feet as a deliberate joke about my ageing self as well as my shamanic crow journeys. I'm going to add my very first blog post here, as it deals with how I came to terms with studying shamanism as well as my own moment of God's Grace.

Dance – 5 April 2007

Last year, I watched a TV documentary series called "Extraordinary People". The episode I enjoyed the most followed the life of a blind, brain-damaged young man who is a musical savant. He has the intelligence level of a four year old and yet he plays jazz like a genius. At one stage, he was given the chance to listen to an entire orchestra. He then "translated" the entire performance into a piano solo. It was awesome!

He flew from the UK to Las Vegas, with his toy beanbag elephant for company, to do a concert to raise money for disabled kids. There he met a blind boy with autism who plays classical music and two other gifted musical kids: a blind girl on a violin and another autistic boy who plays the keyboard. Together, they had a jam session that rocked the roof off. They were brilliant. The one psychiatrist studying them said that science now thinks music is the "universal code" that drives us at a deeper level than language or any other sense-related ability.

Three years ago, I popped on some soothing music to try to meditate. I've always liked the idea of meditating, but it just doesn't work for me. My mind does not understand the concept of emptiness. It is a cage full of budgies all wanting to scream their latest word the loudest. But this one time I actually got it right, one of those rare perfect moments when things click together. Maybe it was because I didn't try so hard.

I was desperate for an answer to a crossroad I'd reached in my life regarding my religious/spiritual beliefs. I was born into a family that, counting both my parents' sides, spans almost every variations of Christianity. As a result, my parents had a more laid-back attitude to religion than many. Being a church-goer was never viewed as the only road to heaven. I grew up with the unspoken message that all religions lead to God and therefore were of equal value.

It was only when I went out into the world that I began to realise that not everyone was as open-minded. I was warned I was "in danger of being a Pantheist" by a teacher when I was in junior school. I had to go look it up in a dictionary at the time. I had to admit, what I read did sound a lot like me. It was the first time I remember feeling both relief and unease at who I was. So I was a Pantheist. Why was that a dangerous thing?

In high school and college, more devoted Christian friends tried to convert me to their "way". Although they meant well, they left me feeling less acceptable and worthy.

Why do some people think they know what is best for you better than you do? It's like they see you happily being a square peg in a perfectly geometric world of your own and simply cannot stop themselves from trying to squash you repeatedly into a round hole. Or, worse still, they whip out all these abrasive words in a desperate attempt to file the corners off your square soul. Words that imply you are "wrong" or "bad" for simply being true to yourself. Ultimately, there are only two people who know you: yourself and God. Other people have a right to their opinions, but that is all they can ever be – opinions.

That was why I found myself trying to meditate three years ago. To try to find the "me" I had lost along the long journey through so many other people's opinions. As a child and in my teens, I'd known who I was and been happy. In my twenties, I'd faced confrontation on who I was and fought back, the way you do when you are young and rather full of self-righteousness.

In my thirties, I'd expanded my friendships to include a wonderful range of equally wonderful people from a variety of different belief systems: Neo-Pagan, Wiccan, Buddhist and Native American Shamanism. My thirties were a time of tremendous personal expansion, but it was also a time where I started to wobble like a spinning top that has hit the edge too many times.

By my fortieth birthday, it was clear I had wobbled so far off the path that I didn't know how to find my way back. A friend suggested meditation to clear my mind and see the way home. I tried... nothing. Or to be exact, too much! I'd sit there and my mind would gabble and chatter about everyday life until I either fell asleep or got bored and gave up.

Then one day, I was pottering around the internet and read a woman asking similar questions. She was a Catholic considering becoming a Neo-Pagan. She was standing at the edge of everything she had been taught to believe was *good* and *evil*. She had left a message asking for help and someone had replied, "Pray for guidance – then listen."

Seemed fairly sensible advice. I decided to try it myself. For once and for all, I needed to know if being ME was okay with whoever was "Up There." I said a small prayer to that extent and sat down to wait and listen... and for the first time EVER all those manic budgies in my brain finally shut up.

Silence

Real silence

Cellular level peace and quiet

Was this meditating? I closed my eyes and let the silence take over. I found myself standing at the edge of a lake at sunset. Someone was walking across the water towards me. A bearded guy in a long robe.

Jesus? Hell... Jesus?

I dismissed the thought as stupid, but as he walked up the shore to me I could see the holes in his hands and feet. I didn't know what to do. So I was honest and I said, "You're the last person I was expecting to see." He burst out laughing and it was such a joy-filled, infectious laughter that we both fell about laughing for a while.

Then he took my hands and we walked out onto the water together and we danced. With stars above and stars reflected in the dark water below, we danced. As we danced, he "exploded" into the stars and became the Universe itself... and then I found myself back on the shore.

I'm not sure how long I stood there before he appeared, walking back across the water towards me once again. This time, he was carrying something. A crow. He said, "This is for you," and the crow hopped from his arm to my shoulder.

I opened my eyes and I was back in the same room in my same house. I have a Native American friend who had sent me an internet link to totem animals a year before. I went and looked up crow. There were stories about how crow was the messenger of the Great Spirit.

So the bringer of the Holy Spirit had brought me the messenger totem of another culture's Great Spirit.

Now, I keep thinking about those "disabled" kids and how they've tapped into creativity and Creation at a level we can only daydream about. Music and Creation. Music and life itself. Dancing on water and amongst the stars. Ancient peoples using dancing and singing to connect to the Source....

Is faith merely (re)learning how to dance on water? Was the world created in seven days or seven notes?

I think I really like that idea! Holy and Great, Human and Sacred exploding together in a universe of infinite possibilities. Different music, different steps, but always the same Dance. I have found my way back to the Dance. I hope you have found yours.

My blog was supposed to be a place for me to talk about my shamanic-psychic self under a fake name, but it quickly became a Scottish travel blog. I'm not complaining. I made loads of friends through blogging and even won the Best Scottish Travel Blog award for two years running. Whenever we went out I took my camera with me, looking for pretty and interesting things to share with my blog fans. I also started to create more art on my computer, simple things to use on my blog or on the forums. It kept my mind off the pain and tiredness.

I'd heard stories of people who'd ended up with book contracts or good writing jobs thanks to being found via their blogs. That really interested me and I did enter some competitions and won a few small prizes. I was secretly hoping for a lucky break and I thought I had found it when another blogger recommended a new publisher that was actively looking for new authors. I had a manuscript for a book that I'd written ten years earlier. I took it out, tidied it up and sent it to this new publishing place.

I was so thrilled when they wrote back that it had been accepted. First Light was about to become a real book. I was so happy, but sadly, my lucky break was not all it seemed. The publishers never seemed to sell any of my books and a few years later I saw a news article on TV about them. Basically, the publishers were a scam. I wasn't the only one caught. My only consolation was the fact I kept full copyright of my book. I took First Light away from them and republished it myself, via Amazon. At least this time, I got to choose the cover art, which had been really dull on the first edition. I used my own art for the new cover.

20

It was while living in the country house that a physical trauma led me to seeing chakras as well as a chakra reading that led me to a great battle. Both events are so intertwined that I'm not sure in which order to write about them. It's a bit like the chicken or the egg. The physical trauma related to endometriosis pain. I've never been a delicate princess type, but that was proving to count against me at the time. I never thought to tell the doctors about my sleepless nights and pain. I simply "sucked it up" and got on with life.

When I did finally go to the doctor, he was somewhat useless. He obviously thought I was over-exaggerating about the pain and sent me home with basic pain-killers. It was frustrating because I knew something was very wrong. I'd had pain from the endometriosis for decades. Given my past experience, I knew this was probably something serious.

While I went back and forth to the doctor, bouncing about the medical system, I tried to find help in other ways. I asked for help on the forums. One friend, Orla, offered to check my chakras and maybe do some reiki. I thanked her and gave her my permission. I was willing to try anything. Orla gave me a specific time and day for when she'd be looking at me. She was in a different time zone, so I'd most likely be asleep when she was working on me.

About two days before that chosen day, I had one of my vivid dreams. This one was a doozy! I was both in it and yet observing it in that weird way of dreams. There was someone with me, talking to me, but I never saw who this person was. I was dressed in old-fashioned clothing. What era? I really don't know. I was wearing the kind of plain, long skirted dress that ordinary women wore for centuries.

There were dirt roads with horses and donkey carts, but that doesn't narrow the time zone down much either. I knew it was cold, but there was no snow. I'd say spring, after a long hard winter. I watched two women walking along the dirt road, a mother and daughter who looked to be in her late teens. I knew they were refugees; dirty, exhausted and starving.

They stopped to examine something dead lying on the road. It was fairly big, but obviously quite light as the two women picked it up quite easily. It looked like typical roadkill, dried out and flattened by a hundred cart wheels. I went across the dirt road for a closer look. It was human. A woman or girl twisted into a foetal position, naked and skeletal thin.

The mother and daughter took it off the road and into the bushes where they started to eat it, tearing shreds of dry flesh from the bones. It was nightmarish watching them. The invisible person with me said this dead female had never been seen by the village as human. She had been insane or mentally slow to the point of walking on her knuckles and behaving like an animal. The village had thought of her as a beast, so her dead body was not seen as the body of a human. That was why the two women felt no horror about eating her, plus they were near starving themselves and had no choice if they wanted to survive.

And then… I was not there any more. I was in our bedroom. I heard a noise, like someone tapping on a window. I got out of bed, vaguely aware that this was a lucid dream and not reality. It was early dawn and the pale, greyish light was just making things visible in the room. I noticed a small, almost smoky shape low down by my cupboard door.

Sandy asked, "What is it?"

I replied, "It's an Earth Spirit with a gift for me."

The smoke became a solid form, a tiny woman about a foot high, roughly 30cm. She was elderly with her hair in a bun. She had a big nose, twinkly eyes and a sweet smile. Something like a friendly witch or gnome lady.

She handed me a piece of a tile, like a bathroom tile. I knew it was ancient and that she had dug it up just for me, to prove that she was literally an "earth" spirit. The tile design was a griffon lying down with a zig-zag pattern behind. I recognised it as being from Ancient

Crete, Minoan. I've been a fan of Minoan art since high school.

I looked up at the little Earth Spirit woman and went, "Oooh!" Sandy asked why and I told him, "Fairies!" All around her I could see these tiny fairies, like dust in the sunlight, but glowing brightly in all different colours.

My mom came into the room and asked me what was going on. I said, "I've been given a gift." and I held out the tile to show her, but it had turned into a photograph. It was an old family photo of my mom in her teens with her mom and sister. They were in swim suits, sitting in a row and smiling at the camera.

As I went to hand the picture to my mom, I realised it had changed. My aunt had turned into me. Now the photo showed three generations of my female family, lined up by a rock pool. This made sense to me. My grandmother's family were British consuls in Crete and Constantinople. My grandmother's grandfather was born in Crete. Three generations of women from that family line, all on a Cretan tile.

The first dream portion was equally disturbing because some of it also fitted family history. That British consul on my grandmother's side, the great x3 grandfather, married a local girl. Her family were Turkish Greek and fled Turkey to live in exile in Spain for 100 years before finally returning.

You read a sentence like "fled into exile" without really thinking about the implications. Fleeing for your life means leaving with nothing and often travelling great distances. My ancestors fled from Turkey to

Spain. That is a long way to go. Did they travel by ship or over land? What had that experience really been like? The cannibalism part of my dream haunted me all morning. Was that real? Had that actually happened?

About midday, the phone rang. It was my reiki and chakra friend, Orla. She apologised straight away, saying that due to some problems at work she'd done my chakra reading that night, days earlier than planned. She said she had to phone me as what she'd seen was complicated and startling. She said she didn't want to alarm me, but I was holding something in my root chakra. It wasn't harming me. In fact, my chakras were in excellent condition. She struggled for a word to fit what the "thing" in my root chakra was.

She said that this wasn't a word she liked using, but the closest description was a family curse energy that ran though my maternal female line. Orla said that this had come about due to some extreme trauma. A maternal ancestress had done something bad in order to protect her family. When she died, like Myrt, she was so afraid of hell that she refused to pass over. Instead, she kept latching onto the women in the family to protect them, but over time this twisted protectiveness had become something completely mad.

I remember I burst out laughing. A curse in the female family line? I wasn't at all surprised. Then I told her my dreams and my maternal family history. That side of the family has actually called itself cursed in old family letters and documents. Perhaps the most famous of that female family line is my great grandfather's cousin, Mary Vetsera, who committed suicide with the

Austrian crown prince Rudolph. There's a heap load of unhappiness in my maternal line, with family feuds and all sorts of dramas.

My grandmother's mother died of a heart attack at age thirty. My grandmother, then aged four, was sent to live with distant relatives who tortured and starved her, probably because they didn't approve of her existing at all. Both my grandmother's parents were married when they met. They left their families and divorced in order to be together. Utterly scandalous and sinful in Edwardian times, especially for my Irish Catholic great-grandmother.

Me with my maternal grandmother, Doreen Ongley.

That side of the family has a long history of conflict, pain and sorrow. And I'd volunteered to hold it inside me and somehow deal with it in order to free my entire female family line? Oh, whoopee…. All I'd wanted was help with my endometriosis pain, not some female version of an Arthurian quest!

As things turned out, I wasn't able to do anything about that curse as my own personal health trauma was about to implode. A few weeks after Orla's phone call, my mom had to pop me in a car and take my writhing-in-agony self to the hospital emergency ward. It had happened again – another ruptured ovary. I was in surgery for hours as they tried to patch up my sad, old body.

I woke to a state of bliss that only a large dose of morphine can induce, but that peace was short-lived. I'll put what I sent to my close friends here to explain:

March 29, 2007

The last ten days have held some strange experiences for me. As I already mentioned, I had bad panic/anxiety in hospital last weekend. Apparently, it was because of the high dose of morphine I was on, but I didn't know that at the time and it was horrible! As long as I stayed active I felt okay, but the moment I relaxed I'd have surreal flashing visions, nightmares, panic etc.:(I couldn't even close my eyes to relax and sleeping was impossible. By the time Sandy visited on Saturday afternoon, I was nearly hysterical.

He suggested I find a way to stop the nightmares using meditation. While he was talking, a crow flew by the window and yelled at us. It was the third time that morning a crow had made a noisy point of getting me to take notice. I started thinking about how crow is said to carry souls from the dark to light. Since I couldn't control my mind I figured maybe crow could help.

After Sandy left, I asked crow to carry me through to the light. That night when I went to bed, I saw a huge crow that took hold of my shoulders. I relaxed and fell asleep. It was the first night since the op that I had no flashing images or nightmares. Since then crow has been in my dreams with a vengeance. He made an interesting demand, too. He's adamant that I need to start writing again. The way I used to back about 5 years ago before my life got complicated.

And there's more!

The first night I slept peacefully I dreamt of this little grey bug-like creature hanging from a conveyor belt on the ward ceiling. Several other bug critters were dashing about the room, watching anxiously from below. I asked if the hanging one was sick because its eyes were half closed and they told me yes.

I realised that the little guys below all had

different colour antennae. Bright coloured bobbles at the end. It took a few moments more to figure it out. They were the rainbow colours; they were chakras! The six little ones watched as number 7 got whisked away to be healed. I asked if they were mine and they said no. I asked where the ill one was going and they said, "County Cork, Ireland". Then I woke up.

That evening, a lady in the neighbouring ward was transferred to my ward. She's from County Cork, Ireland and I think the sick chakra bug is hers. So, I tried to see my own chakras and I saw seven rainbow ladybugs! When I first came home from hospital, orange ladybug was a bit dull and had the shivers, but I gave him some extra energy and he perked up a lot.

Last night, hubby posed the question whether or not I could see his chakras. I tried... and I can. His chakras were slightly different. Mine are kiddy's crayon colours, but his are deeper, jewel colours. I felt this was because of our personalities rather than a sign of anything wrong with his chakras, but I started doubting myself and asked for confirmation. I asked to see someone else's chakras to compare.

Minna – I saw yours. Sorry for intruding without asking first. It wasn't intentional. I just thought of your name and *zap* - there they were. I took a quick peek to be sure there are characteristic differences and then I left them alone. I'll not write what I saw without your permission, but I will say they are so CUTE which doesn't surprise me :)

I have been able to pinpoint which chakras hubby has weaknesses in, which was quite fascinating. I've never felt ANY connection to chakras before now. Quite amazing. And there's more! My abilities to connect to passed people might be changing, too.

I have never seen a passed relative while awake. I get emotions and pictures/symbols and that's it, but the day I came out of hospital that changed. I was in the lounge, lying on the couch. My mom pointed out that I'd lain on that couch sick several times over the years (we've had the couch 27 years). It brought back the memory of my one cousin sleeping on it. We have photos of him fast asleep when he was about six. So cute and especially poignant as he died at the age of twenty-three.

I thought to myself "We can never get rid of the couch. Frank slept on it."

...and I heard his voice in my head say loudly, "GEEZ, Shell!" in a half joking, half exasperated tone of voice. I looked up and there he was, standing there grinning and rolling his eyes at my stupid sentimentality. We shared a laugh and he mimed a message just for me. Then he waved and left, but just an hour later he was back and once again he spoke. He gave me a message for my mom and another for my dad. I told them as he was saying it to me and to be honest, all three of us were shaken up and in tears.

I don't know if this is a one-off or a new development. Hearing words and seeing his wonderful smile was a lot better than just getting symbols. I wonder why being in hospital seems to have turbo-boosted me onto a new level?

It was Orla who proposed a theory as to why things changed. She thought that the anaesthetic had worked on my brain the same way South American shamans use all those weird hallucinogenic plants. I suspect she was on the right track there because from then on, my abilities were completely different.

21

And where was my elephant-now-spirit guide, Sol, during all of this? He was around, but not particularly noticeable. On the forums, when I spoke about Sol, some people felt the fault lay with me and that might have been true. I did ignore him at times, especially when I was sick and in pain. It took too much effort to try to figure out what he was miming and trying to tell me. One forum friend, James, suggested I try a type of automatic writing I'd describe as spirit dictation.

I did give it a try, but mostly I'd end up sitting staring at an empty page feeling bored. James nagged me a lot to keep trying and I did a splendid job ignoring him as well. I did finally manage a small spirit dictation breakthrough. Sol managed to get through an entire sentence: "Chicken smells good."

Really? I mean, I know I was roasting a chicken at the time, but you FINALLY make contact with your spirit guide and all he has to share with you is that he likes the smell of roast chicken? I was beginning to wonder if I had the last one left. You know what I mean? At school when kids pick others for sports teams there's always the goofy kid no one wants. The one left. Come to think of it, that was usually me at school. Maybe I was paired with my perfect soul mate in the spirit world.

The goofy kid gets the goofy spirit guide? I started to laugh writing that! The elephant in my mind just did the whole regal flourishing bow in my mind. He likes that goofy tag. Oh yes, he's still around, but... well, you'll have to wait to find out what he's up to now. A lot has happened between then and now.

Let's go back to the "then" of 2007, when we were still in the country house. I was juggling my health, a new blog and trying to self-advertise my newly published book. And then, as if life couldn't get any more frantic, our landlord decided he not only didn't want to sell us the house, he wanted it back. We had three months to find a new place. Three months to find a new home would be stressful in normal circumstances, but I was recently out of surgery and not in the mood to go house hunting. Also, any house we rented had to be disabled friendly for my mom who can only stand and walk with crutches. It was a frantic time and rather a blur now. The old saying that you only remember the good times it mostly true. This was not a good time and I remember very little of it now.

Thankfully, I did save things to Word documents so I still have all my attempts to let Sol dictate to me. I put my questions and replies in italics and Sol chose a colour for his portions. His favourite colour – pink. Pink has to be the most eye-watering colour to read and not at all book friendly, so I am going to use a different font for Sol. I chose comic sans since it seemed the most apt!

11 October 2006

Chicken smells good.

25 Oct 2006

Listen with your heart. Trust more. Life is good. Enjoy. Live.

When you trust, believe, you will hear clearly.

8 Nov 2006

Listen to me. Do not be afraid of what you hear. The more you listen the easier it will become. Stop worrying who is talking. Turn off your head!

Yes. I have more. Stop worrying about typing. Leave it. Life is challenging. But you can overcome anything.

30 Jan 2008

Welcome back. You are hearing me better than before. Good. This is good. I am annoyed with you for leaving me alone here I have missed you.

I'm sorry

I know you are sorry.

Forgive me?

Of course!

Your mind. Oy, Your mind gets in the way all the time.

Poor Sol, he was right about my mind. I was thinking about all I've written so far, and I realised there's a pattern. I'm lousy at meditation. I can't turn my mind off. I think-think-think constantly. As a result of that failure, most of my messages have come through when I am in my own "the zone" variation of the meditative state; on awakening from sleep, showering, watching boring TV, sitting in nature or being a passenger in cars.

Showering and long drives are particularly good empty-mind moments. The first time I saw dead people was in the shower. Not one of my best moments! I was thinking about a friend whose father had just passed and there he was. In fact, it was both him and his wife standing there smiling at me. No, no, and NO! I really am glad they found a way to drop off a message for their daughter, but in the shower? Standing wet and naked talking to strangers is NOT my idea of fun!

That experience was a confirmation that this was real. I'd never met or seen my internet friend's parents. When I described them to her, including what her mom was wearing, she sent me back a photo of her parents. Her mother was wearing the exact clothing I'd seen and they looked... well, they looked exactly like the people I'd seen. An alarming confirmation that I had seen real, dead people while naked.

I've since demanded that my guides keep dead people away when I'm in the bathroom. Needless to say, the Elephant in my head completely disregards this rule. He'll pop in any time he wants and if I act embarrassed, he'll crack really awful jokes. Really... awful... jokes. We won't go there. Trust me, you don't want to know how bad a mimed vulgar joke from an irreverent Jewish Elephant can be.

I must admit, as much as I loved the old rogue, there were times where I wondered about him. I thought spirit guides were these higher souls sent as teachers. Surely such beings would be noble and dignified? An elephant just blew a raspberry at me as I wrote that. Everything changes and nothing changes!

22

That wondering about Sol reached a climax for me around the time our landlord demanded his house back. All of us loved that house and Sol had constantly sent little confirmations that this was to be our home, but now it was all being ripped away. How could Sol be so wrong? Had he deliberately lied to me? Interestingly, it didn't shake my faith in him being real, but it completely shook my faith in him telling the truth. Was he really all he pretended to be?

I'd read enough books to know that famous psychics had spirit guides of a completely different calibre. Their guides gave them deep, meaningful messages and were serious beings, not twinkly-eyed Jewish elephants who danced in hula skirts, letting it all wibble and wobble.

Take James' guide for comparison. He was an impressive higher being. It was James' guide who led me to trust that my abilities were real. This happened in the best way as always: through conflict. Without a doubt, the only way to deal with fears is to face them and in my case, life has always shoved me face first into anything I try to avoid.

It started with what the internet calls a troll, a person who deliberately causes trouble for their own amusement. This particular troll came onto the shaman forums pretending to be interested in shamanism, but then began systematically picking apart every idea and person on the forum. Personally, if I'd been a moderator I would have banned her, but perhaps it's a good thing I wasn't as she led me to finally having faith in myself. The gifts of life lessons often come packaged in the most surprising ways.

Traditional psychics say that you can only see or hear your own spirit guide, but I was about to prove that theory wrong. It started one day when I was in the car (in the zone) and thinking about James. He had been having some health problems and I was worried about him. As I thought about it, a voice ripped through my head, loud and clear with a posh British accent. This male voice said, "James brings it upon himself. He does not deserve your sympathy."

That was the first time I heard James' spirit guide, Eagle. I was completely awed. While Sol struggled to get through to me, elbowing his way between the thoughts in my mind, Eagle had cut through like a laser beam. He was and is one of the most powerful higher beings I have ever had the honour of talking to. He has never been difficult to hear.

Of course, the first thing I did was to go onto the forum to let James know what had happened, which brought a deluge of abuse from the troll. This led to a few others voicing doubts as well, which unfolded into a long and tiresome bickering fest. At the same time that this was happening, someone else on the forum asked for advice. I was going to see if I could get Sol to help me reply, when Eagle was THERE in my mind. Clearly and precisely, he dictated a perfect answer.

I wrote this into a word document as I don't trust forums. I've had long posts vanish due to a glitch or hiccup. I write, save and then copy-paste. I wrote out Eagle's response, copied it to paste into the forum... and found it was already there. James had left a reply while I was away and it was word-for-word the exact same as mine. I added my reply, explaining that I'd had mine dictated to me by Eagle as well.

This shook James and led him to believe I was telling the truth about hearing his guide, but the troll simply saw it as the two of us conspiring. That was to blow up into a battle that destroyed one forum and damaged another, but for me it was a wonderful, pivotal moment. Not only that, it also led to James and I forging a strong friendship that would prove invaluable over the next decade of my life. But it did nothing for my trust in Sol.

If I could hear Eagle perfectly and receive impeccable advice, why was Sol so vague? In fact, the more I thought about it, Sol seemed almost reluctant to give advice or instructions. My doubts built up steam as I went over all the events of our shared time together. One day, after an unsuccessful attempt to communicate using mime and the pendulum, I completely lost my temper. I shouted at him in my mind, which was most unsatisfying, and told him to leave me alone and go away. He did as I asked and vanished.

I was too busy to feel the emptiness in my heart of him not being there. Once again, we were on the move to a new house. This time, none of us wanted to move and we were all unhappy about it. Over the past six years, I had packed and moved six times. It was stressful and exhausting. On top of that, I was waiting for more surgery for a hysterectomy and a hernia. All those operations had taken their toll; my stomach muscles were shredded. The hernia was uncomfortable and made me look several months pregnant. I felt a thousand years old.

Since the country house landlord had changed his mind suddenly and without warning, we were completely unprepared. It was a case of moving to whatever was available rather than picking a house we liked. We moved in 2008. It was early spring, but the weather was still wintery with sleet and strong winds. It fitted the mood perfectly. We had left our picture-perfect countryside on the edge of our favourite town to move onto a wind-battered hill above a dull, little fishing village.

But the best gifts of life often come to us in the most unlikely packages. Nine years on, I can tell you we later heard that the perfect country house was sinking. Literally. The walls were beginning to crack when we were there and a small but extremely scary sinkhole had appeared in the back yard. It seems the foundations are unstable due to erosion from an underground stream. Would I really have wanted to buy it, knowing it was built on unstable land? Absolutely not!

And there's more. The unpleasant medical practice we belonged to at the time was now a lot further away. We eventually joined a new, closer one. At this new place, which had happier and thus more helpful doctors, I discovered that I'd had two problems misdiagnosed. Sadly, these had both already caused me permanent physical damage, but it could have been a lot worse.

Best of all, the colder, harsher area we moved to is populated with some of the warmest people I've ever met anywhere. The country house was gorgeous, but our closest neighbours were cold and unfriendly. In our present home, the hill house, the locals are not only friendly, they have become friends. I could feel Sol smiling at me as I wrote that.

It would take me eight years to fully understand why he'd lied about the country house. Now I understand that if he'd told us that it was only to be a short term rental, we would not have relaxed and had all the fun we had while living there. Instead, he pretended it was our forever home to stop me worrying about moving again, so that I could focus fully on my personal health.

We spent two wonderful summers in that house. We had loads of barbecues and often ate outdoors on the back patio. Looking back, I can see how much we needed that breathing space between constant moving house. Like parents, guides and higher beings sometimes tell the odd white lie if they know it's better for you in the long term.

23

At the time we moved into the new house, which I'll call the hill house from here on, none of us was in the mood for such a philosophical thought as *this is for the best long term*. All the drama of house moves plus my health and other problems had led to us all becoming so stressed out that we did the thing all families do under stress – we fought with each other. I figured we needed a holiday. No, I *knew* we needed a holiday! My parents last holiday was in 1981 and Sandy and I hadn't had a holiday since our honeymoon in 2003. I began to plan a holiday. I was still waiting for hernia surgery, but knew that could take a long time. I wanted us to have some fun before the summer was over.

I had hoped to plan a full week away, travelling through England to see all the famous sites, but that wasn't possible. Around the time we were looking for a new house to rent, my dad was in the process of looking for a new job. The place where he'd been working had made major cutbacks, the first signs of the recession as it turned out. He had only been at a new job for a few months, so he wasn't able to ask for holiday leave, but he did manage to get a Friday off. That gave us a long weekend to plan around.

We managed to see a lot in three days, but it was a bit manic. We left early on Friday morning and Sandy drove straight down as far as possible through central Scotland and on along the west coast of England. We crashed each night at those travel places. Over the next two days, we saw Stonehenge, Salisbury Cathedral, Glastonbury, Avebury, the White Horse, and all sorts of unexpected delights, like Cheddar Gorge.

It was in Glastonbury that my dad took a photo that came to be the way I described my abilities. He was taking a photo of a gold altar cloth covered in embroidered angels. In the photo the cloth is only faintly visible because the camera also captured the reflections in the cabinet glass. As a result, you can see me as well as the altar cloth in the layers of reality. I love that photo because every time I look at it I feel like who I am makes sense.

On the way home, I had a most amazing experience. I wrote about it for my blog, using that altar cloth photo:

> Sometimes the reflections on the glass in my mind obscure parts of what I get and I'm left with pieces and fragments. Other times it all just "clicks" and the reflection fades... and I see through the glass in perfect clarity.

Those perfectly clear moments are a high that cannot be matched. I had a moment like that on the way home from our holiday. Usually I don't share things like this in public, but I think I need to be true to who I am.

On the way home, I was drifting as I listened to music on the radio. We were going north on the motorway. It was mad busy and the traffic was moving slowly. As I drifted, I kept seeing this angel sitting on our car roof. It looked bored, chin in hand, sitting sideways with his feet dangling over my window. A guardian angel, for want of a better description. I tried to see if I could see anyone else's guardian angels. What I got was a lot more than I expected.

I saw my husband's angel and I also saw the wings of my mom's angel and my dad's. No more than that, though. I got a bit frustrated that I couldn't get more detail and kind of gave up... started watching the scenery and passing cars. That was when I realised I could feel angels everywhere and then I started to see them. Not clear, but clear enough to say there was an angel sitting in the lotus position on top of the large lorry/truck in front of us.

I even saw two angels playing dominoes on top of a car full of a mom-dad-kids family. These angels realised I could see them and waved. I did not wave back! All the angels seemed to realise I could see them at that moment and for a while the sensation was intense. A wonderful feeling of everyone being connected. Like a huge, crazy web of light threads from every car and person and angel. Then we pulled off the motorway to have a meal and I lost the connection, but that vision of all those angels above every car will never leave me.

Looking back at that photo, I had another idea. Maybe the glass is more like the mirror glass that becomes transparent when light shines through it. Without the light, all you see is your own reflection, then someone turns on the light and *BANG* you can see straight through to those other realities.

I even know what acts as the switch that flips on the light. The switch is always Love, one way or another. Which makes perfect sense really – Light is just Love made visible. :)

Some of my blog readers wanted to know more and asked me what I thought about angels. I wrote another blog post, going into more detail about what I'd seen as well as some other stories.

What do I think about Angels? I think they are not human, nor ever were human. These are not ghosts or spirits. They are a higher energy/life force than us, but "higher" doesn't automatically mean more advanced or superior. They're just different. They do seem to watch over us and even communicate with and protect us at times.

They have been called many things by many different cultures, but the basic concept is always the same – they are messengers and protectors who work for God. Depending on your spiritual/religious faith, you could call them Higher Beings or Light Beings and change the word God to Creator, Source or Great Spirit or... it's all the same really.

I think the wings and body shapes are purely symbolic. It's no more than a way to convey an idea or a message. It is interesting to me how angels are shown as winged and pretty in religious Christian art, since the Bible makes no reference to angels having wings or being pretty! In fact, some biblical angels are downright scary.

I'm not even sure Archangels are ever described as winged. Cherubim were described as having wings, but in their case this is multiple wings and even multiple heads! Our modern image of a cherub as a fat baby is actually based on Cupid, the ancient god of love. Biblical angels looked either completely human or extremely inhuman. I believe the inhuman versions, such as cherubim, are simply symbolic.

The most vivid example of how this is purely symbolic was my husband's guardian angel that I saw when we were on holiday. I saw a female wearing a golden mask. The mask changed twice and both times the symbols were things that relate very personally to my husband. I asked this angel to show me her face and she took off the mask.

For a few seconds I saw a woman's face, but then it began to change. The face became another woman, then another: black, white, Asian, old, young, pretty, plain, even famous – I saw Cher's face in there! The faces were changing every second and grew faster until they were just a blur. That was when the angel put the mask back on.

I think the faces, wings, and even body shapes are just make-believe. I suspect that human minds can't cope with a creature that has such a vastly different make-up to us, so angels create these masks of symbols and shapes we find easy to accept.

I also think/believe we come into contact with the human shape angels in our lives without realising it or only realising it later. I have had an experience like that. In hospital about 15 years back, a nurse came to me after my operation and told me, "Don't be afraid. God is taking care of you."

This male nurse was distinctive and easy to remember. Firstly, male nurses are fairly rare in South Africa and this guy was tall, well-built and black. He looked like a Zulu. I waited to see him again to thank him, but he never returned to my ward. Eventually I asked about him, but the doctors and nurses said no-one like that worked at the hospital. He did not exist.

I was completely awake when he spoke to me. Admittedly I was in a lot of pain, but not to the point of hallucinating and creating big Zulu guys in nurse uniforms! Was he an angel messenger? I like to think so. He's not a unique story either. I've heard so many stories of people who have been helped or warned by strangers who just seem to appear and then... gone. I have no firm explanation on what they are, or why they sometimes step in to help us, but I'm glad to know they do seem to watch over us.

Reading that old blog post now, I'm smiling to myself. Most of my hunches and deductions were correct, but some were way off. But that is another story....

24

Before I continue the story of higher beings and angels, I need to deal with the other side. The things some people call demonic. Oh yes, I've experienced both sides. All psychics do. Is there Good and Evil? Yes, but there is a huge layer of grey between those two and the lines can be blurry. Myrt thought he was a demon, but he was simply a human soul lost in his own anger and fear. The family curse energy that my friend saw in my root chakra seems to have been similar, something that once was human, but had turned dark.

I don't have all the answers. All I can share are my stories. To do that, I need to go back to the first time I came up against the other side. That was when I was a teenager and completely clueless. I was thirteen and we'd recently moved house. I had a new bedroom with its own bathroom and a view over trees. I loved the view and my room, but the rest of the house... not so much. We lived in that house for 30 years so the exact dates of some of these events are a bit vague, but one thing I do know is that the weird neighbour was there when we moved in. Before I get to that story, I'll deal with the house itself.

Our house, 1980s.

That house was haunted. I'm not sure if it was a ghost or a poltergeist. We got so used to it over the years that we mostly ignored it. Every night, my mom would hear digging and scraping outside her window in the early hours before dawn. My mom suffers with insomnia and the noises didn't help. She used to get up and try to find the source of the noise, but there never was anything to explain where the sounds came from.

The most spectacular strangeness in that house was the crashes. The first time it happened, it gave us a huge fright. My mom and I were watching TV when there was this sound like a wardrobe had been pushed over with a loud smash and bang noise. We leaped to our feet and checked every room, but nothing was overturned or damaged. After that night, the loud BANG and CRASH would happen at random times. Not often and always at night.

There never was any sign of what caused the noises. We eventually reached a stage of becoming so used to it that we'd just ignore it and keep watching TV. I joked that we probably had the most frustrated ghost or poltergeist ever, probably sitting in a corner crying at our complete lack of interest.

The worst feeling room in the house was the bedroom my dad used as an office at the back of the house. I didn't like it, especially at night. We kept the door closed when we weren't in there because I hated going past it at night. It always felt like I was being watched from the darkness. Something did eventually happen in that room, but I'm not sure which story that relates to as this may connect back to the weird neighbour.

The weird neighbour was a woman with far too many cats. There's nothing particularly odd about that, except she gave me that prickly-neck feeling of animal distrust. I had no logical reason for feeling negative about her. She was one of the quietest neighbours on our street. She worked long hours and was rarely home, but whenever we did see her, she always smiled. She never spoke or said hello... just smiled.

Her cats ranged the neighbourhood. They were fairly average cats, except for one. He was a huge tomcat and extremely aggressive. He killed birds in our yard as well as attacked other cats. I think he even had a go at a few dogs. I suspect he was the cat who left my poodle with slash marks across his nose.

I was out in the garden one day when I saw him stalking a bird. I chased him away and he ran and leapt onto his home wall. I was still in full out run and yell mode, too late to stop, when I saw his owner stand up from behind her garden wall where she must have been gardening. She picked him up and I waited for a reprimand. I was only fourteen and always looked younger for my age. But instead of being annoyed, she cuddled her cat and smiled. She stood there, staring at me. She had this wide, smug smile, as if she was pleased I'd chased her cat. I went back to our garden thinking, *Creepy woman*, then forgot about it.

The dreams started some time after that. I'm not sure of time spans, but I do remember I was still in high school when the dreams began. At least once a month, I'd dream that her cat was trying to get into my bedroom. I remember a particularly vivid nightmare where the cat was trying to enter through my open bedroom window as I was trying to force it back out. I had its head in my hands and it was biting me. As we struggled, I actually broke its jaw. I felt and heard the gristly crunch as I pulled the jaw down. I woke up thinking *GROSS!*

Years passed and I moved bedrooms. The front room was always cold. It had three outside walls, being attached to the house. It can get cold in Africa and that room was freezing in winter. I finally decided to move into the bedroom that had been my dad's office since it was much warmer. I wasn't bothered by the fact I'd found the room creepy as a teenager. I was twenty now and I figured new paint and curtains would end the creepy vibe.

This back bedroom was on ground level, which would become a problem. The neighbour's cat could now reach the window and it actually did try to get in. I wasn't scared, I just found it annoying. I love cats, but I'm highly allergic to them. As a child, I would get asthma by simply having a cat walk past me. So here I was in a warmer room, now unable to open a window.

With the window closed, the cat would sit on the window ledge and watch me all night. The way my bed faced meant that the first thing I saw every time I woke up was the cat staring in at me. I started keeping the curtains shut because the cat constantly watching me was a bit odd, but sleeping in pitch dark was equally unpleasant. I'd often wake up and turn the light on to ease my feeling of claustrophobia.

One night, I woke up in a state of sheer animal terror. Even weirder, I was reciting Psalm 23, The lord is my Shepherd. I spoke the whole psalm out loud, word perfect. I know it was word perfect because later I went and looked it up. The moment I finished saying the psalm out loud, the terror eased off. Was it me reacting to the claustrophobia, to the resident ghost or to the cat? I don't know. I had recently started working at our local library and I got to know our weird neighbour better from the other librarians. She was an avid source of interest, living unmarried with a much younger man which made for great village gossip. Our neighbour regularly came into the library, but I never dealt with her at the counter.

This was deliberate. I always found some excuse to be busy elsewhere. The reason for this is something I cannot explain in any sane manner. For some reason, I could not look into her eyes. I felt that if I looked into her eyes she would SEE me and I wanted to stay invisible. She felt sticky sweet and poisonous, like a Venus fly-trap.

The story of our neighbour would get a lot weirder before it ended. A wave of hysteria was about to hit our town as South Africa discovered Satanism. Our conservative Christian country was suddenly seeing monsters under the beds and signs of the devil in songs played backwards. Most of it was complete nonsense. I remember upsetting a woman I baby-sat for by bursting out laughing when she told me she'd heard they were on the hunt for children to sacrifice. I thought it was the biggest load of stupid ever.

The gossip about Satanism flew around our small town like fire. Hell fire? Ha! The biggest story was that our little village had an active Satanic coven run by a man who was reported to be the leader of the whole South African Satanic scene. *Mmm… yeah….*

It was around this time that I had a plague of stinging ants come up through the floor in my bedroom. We did eventually get rid of them, but I had to move out and return to the cold, flat-let bedroom. The first few nights after I changed bedrooms, the cat went mad with frustration. It could get onto the roof, but thanks to the roof overhang it couldn't get onto the window ledge from above and the window was too high to reach from the ground.

The cat took to pacing up and down on my bedroom roof. It's amazing how noisy small paws can be, not to mention the wailing and growling. Did I mention that this cat growled? It's the only cat I've ever heard growl. It would sit on our fence and growl at me as I did the gardening. I'm an animal lover, but that cat... nope.

The strangeness of it all finally began to weave together one weekend. I was in our front garden pruning a hedge when a man driving by stopped, reversed, and then asked me a few casual gardening questions. He was exceptionally handsome and I was twenty-seven, single and suddenly aware I was in my old gardening clothes.

He said he was new to the area, having just moved into the old house at the end of the street. he said the garden was a mess and he was looking for a garden service. We chatted a bit. He smiled a lot, but I remember thinking that he felt like the kind of person your mother warns you about. The "don't get into the car" stranger.

A short while after that, someone at work had new

gossip. She said that the high leader of South Africa's Satanic Church had apparently moved into the house at the end of our street. I must admit that did unnerve me. I was in the library one day when our weird neighbour came in. I backed off as I always did, went and started sorting the filing cabinet. I let another librarian deal with her. She said she was there to help a friend join the library. He was just parking the car. A man walked in as she was speaking. It was the handsome man I'd chatted to in the garden.

The other librarian was clearly smitten by his good looks and dazzling smile. She kept stammering as she helped him fill in the library forms. It would have been funny, except it was too surreal. Here was our weird neighbour cuddling up to a man the village gossip had tagged as Satan's pope. I was busy putting books back and when I came around a corner, there the two of them were, arm in arm.

Our neighbour handed him a book she had taken off the shelf. She leaned in to whisper to him as he paged through the book and they both laughed. No... they sniggered. That's the more appropriate word. They clearly thought the book was ridiculous or rubbish. I backed off and hid around the corner. Their behaviour felt unwholesome. They left soon after and I went to where they'd been standing and took down the book they had been paging through. It was an autobiography titled "My Life as a Witch."

25

Now that we have dealt with the fact I have had some dark experiences in my past, I can return to Orla warning me that I was holding a dark energy in my root chakra, a family curse that ran through the female line of my family. I mentioned that the photo I saw in my dream on the night Orla worked on me in 2007 was of my mom, her mother and sister. There were other females in this family line.

It just struck me now, the quirky coincidences of that feminine line. My grandmother had two daughters born 11 years apart: my mom and my aunt. I was born to her first daughter and years later my aunt gave birth to a daughter, just three days after my 18th birthday. My baby, my unborn daughter, was due to be born the same week as my grandmother's birthday. My cousin would give birth to her daughter the following year in the same due date week as my child. My cousin and I seem to echo each other and yet in many ways we are chalk and cheese. I take after my grandmother in looks. I am short, dark haired and curvy. My cousin is like her mother, who took after our Scottish-Dutch grandfather. She is tall, slender and very blonde. We are just as different in personality as well. Complete opposites.

My mother and her sister were also the opposite of each other in looks and personality. My mother, as the eldest child, was the one who was given all the responsibilities and chores. Her sister, the youngest child, was indulged and became the family princess diva. My aunt is not an easy topic to write about. She caused heartache to everyone who cared about her throughout her life. My aunt was rebellious, demanding and headstrong and she raised her daughter as a mini version of herself.

At the time of the Satanist scare in South Africa, my cousin was in junior school and I think she began using the idea to scare the other kids. My cousin liked to be noticed and enjoyed holding power over others. She set up a dark altar in her bedroom with a silver cloth and black candles. My aunt saw it as amusing and indulged her. Was my cousin genuinely dabbling in Satanism? I do not know. I do know the last time I saw her in South Africa she was dating an ex-Satanist. I actually liked him the best of her boyfriends. Kind of ironic.

Our lives went different ways and I haven't seen my cousin since 2003. I saw my aunt in 2006 when she came over to visit us, but she also vanished out of our lives a few years after that. This led to my mother asking me for help. I had begun seeing chakras and my mother asked me to try and use that ability to find out how her sister was. My mom was really worried about her baby sister, so I agreed to try.

I took a quiet afternoon to send my mind out and I connected to my aunt fairly easily. I saw her chakras, but they were different. Since my surgery, I had been practising seeing chakras, using all my friends and family as test subjects. As I said earlier, I saw chakras as little rainbow coloured creatures; butterflies, wolves, ladybugs, teddy bears, bees, and even little dragons. But I saw my aunt's chakras as coloured spheres, like clear glass balls.

Within each sphere was a scene that I was able to enter into. Some were real places and some were set up more like a scene from a play. I can't remember much now, but I do remember the last one I looked at. Back then, I had no ability to control the order I saw them in. They'd pop into my mind randomly. It took me a few years to control when and how I see chakras. Nowadays, I see them in order from the 1st Root Chakra at the base of the spine all the way up in tidy order to the 7th Crown Chakra at the top of the head.

The last one I saw for my aunt that afternoon was actually the 1st root chakra. This red sphere held a countryside scene with farm fields edged with trees and a dirt road. It was very pretty, if a bit quiet. As I looked around, I realised there were no birds or animals. Was this based on a real place or merely a theatrical scene? And then I saw it... an animal coming down the farm road. It was dark in colour, running at an easy gait along the dirt road. It was about the size of a really big dog. A wolf? It ran strangely….

I studied it, trying to figure out what was wrong with the way it ran. Loping would be a better word. As it came closer to where I was standing, it stopped and stood up to look at me. It wasn't an animal. It was human in shape, but dark and hard to focus on. I knew that it had stopped because it realised I could see it and it wasn't at all happy about that. I felt rage coming from it. I panicked and severed the connection. I remember sitting there, heart thumping, thinking, *What the hell just happened?*

I'd never before come across a sentient creature during a chakra reading. What was it doing in my aunt's root chakra? I held the ancestral curse in my Root Chakra; the same chakra and same family line. Was this thing related to that in some way? I called on Myrt to protect me, used some shielding concepts I'd picked up on shaman forums, then I wrote the reading out before starting dinner. I didn't tell anyone what had happened. I wanted to forget what I'd seen.

After dinner, Sandy asked me to meet him upstairs. He vanished before I could ask why. I found him sitting on the edge of the bed, white and shaking. He said something very strange was going on. During dinner, something had kept urging him to hurt me. He told me that there had been no words, just a raging ANGRY force trying to make him stab me in the eyes. He was completely freaked and so was I!

I told him about the chakra reading and what I'd seen. Sandy agreed with my hunch that his angry force was the same angry dark thing I'd seen in my aunt's chakra. I felt very aware that what I had done was wrong, even if my intentions were good. I had spied on my aunt and invaded her personal space. If I'd been seen by something that did not want to be seen, that really was my own fault.

The next morning, Sunday, we decided to get out for the day. We had a lovely time out in the countryside. Sandy was completely relaxed and fine until we got home. The moment we were back, the feelings returned. Sandy explained it as an incredible feeling of being under pressure, as if something was within him and trying to use him. Every time he sat down to eat, this intense pressure to stab me in the eyes would hit him... because without eyes I wouldn't be able to see It?

That dark thing had been extremely angry about being seen, but I, in my fledgling ignorance, had thought I was safe because I used shields to protect me. I never thought that this thing would then look at some other way to get to me, in this case via my own husband. For the following days and weeks, we tried everything from prayers and smudging with sage to encircling the house with salt and purifying herbs.

Through it all I made sure we ate with the steak knives every night. The really sharp ones. Was I scared? A bit, but there was no way I was going to allow this thing to bully us with fear. I'm not sure what made it stop. We were trying everything we could think of and asking our friends for help as well. Sandy did find one thing that helped him. Before meals, he'd imagine himself encircled by angel's wings. He said that the first time he tried this he felt queasy and "sort of fizzy from the inside outwards" and then really good and safe.

Poor Sandy. He had borne the burden of my stupidity. It was a harsh lesson in not taking things seriously, especially things you don't understand. I had never taken much interest in the idea of shielding. I'd even wondered if Myrt really was protecting me. I certainly learnt my lesson on that! I had been so well protected that this thing had to turn elsewhere to try to get to me.

I never again went into a chakra reading without first asking my guides if it was okay to do so. I'm still not sure what that thing was. I have done many more readings since that day and I do sometimes find things attached to people. I call them feeders. They are parasites who take energy from the host in the same way fleas live off an animal. Strong emotions create the most energy, especially hate, fear or anger. Some feeders will try to provoke the host person in order to have more emotional energy to feed on. It's possible the thing I saw was a creature like that, which would explain why it was angry to be seen. Or was it related to our family's ancestral curse? I still don't know.

There is one final chapter to this story. A few years back, my guardian angel came to me as I was getting ready for bed. He said he would stay with me all night and sat at the head of the bed with my pillow in his lap. Twice that night I woke up and could see/sense his presence. He stayed with me until dawn.

Later that day, we had a phone call from Africa. My aunt had died of a heart attack the night before. The angel never explained why I needed protection that night. Was it because that thing attached to my aunt would have been set free when she died? Would it have come looking for me once again? I am so grateful I was watched over that night.

Since those first experiences, I have learnt a lot (mostly the hard way) about dealing with dark entities. I can now say, with reasonable confidence, that the worst possible human emotions for drawing in dark things are hate and fear. A lot of religions put anger at the top of the list of the bad emotions, but I've found anger to be cleansing and useful if used responsibly. I think of anger as a knife: it can be a weapon or a surgeon's life-saving tool. It all depends on how and why you use it. Hate is worse and fear is just as bad. In fact, for me fear is the worst, but more on that later.

Thankfully, my experiences have mostly been positive, but far too many New Age enthusiasts think it is "all good" and are far too trusting. I once met a New Age psychic in South Africa who connected to something unpleasant during a channelling session and threw her boyfriend across the room. Thinking everything out there is warm-and-fuzzy is on the level of the naive tourist who ends up mauled by a wild animal while trying to take a selfie together. Is it the wild animal's fault or the tourist's for dismissing the animal's natural instincts? The best rule of survival is: if you're not sure what it is, approach with caution. There's no harm in being careful.

Which reminds me: I completely forgot the finale to our haunted house in Africa problem. My mother and I got rid of it. After twenty odd years of putting up with it, we decided it had to go. My aunt got us a vial of Holy Water and I had a Jewish prayer of house blessing. I know, a rather eccentric combination, but it worked. We started at the back of the house with my mom sprinkling Holy Water as I said the blessing in each room. We worked our way to the front door, hoping that it might force whatever was bothering us to leave that way. The bangs and crashes stopped. Not only that, the weird scraping noises in the garden stopped as well.

My psychic friend James was horrified when I told him this story years later. He felt I should have tried to connect to our problem-maker, find out what/who it was and why it was there. James said I should have coaxed it to go into the Light. He has worked with a psychic who removes spirits in this humane way. I never knew there were other ways to deal with spirits back in the 1990s. And honestly, if I had thought to communicate I probably would have told it, "NO TRESPASSING – move on!" I'm afraid I wasn't a very compassionate psychic in those days.

Another friend recently asked me what my opinion was of a TV show she had watched about exorcisms and removing demons from houses. She said that in many of the cases the dark thing returned after a while. I said I wasn't surprised. From what I've witnessed in my own life, it's not enough to call in a priest to bless your home.

Fear is undoubtedly the most weakening emotion. A fearful person has no ability to protect their personal space and that includes their spiritual space. All fine if you've got a great exorcist, but when he/she leaves it is then up to you to keep the door closed. Anyone praying in fear or still fearful after the exorcist leaves is doomed to pull whatever is bothering them straight back. It's about what you are *feeling* as well as what you are saying when it comes to prayer.

I think this might be what Jesus was getting at when He said faith can make you walk on water and move mountains. Faith and trust are emotionally calming and calm people are able to focus their own power in order to send clear messages outwards. Add Love and you have an intent energy that is powerful enough to travel through time, space and dimensions.

26

When I describe beings or things I have encountered, I use names that work for me, not anything official. I'm figuring this out as I go and I tend to use terms that feel right to me. I'd say there are as many variations on life in other dimensions as there are life forms on this planet. But as to phylum, genus, species? I haven't a clue. I often end up realising I was on the wrong track when I look back, just as I did with the pesky elephant that turned into a spirit guide. Ah, that pesky Sol. He was still a conundrum. He had refused to fit the box as a totem elephant and now he was refusing to fit as a spirit guide. Unlike my friends' guides, he never seemed interested in teaching or offering advice. He'd give advice if asked, but it clearly wasn't his thing.

But if my spirit guide experience was in limbo, the rest of my psychic life had ramped up a gear. One of the loveliest experiences I've had was in May 2009.

Sandy had decided to go look for his father's grave. It had been 35 years since his dad was buried at Tomnahurich cemetery in Inverness. Sandy was a teenager at the time and had never been back, but this particular May weekend he felt a need to return. We drove through to Inverness, parked the car by the gate, and then Sandy set off in the direction he vaguely remembered. I browsed a bit, then went to stand higher up where I could enjoy the bright, sunny day and take some photos for my blog.

I watched Sandy wandering about to my right in the area he was sure he remembered. He was busy going up and down the rows and rows of graves when I saw something. To my left and near the entrance gate, there was a man standing by a grave. Not a literal man; this was an image of a man superimposed over the reality before me. He was standing with his arms at his sides, fairly relaxed. He was wearing grey trousers and a long-sleeved white shirt with the sleeves rolled up to just below his elbows.

It was only vague and he faded fairly quickly, but I was curious now. I went down to where I'd seen the man. It was over in another area of the graveyard far from where my husband was looking, but it was a nice day and I enjoyed the walk. I went down the path and looked at the grave where the man had been standing... and there was the name of my husband's father.

It felt strange, but good, to call my husband over and tell him I'd found the grave site... with a little help. The man was too vague to swear he looked like my husband's father. Later that week, my husband went home and got his mum to take out the old photos and there were pictures of his father dressed like the man I'd seen. All in all, it was a perfectly lovely day.

Not long after that, I was back in hospital again for hernia surgery. The surgeon warned me not to do anything strenuous for a month: no lifting, bending or stretching. Thankfully, I had my mom and Sandy to take over the chores and they did a fantastic job. Even sitting at the computer was painful at first, so I had about two weeks of not being able to do much of anything. In that perverse human way, I had all the time in the world to read and I did not feel like reading. It was during a long day of lying on the bed pretending to read that a word kept popping into my head – *MOTHER*.

It slowly dawned on me that it might have meaning,

so I asked for more information. I saw a woman's face. She had long, silver grey hair, but her face looked young. She smiled at me before she faded away. It was in September 2009 that I saw her again. I was in my bedroom trying to write the sequel to my first book when her face appeared in my mind. I tried harder to keep my brain quiet and allow myself to see without questioning the how and why.

With simple acceptance and a quieter mind, I was able to see all of her this time. Once again, she was smiling at me and she gave off this strong feeling of gentle, tender love. She was a woman of average build with an oval face and long, straight hair. Her hair was impressive, thick and silvery grey in colour. She was wearing a long dress, but I could see her feet were bare. She came closer so that I could see more details and I realised her feet were actually the base of trees. Her toes were like gnarled old roots. She even had little branches with leaves sprouting from her toes.

She lifted the skirt of her dress so that I could see her legs. They were a deep, dark blue. As I looked closer, I realised they were made of water. I could see tiny whales and other ocean creatures swimming about. Her legs were the oceans. From there, she showed me the rest of her body as if her clothing dissolved away. Her stomach was molten rock and swirling fire, like the Earth's core or a volcano. Her upper body was vague, but I could clearly see that her breasts were dripping bees instead of milk. This seemed really odd, but it kept being repeated when I questioned what I was seeing. Moving upwards, her throat was pale blue and full of flying birds. Her face was a normal human face, except that her eyes were dark and full of stars and that grey hair was actually heavy, falling rain. She was amazing.

I told a friend in India who had sent me information on Durga, the ultimate Mother Goddess. After talking to him, I realised that I was now getting two words in my head, over and over: *EARTH MOTHER.* I now had a name for who she was.

Another friend I spoke to asked me why I hadn't seen her heart or asked why bees were coming from her breasts. Good point! I tend to overlook the obvious. I took some quiet time to try to connect with her again and ask about those bees. She returned to show me that her heart was a beehive full of honey. It was warm and buzzy and gave me this mellow feeling. She showed me that a hive holds all the seasons from spring to winter. I thought about how bees are a matriarchal society. She had shown me the divine feminine hidden in her beehive heart.

I saw her again about a year after that, but at the time I didn't put the two visions together. It was only after I started writing this book and was going through my saved notes that I saw this connection. My life was so busy at times that I regularly saved things and then forgot about them. This next passage is one of those forgotten stories.

It was December 2010 and a blogger friend had asked me to try an experiment. She had been to a specific place in America and had a vision there. She was curious to see if I could meditate and travel to the place in my mind. If I did manage to do that, would I see the same things or similar? It was a place I had never heard of, which made this experiment all the more interesting, called Mount Shasta. The blogger friend gave me that name, nothing else. I found the email reply I sent her (Friday, 10th December) saved with all my other oddments:

Well, I'm back from seeing where Mt Shasta might take me. I didn't get much except I suspect I got more than I realise and just need to set it out to look at it. It's a bit like beach-combing – you find your pockets full of surprises when you lay it all out at the end.

I was afraid I'd fall asleep, but I never slept because I got colder and COLDER. Although our house is chilly, I got the feeling this cold was from the experience. I never got my mind totally out of "here" to "there", but in brief hiccups I kept seeing a mountain covered in snow and snow all around. I twice saw buffalo in the snow at the base of the mountain and had a sense of two time eras superimposed as the buffalo were translucent and I could see city lights through them.

Other vivid images that were interesting: a black wolf running in the snow and a white hare or jack rabbit. The white hare led me to a woman dressed in white skins with long, silvery grey hair. She looked like a Native

American version of the Ice Queen, but she felt nice. She gave me a cloak of black, edged in a design like flames in red and gold.

Two last things. I saw myself (and this sounds awful, but wasn't at all) as a skin. I was pulled tight as they do to cure a skin and I was told I was going to be made into a drum! It should have been a horrific sight and idea, but it wasn't. Oh, and I realised something when I was with the woman. I saw the words "crow of bones" and then they melted together and became -"crones".

The blogger friend was pleased with my results. She had seen the same woman in her vision. I don't remember anything beyond that and I completely forgot that this woman also had silvery hair. Her nationality might have been different, but I think she was the same woman with the beehive heart. I clearly didn't think so at the time, but looking back I can see patterns I had no idea about in 2010.

Both the woman and the animals would make more sense as the years passed. Being a drum is similar to other things I've been told: that I am a bridge and one who speaks out. I could have picked a less stressful vocation, but I suppose that's the whole point of a vocation – it picks you. The dark wolf was Myrt and the hare is the symbol of the Goddess. I've seen the white hare depicted with her since then. And the crow of bones? Ah well, you'll have to wait to find out how that story turned out!

In 2011, the friend who originally told me about Durga emailed to ask a question. He was wondering what the future held for our planet, considering how weird the weather had been that year. He wondered if I'd seen or felt anything. I told Sandy and he suggested I try scanning the planet in the same way I scanned people's chakras.

That seemed a bit too much to take on, but it got me thinking. Could I ask Earth Mother herself what was going on and would she reply? I decided to give it a try. Well... I got an answer. I shared it with a few friends and they wrote back to suggest that I put it on my blog. At that time, I was nursing a new health issue that was causing me extreme hand pain, so I put off blogging, but did eventually put it up for my New Year's Eve post. Here is my original email:

> I managed to find some quiet time this morning to meditate and asked Earth Mother what all our weird weather means. I was taken down into the ground. At first, it was like floating-plummeting down a mine shaft or a deep hole. I came into caves or caverns, all very dark! It was as if I had a tiny torch, so I could only get small glimpses of what was around me.
>
> I saw pictures on the walls. A flash of a face that reminded me of Tutankhamen. More "bits" that looked Egyptian, but then pictures that reminded me of paintings or mosaics I've seen from ancient Crete. The one I saw

clearly was a big fish, like a tuna. Above and below were bands of design, like Cretan or Grecian geometric patterns.

I floated on into a new cavern, carved like a giant room. There were pillars that seemed made of clay or stone. They were Cretan in design. In the corner of this cavern room was a big, raised, oblong like the base for a bed, but moulded or carved from the stone floor itself. I tried to ask about this oblong and the place, this room. When I thought *room* I heard, "womb, room, tomb".

I felt amusement from whoever said the words because of the fact I couldn't get it clear which word was right. In a way, they all were right because a "room" in the centre of the earth is both a "womb" and a "tomb", really. I heard, "ATLANTIS" softly spoken, but clear. A woman's voice. I think part of what I was shown were ancient ruins yet to be discovered and I think part of them was a tomb and part a temple.

I went down deeper. I saw lava at times, but it was far off down side tunnels I wasn't travelling through. I saw white cities in the dark, but I knew they weren't here. They were little pictures, almost like bubbles or TV screens, on which I could see another world. Another Earth. These cities were all white buildings and above them there were orbs of light that lit up these cities the same way we use street lights, but these lights were floating and they seems to sparkle slightly, a bit like some fireworks.

Down deeper, I saw the belly of a huge, white reptile above me. It was as wide as a bus and looped up into the endless darkness. There was a line of red along the belly crease and some blood dripping. I realised it had been cut. Then I was standing further back and could see that it was an enormous, white snake curved up into a loop.

I got the word "OUROBOROS", which I know. The snake holding its tail is in every culture of the world and in most cases represents the continual cycle of Nature, Life, Seasons. It can symbolise all-being-one or reincarnation, as well. I saw who had cut it. It was one of the forms I see Mother Earth/Earth Mother as: the goddess Durga. In one of her hands, she held a silver sword and I knew she had cut Ouroboros.

I could see the cut in the snake was very fine, but had still managed to sever the snake almost through. Only the skin on its back was holding it together. There was no anger or fear in this cutting. Nothing 'bad' in either her or the snake. It was more like seeing a surgeon cut into a patient. I think the Earth cycles, weather cycles maybe, are being cut through, but this isn't something bad or fearful. It is necessary.

Then I saw the oceans and all the fish and dolphin were swimming in one direction. They were swimming into a huge spiralling "hole" like when the water spirals out of a bathtub, except this spiral was on its side and within the ocean! It was huge. A whale could easily swim into the spiral hole. I was taken with them and found myself surfacing on a coastline where the water around me was so pure and pristine it sparkled. And then I was back in the dark hearing "womb" and it was over.

I still have no idea what some of that meant. Symbols can translate in many ways. At the time, I added this on my blog:

Wombs and tombs? Birth and death, or maybe just a doorway? The fish and dolphin went through a kind of doorway. What lies behind the door for our planet and us? The unknown can seem scary, but the unknown is also exciting. After all, it's the way every adventure starts.

27

Adventures and how they start.... Oh my, what an adventure still lay before me that I had no idea about back in 2011. I've tried remembering what specific events happened during 2010 to 2012, but it's a bit of a blur. The main event that stands out is September 2010 when my dad was supposed to die. It started so unassumingly. My dad had to take his car in for repairs and was off work for the day. He came home feeling very out of breath and mom suggested he go to the doctor. She feared it was his heart as he'd been under a lot of stress.

Dad was working on a contract that was due to run out that week. My dad's an industrial electrician. The factory he was working for back then dealt with processing organic vegetables, which were cleaned for packaging with water and chlorine. It was this machine that was causing problems, spewing clouds of chlorine steam vapour into the factory. Staff had walked out a few times, complaining they could not breathe.

My dad had been assigned the task of balancing the chlorine dosage, which really wasn't his job. He spent weeks struggling with the machine and this had led to several arguments between my dad and factory management. Hence his stress about them renewing his work contract. So that day, dad went off to get his heart checked while mom and I stayed home to help a plumber who was there to check and fix the radiators. We were so busy that we never noticed how many hours had passed until the phone rang. Dad was at the hospital. They wanted to run a few tests.

Sandy took us straight to the hospital, where dad was in the process of signing himself out. His heart was fine, but he had a high temperature and the doctors suspected he might have pneumonia. They wanted to keep dad in, but he told them that was rubbish, he was fine. The hospital allowed us to take him home as long as he agreed to rest, take his antibiotics and be booked off work for a week. For the following week, dad was ill with what seemed like a typical chest infection, except it showed no sign of improving.

Dad's work mailed him a letter saying that he had to come in for a meeting about his contract the following week, but he never got to go as his doctor booked him off for another week. Then suddenly, dad's health went downhill fast. By the morning of the 17th of September, he could barely breathe and we called for an ambulance. As they were loading dad into the ambulance, a delivery man arrived with a letter to be signed for. It was for my dad, but he was already in the ambulance so Sandy signed for it. We left it unopened and followed the ambulance to the hospital.

And our lives fell apart. Within hours, dad had gone from sitting in a ward to lying in bed with an oxygen mask to High Care with all these tubes and machines. My dad's main concern was that we let his work know. Sandy asked the hospital for a new letter, booking dad off for a third week. Then he drove through to dad's place of employment and gave the note to reception, telling them what had happened and asking if they could they please reschedule dad's meeting.

It was only much later, when we were back home, that my mom opened dad's registered letter. It was from his employers and said he had been dismissed for refusing to attend the meeting that week. At the time, it felt like the ultimate slap in the face. We didn't tell my dad about the letter, as the specialist warned us not to stress him in any way. His lungs were in a terrible state and they had no idea why. They ran every type of test, completely bemused by my dad's condition.

A lovely consultant, who I only remember now as "Call me Joseph", sat with us and wrote down dad's entire life health history. He was the first one to look alarmed when we mentioned the chlorine steam at dad's work.

That week is a blur of constant hospital visits and seeing my father deteriorate daily until the hospital decided to send him for specialised care at the ICU in Aberdeen. We followed as soon as we could, arriving at Aberdeen Infirmary to find dad in the highest level of care with tubes and machines everywhere. The doctors still had no idea what was wrong with him and nothing was helping. The specialist took us into a room and told us the next 48 hours were crucial; either dad started to improve or he would die.

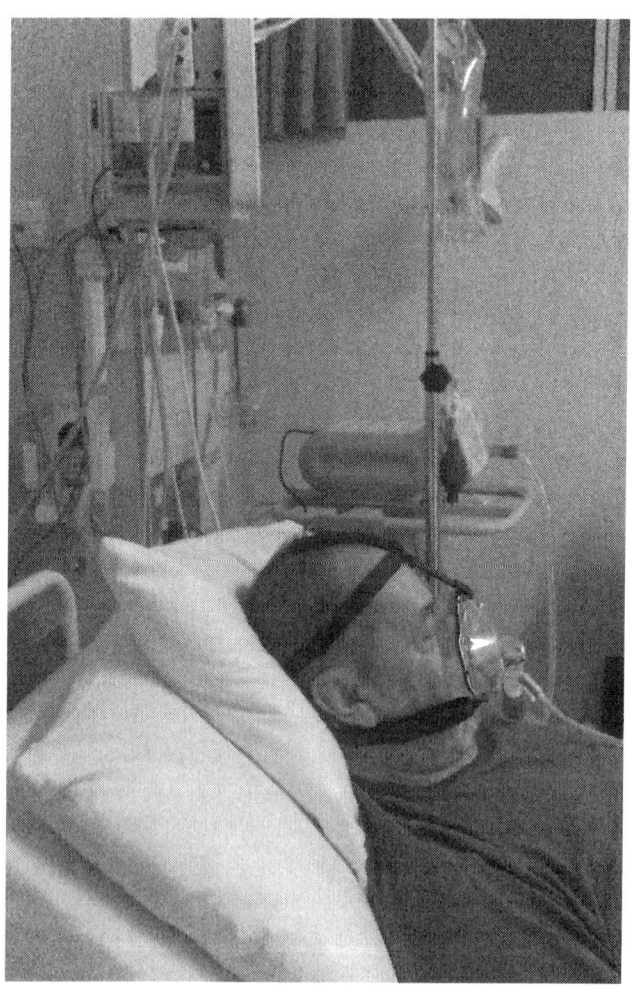

In a daze, we sorted out a place to stay, booking into a holiday cottage outside of Aberdeen.

My dad was always exceptionally healthy, looked ten years younger than he was, did sports and had barely ever been ill. None of this made sense. It felt like the worst bad dream. I still remember the waiting room for ICU. They had made it as nice as possible with soft, comfy chairs, tables and a coffee machine. I particularly remember the lighting. There were ceiling lights made to look like skylights with fake blue sky with white clouds. And I remember the phone on the table. No one was allowed in to the wards until they called for you.

It was so quiet. I remember the huddled families talking quietly and I remember passing beds where you knew at a glance... this person is never leaving here.

One young teenage boy we passed every day still haunts me. No young person should be in a place like that. He and his family moved me so deeply that I wrote a poem about it while I was there in that waiting room. I don't know who those people were, but I would still like to dedicate this to them and their beloved son/grandchild.

In Passing

I passed by your bed
and wondered your story;
Tattoos and T-shirt
completely out of place
amongst the tubes and wires.

With arms so thin and eyes so tired,
watching the TV without seeing,
seeing me without watching
every time I passed through.
Watching you waiting…

I knew. Did you?

Did she know too?
I watched her pass through, with
rucksack and Thermos, packets of snacks.
All the signs of the long term
traveller of wards and waiting rooms.
Holding herself together with
the busy brightness of a mother's love.

Others passed by too.
I saw them take turns
to hold your hand as you waited,
and passed them
as they waited, in crooked huddles
over half cups of coffee.
Women talking; a man hiding
tears in a corner, as I passed through.

And I knew they knew too.

Though none of us spoke
in passing, in waiting.
Connected in such disconnection.
Brief greetings and smiles
in hallways, in passing,
and then they were gone.
Empty chairs.

Empty bed.

I passed by your bed
and wondered your story,
and wished you
safe journeys
in passing.

For about three or four days, we went to ICU every
visiting time and then one day we went in and dad's
bed was empty.

A nurse told us dad had been moved to another ward. At first we were excited. If they'd moved him out of ICU, that was good news. Right? We followed the instructions through the labyrinth of the hospital and found dad at the far end of a small ward. But instead of looking happy, dad was in tears. It turned out that the doctor had told my dad he was dying and would probably not last more than a day. My dad was, not surprisingly, a wreck.

An elephant-man in my head pushed through it all to take my hand and whisper in my ear, "No, not yet. He has at least fifteen more years." I leant in and whispered it to my dad, who burst into tears. Then Sandy demanded to see the doctor. We left my mom with my dad and tackled the doctor together. Sandy reprimanded him for telling my father he was dying in such a callous way and then Sandy demanded a second opinion. The hospital sent us an apology and promised us a different specialist.

As we were leaving that day, something bizarre happened. Sandy was walking ahead with my mom. She was in a wheelchair as the long distances to walk in the hospital were too much for her. Sandy was pushing the wheelchair… and then he wasn't. This wasn't a superimposed vision in my mind. This time, the image in front of me actually changed.

It was barely a few seconds long, but quite vivid. What I saw was my mother walking with Sandy, leaning heavily against him and they were both crying. My dad was dead. Then a whole rush of images flashed through my mind. I don't remember much. It was too fast, but I do remember that I was seeing multiple realities laid out side by side. Multiple possible futures to this life story.

I remember clearly seeing Sandy, my mom and I standing outside a funeral parlour. I thought, *No, I refuse to accept this!* My refusal to accept his death was as if all of me, from molecular level up, dismissed that future possibility utterly. And something... changed. I can't explain it. I just felt the shift, like that feeling you get of dropping when you're falling asleep. It was as if I had pulled myself from one reality time line onto another.

That night was dreadful, but we got through it. In the morning, dad had a new specialist who was the first optimistic person we'd met in over a month. He was excited by the fact that no one knew what was wrong with my dad and asked permission to try a new experimental drug from Germany. We said, "Go for it."

We had to go home that day to check the house and sort out laundry and household bills. Before we left, my dad took my hand and asked me to please check his chakras for him. I decided to do that during the one and a half hour drive from Aberdeen to home, but once I was in the car I just felt so exhausted. For a month, we'd been visiting my dad two to three times a day. I thought, *How am I going to do this?* I was so afraid of what I might see, so afraid I'd fail.

I tried to focus and my dad's chakras appeared easily. I saw them as coloured bumble bees and I could see at a glance that several looked weak and exhausted, plus some had dark patches on their bodies. As I was trying to think what to do next, Earth Mother appeared. With a gentle smile, she held out her arms and gathered up all the tired little bumblebees like sleepy puppies. As she held them, flowers grew from her arms and the bumblebee chakras settled into them and fell asleep. And that was exactly what I did, too. I slept all the way home.

Within a week, dad was showing such good progress that they sent him back to our local hospital. Within another week, he was home. They told him he'd be on oxygen for the rest of his life, but he had stopped using it by that Christmas. They called it a miracle and I think it was.

For the first two years after that, my dad had to return to Aberdeen regularly for check ups. On one of those check up visits, we decided to go do a bit of shopping before heading home. As we wandered around Aberdeen, we went down this new unknown road and there on the right hand side was the funeral parlour I'd seen in my vision. It actually did exist. It was one of the most haunting moments of realising that the things I see are real and how different the outcome could have been.

My dad is still busy proving everyone wrong. He was warned that lung tissue never heals, but X-rays have shown that his lungs have done the impossible – they have regenerated. Oh, he is not back to perfect health. He still has breathing problems, but he's alive and much better than the doctors ever expected. As for what caused the damage? Dad's miracle-working specialist is convinced it was the chlorine.

That specialist was willing to testify if we took it further, but by then the factory had quickly dealt with the machine and health and safety officers refused to get involved. We gave up on that idea and focussed on getting dad the best results for unfair dismissal. We weren't in a situation where we could afford an attorney, so Sandy offered to speak for my dad. He read up on similar cases on the internet. The tribunal was held by phone meeting and Sandy won. It wasn't a big amount, but it was the highest allowed pay-out and that was most satisfying.

While all this was going on, I was in the beginning stages of a new health problem. It started in Aberdeen where the long hours spent walking and standing in hospital became more and more painful. By early 2012, my life was a blur of pain and I'd blown up with so much water retention that I couldn't fit into any shoes or bend my knees. The worst was the hand pain. It left me unable to do anything. Sandy had to wash, dress and feed me. Even the vibration of the car made my hands hurt, so driving to the doctors was an ordeal as well. On a scale of 1 to 10, bearing in mind I've had an ovary rupture with internal bleeding and a miscarriage, this pain was a full 10. It's the only time I've had pain so bad I could not talk or breathe.

Over the next six months, I had 18 blood tests and 4 scans, but it was Sandy who figured it out. My water retention and extreme hand/feet pain was listed as a potential side-effect to one of my medications. At Sandy's urging, I changed doctors to the new place we use now. The doctor stopped my medication and the pain and swelling began to ease, but it has left me with permanent nerve damage in my hands and feet.

One really funny realisation did come about through that experience. As bad as the pain was, I kept writing, mostly using one single finger to painfully plod my way through blog posts and emails. Clearly, I am and always will be a writer at my core. And 2012 did have one brighter moment; I made a new friend from an old acquaintance.

28

For several years, I had been using an online website to find free-use photographs for my computer art projects. A photographer there also worked on the site as admin. I'd used some of her photos over the years, but we'd never spoken. Then, in June 2012, we finally started chatting and what a revelation that was. This photographer was a kindred spirit who had written a book about her own psychic experiences.

She had put her psychic life on a back-burner for years, but was now ready to start over. At the time, I was working with my friend, James, via email. He was trying to help me improve communications with my elusive and irrepressible spirit guide, Sol. We decided to invite Emily to join us.

Our small email study group of three was great fun. We discussed all sorts of topics, not just the esoteric. Em surprised herself and us by leaping forward in her abilities, much the same as I often do. James and I were left eating her dust as she zoomed into a better relationship with her own spirit guide as well as reinventing herself and her life. Spurred on by this new wave of energy and with the pain in my hands finally receding, I began thinking seriously about writing the sequel to First Light. I had already had a dream message that I should start writing again. Oh yes, I was still having dreams. This one happened back in January 2011:

I dreamed my soul was being moved into a new body as my old one was dying. I hated my new body. I wanted to return to my old body and die naturally, but my parents were horrified as they didn't want to lose me. I woke up crying as I told them I was going back to my old body to die... except I was still asleep. I lay in bed, in this dream within a dream, thinking about two new books I was writing. I was really thrilled with both and really excited. Then I heard a noise downstairs.

I went downstairs to check. It was summer, so already dim dawn light. As I stood half way down the stairs, I realised there was a wild crow flapping about the living room. The front door was open, but only a few inches, not enough for the crow to get back out. I realised that the wind had blown the door open and maybe blown in the crow, too. The crow flapped about a bit before settling on the back of a chair. I went down the stairs as quietly as I could and managed to get into the room without scaring it. Then, with that perfect logic-illogic of dreams, I started to put on moisturising cream!

The crow watched me rubbing cream into my arms and started preening itself. My thought was that it felt relaxed that we were both preening. I managed to walk over and stand closer. I could see the crow was dusty or old; its feathers were dull. Then I noticed the one wing had bones showing at the end. The wing tip was dead? No, as I watched it preening I realised I could see the rest of the feathers on that wing. It was a dead crow.

I woke up for real at that stage and went onto the shaman forums to ask advice. A friend told me a legend of Dead Crow who was eaten by her shadow. She suggested I journey-meditate and ask crow what the dream meant. I did as she suggested and the dead bone crow returned.

This crow told me I was here to help others heal themselves. She pulled a feather from her own wing, handed it over to me and said, "Write." Then she took off, flying up into the sky and growing bigger until she was huge, as big as a condor.

She swooped down and came up really close. Her eye was about the size of a baseball. She made me look deep into her eye and I felt laughter in there.

I thought, *Dead Crow's eyes are full of laughter and in her black feathers I saw stars and constellations. The night sky lies within her, the light lies within her. She is the sky.*

She laughed at me as I thought that and opened up her wings, so that the sunlight turned each feather into a rainbow. She said, "The wings hold all the stories," then, "Enough," before flying away.

Dead Crow, bone crow... I felt something strong there. The goddess with silvery hair at Mount Shasta had said "crow of bones" when she turned me into a drum skin. A drum. A voice. A writer of words. I remembered African sangomas throwing the bones to see the past, present and future. I got out of bed, grabbed a pen and wrote down this poem:

> Crow of bones...
> older than dirt
> and smarter
> sharper
>
> dry as old man's laughter
> who will you become?

Who would I become? I had no idea, but I did know that I had to start writing again. All the pain and illness in 2012 had set me back, but finally, in February 2013, I started to write my second book. Once I started, I could not stop. I was up at 4:00am in the morning to start writing and I went to bed after midnight. I had been similarly obsessed when I wrote the first book, barely leaving the computer, but writing the sequel was beyond anything I'd experienced before. Every change of scene was a roller-coaster of emotional highs and lows. It was as if I wrote parts of my soul into that second book.

James and Emily offered to be my proof readers and editors since I had decided to self-publish. I had taken back full control of my first book and self-published a second edition with Amazon. I had everything set up there to add more books. It took me roughly five months to write and another six months to edit and prepare for publication. I remember fearing writing the last word because finishing a book is both a birth and a death for a writer. This time, I hoped to avoid that by beginning another book at the same time. I had other story ideas sitting in another computer folder for when the story-writing withdrawal hit.

The day I wrote the last sentence of book two was the 7th of July 2013. My family opened a bottle of fancy wine to celebrate. I decided to take a few days breather before sending it out to my friends for editing. It had been a cathartic experience, but I felt quite shattered. Even though I'd hoped to avoid the withdrawals, I still felt lost and empty. I was in the shower on the morning of the 10th of July when it really hit me.

In fairness, it wasn't just the book. It was as if all the struggles of the past few years hit me that morning; my health, my dad nearly dying and Sandy's mum passing from leukaemia in 2011. It had been such an extreme time. That morning in the shower, I started to cry and just could not stop. I could feel Sol there in the bathroom, standing and watching me. He seemed glum, not his usual perky self. Then suddenly, I *heard* him clearly in my head for the first time.

How can I explain how different this voice in my head was that morning? Even though the things I hear are in my mind, they still vary in strength and clarity. To use an analogy, psychic hearing is often like tuning in to a bad radio station. It crackles and fades, you lose words or mishear things regularly, and sometimes it's like someone stuck a blanket over the radio and everything is muffled and faint. But on the 10th of July 2013, Sol's voice in my mind was as clear as if he were standing beside me talking. He said, "You deserve better," and he sounded so sad.

I turned towards where I could feel him standing and asked, "What do you mean?" because under the sadness was something else, something I had never felt before. As I asked, this PUNCH of emotion entered my heart; deep and overwhelming LOVE. So much love that I was in tears again, but a very different kind this time. Tears of wonder. Even after all those years of dealing with that imp of an elephant, I had never truly felt him emotionally. And now, this love? It was huge, sweet and deeply personal. This wasn't some spiritual agape, some all-encompassing love. This was one living being showing his heart to another.

The moment I responded back with love, because I already knew I loved that silly ellie man dearly, he transformed. The cartoonish ellie/man vanished and became a real man. I stepped out of the shower and stood, dripping water on the bathroom floor, bewildered and dazed as he spun and danced with joy. He YELLED in my head, "You can see me!"

He was amazingly vivid and real, a tall man with shoulder length, dark blond hair and a distinct face. I could see every detail, even the dimple on his chin, still visible through faint beard stubble. I'd put his age at mid-thirties. He had high cheekbones, a wide mouth and deep, blue-green eyes. His clothing was old-fashioned fitted breeches and a loose shirt, but no shoes. In all the time I have had this man with me since then, he never wears shoes.

I could hear him perfectly. Now, with no fumbling to understand or need to mime, he was a deluge of words. He flooded me with love, joy and information. It was completely overwhelming, but in the best possible way. He told me that he'd been alive a long time ago, but now existed on the other side.

I asked for his true name and he told me it was Tiernan. *A Scottish name?* He laughed and told me he wasn't Scottish, before continuing to dance around the room like a madman. *Then where was he from?* He shrugged and winked, still the tease, still the joker. Now, in fiction this would be a turning point where it all moves forward smoothly to the next adventure, but this was real.

Oh... my... GOD. This was real. Dancing, joyful dead men throwing their heart into yours was just a bit too much to cope with. My brain went into panic melt-down and Sol-now-Tiernan reacted with horror. Taking full responsibility for overwhelming me, he backed off and vanished, but then returned instantly to see how I was... then vanished again with the same look of horror. For the next few days, this was the pattern. It was during one of the upswing moments of him being around and full of joy that he gave me my first dictated message to share with my friends.

> **Sent:** Friday, July 12, 2013 9:34 AM
> **Subject:** Message from Sol
>
> *Never be afraid to love. It is the greatest gift you have to share. It knows no boundaries of species, space or time.*
>
> *When everything else fails... love remains.*

Being afraid to love him was exactly my problem. I was zooming up and down like a yo-yo between fearing I loved a man who was only my imagination to fearing I loved someone real, which meant I loved a dead man... and what did I do with that? By the end of the next day, we were both a complete mess. That evening, Tiernan arrived in tears and rather melodramatically said that he was going, this was all his fault. But within minutes he was back, wailing that he could not go. I needed help. I sat down and wrote to Emily and James:

Sent: Saturday, July 13, 2013 1:16 AM
Subject: Angel Numbers 1515

The 1515 is an actual number I got yesterday and I can't think of anything else to title this email. I think my spirit guide is having a breakdown. No, I'm not joking and I'm in over my head super big time here.

Would you do me a big favour... which might get a resounding no from your side, but will you see if Sol is okay? As in emotionally/mentally okay. Yeah, I realise that's liable to sound very odd in itself and by now you're probably mad curious. My apologies. Eagle has been super kind and helpful, but I'm not trusting my judgement on this.

Sol's real name is Tiernan. He's fine with me telling you. I want to help him, but that in itself sounds insanely laughable.

help

Emily and James were sympathetic, but as puzzled by Sol-now-Tiernan as I was. This wasn't how things normally went with spirit guides according to the literature. Spirit guides are teachers and mentors, used to staying cool and calm in any situation. This emotional, very human man (who had once been an elephant in my mind) was nothing like that.

It took a while longer for us to both calm down enough to communicate. Sol-Tiernan continued to use pictures and songs to tell me things because talking was overwhelming and confusing for quite a long time. This was a lot more invasive than merely having images pop into my mind. This was a voice that could start talking at any time, butting into my own thoughts. Try imagining that for a moment and then imagine those first weeks where that chatty man was constantly in my head from my waking to falling asleep. No surprise that I was alternating joy and awe with panic attacks.

James admitted afterwards that he thought I'd gone a bit mad or had a break-down when it first began. It certainly felt that way at first, but Tiernan found ways to calm me down and then began working on small but significant ways to confirm he was real. The first way he did this was with music. He'd used songs before; popping tunes into my head that had the perfect lyrics to match whatever he wanted to say. Either he would ask for a specific song by name or it would be *there* as an annoying tune stuck in my mind, a tune to a TV advert, a video on Facebook.

They were often songs I'd never heard of before. He'd say something like, "Go to YouTube and type in BLUE. Pick the 3rd song and go there. The 4th song in the side bar is the one for you." It always worked. Either the lyrics, the video itself or both would have deep personal meaning, quite often on several levels. I can't share all of those songs here. There are too many and some have such complex personal meaning it would take forever to explain. I've used my discretion and only shared the ones that make this story flow.

Sol-Tiernan would also send me pictures or symbols. These might be images in my mind or literal pictures I'd find in some way such as something that would stand out in a book, on TV or the internet. They would be things that connected to something he had just told me or I'd go look up their meaning and find that they fitted perfectly.

Some of the ways he confirmed he was real were quite quirky. All together they explain how this adventure unfolded from a crazy, exuberant elephant in my mind to what our relationship has now become. The pictures and symbols are easy to share as I saved a lot of them to file as they happened. One of my favourites came about during one of my many "meltdown" panic attacks. I was going through another wave of *Am I mad? Is this real? Is he real?* terror, when Tiernan said sarcastically, "Oh course I'm not real. I'm George, your imaginary friend."

George?

"George," he said firmly.

I told him to go away and he vanished. Yes. He was just in my mind. Just my imaginary friend. I needed to calm down somehow, so I went onto Facebook to chat to friends. At the top of my Facebook wall there was a joke picture from a Daffy Duck cartoon. I adore Bugs Bunny and the Road Runner, but I never liked Daffy Duck. I never watched his cartoons, so I did not recognise the picture. The picture was of this giant white monster thing holding Daffy Duck in one hand. Beside it was written this:

I WILL NAME HIM GEORGE, AND I WILL HUG HIM, AND PET HIM, AND SQUEEZE HIM. Share if you remember this...

I felt Sol-Tiernan's laughter before I saw him, arms crossed, leaning against the wall beside me, one eyebrow raised as he grinned at me. *Yeah right, imaginary friend my....* I shouldn't have thought that! He turned and dropped his breeches to moon me. Still vulgar. Still the tease. *Damn you, you annoying elephant-in-my-head, you overgrown imp in a man-skin!* What had I let myself in for?

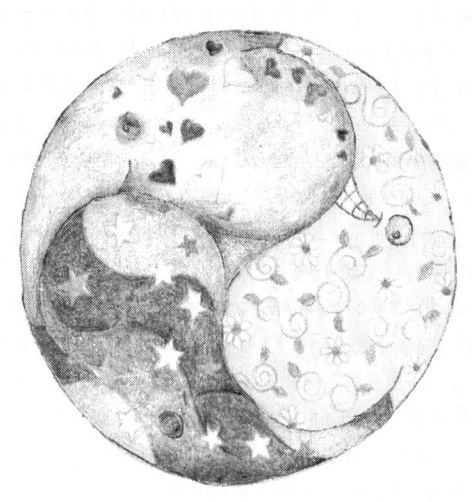

29

Once again, the elephant in my head had completely taken me by surprise, but the puzzle pieces were beginning to click together now he had a clear voice. Elephant... how had I never noticed it before? Of course he would have picked an elephant. It was my favourite animal. Oh, I told people that my favourite animals were cats and horses, but if I looked back at my life there have been elephants all the way.

One of my first favourite toys was a pink knitted elephant. I loved him so much. He died most traumatically when my mother washed him and his body flobbled while his legs stretched into flamingo stilts. So my parents got me a tiny, velveteen ellie. I used to throw him up into the air and catch him, until the day he got stuck on our tile roof. Dad got him down, but he was forever stained pinkish from rolling around on the clay roof tiles.

We went on holiday to the seaside when I was eight. My grandpa came with us and he offered to buy me a brooch from a tourist shop. They had all sorts of cute little animal brooches. I remember the grown ups pointing out all the pretty colourful animals, but I picked a little grey elephant. I still have it in my trinket box. And when I started school in South Africa, my new art teacher encouraged me to enter a craft competition. I won third place with my wall-hanging of felt elephants.

Elephants have been wherever I go. At art college in 1981, my first oil painting was of Ganesh. I'd met him for the first time during an art sketching trip to a Hindu temple. It was love at first sight for me; that gorgeous, chubby, elephant-head god with his pinkish marble body and twinkly, inlaid eyes…. I remembered my first attempt at a journey meditation to find my spirit guide, when an elephant had led me to that old bearded man who laughed till his belly shook as we played tic tac toe with daisy doodles and hearts. I have no doubt now that he was Sol-Tiernan.

I burst out laughing as I wrote that! I was listening to a stream of Enya on YouTube as I write, but right there the music suddenly changed to Pentatonix singing Leonard Cohen's Hallelujah. My ellie-man is still a tease!

But let's get back to the semi-hysteria months of 2013 when my mind was still struggling to cope with a miming elephant turning into a loud and chatty blond man. I need to explain how Sol-Tiernan talks to me because it is the foundation of how I communicate with all the various beings and people I deal with nowadays. It has taken me a few years to understand how he and others manage to speak to me. I wish I knew back in 2013 what I know now. I'd have coped a lot better.

When Tiernan accessed my mind, he could only use what was in there to talk to me. It's like using a computer to talk to others, except this computer is my brain. Just as any conversation on a computer will be limited to the software installed, Tiernan was limited to my languages and vocabulary. He cannot talk to me in French or Swahili, not because he doesn't speak them, but because I have neither of those languages in my mind for him to access. It gets more complex as well. Tiernan wasn't actually sending words into my mind, but rather his thoughts which my mind would take and make into words.

As a result, if I was too tense or tired, words became clichéd and repetitious. Even now, if I'm calm and shut my own mind down, what I hear becomes more varied and unique. A simple example: Tiernan's favourite term of affection for me was "little bird", but if I was tired I would just hear "sweetie" because that is a word of endearment I use a lot myself. It's as if he would send out a thought of affection and my tired or lazy brain would just shoot out my most used term. This would lead to extreme frustration for Tiernan when he knew exactly what he wanted to say, but I didn't have the patience or mental energy to allow those words to appear in my brain. At times like that he would revert to mime, symbols and pictures.

So much happened so fast in 2013 that I am

struggling to know how to continue. In the final months of 2013, I was flung down the rabbit hole and, just like Alice, I was shrunken, expanded, mangled and re-assembled. All of that has led me to become a better person, but not all of it was fun to go through. Perhaps I have used the wrong Alice story as a comparison. I think I went through the Looking Glass. Sol-as-Tiernan showed me my reflection, this self-image I had built up over 50 years, and then he pushed me through it to face my true self. In doing that, every fear, weakness, and amazing miracle that was ME was laid bare. Trust me, it's not an adventure for the faint-hearted! But oh my God (and I say that with complete reverence), what a privilege and a blessing that has been.

I've sat chewing over the next part of this story for quite a while. I eventually asked Sandy's opinion. He thinks I should be honest and tell whatever feels right to tell. Ah well.... When I'm calm, most of this feels right to tell and when I'm anxious I'd much rather not tell ANY of it. Ultimately, I have to trust my heart and trust the invisible ellie-man standing behind me right now with his hands on my shoulders, smiling at my words on the computer screen.

I just pulled a tongue at him. Now I can continue.

What added to the panic was the fact that when Sol punched all his love into my heart in July 2013, a part of me fell in love with him. It was inevitable, I think. He was more deeply a part of my life than any living human. How could you not fall in love with someone that close to your soul? Part of the reason for his joyful dancing about the bathroom that morning was the fact

I realised I loved him too. As far as Sol-Tiernan was concerned, there was no reason for panic, but my Earth-based mentality threw a fit. When he reached out to me in pure love, I pulled away, my mind yelling, *OMG, no! I am MARRIED.*

My reaction left him bemused. He said that he had known and loved me through lifetimes, pointing out that my marriage to Sandy was only for this single lifetime. There he was, radiating joy, while my mind spun out of control on a mad little hamster-wheel of terror. When Tiernan finally realised how shaken I was, he backed off and left. That was when the whole leave-then-return thing started, which led to me writing to my friends for help.

I told them my guide seemed to be having a break-down, but I didn't tell them the full story. How could I? My rational mind understood that if there was an afterlife and reincarnation, then the possibilities of how many people we've loved is endless. But this wasn't an interesting theory to debate. This was happening to me. Finding myself stuck in a love triangle that spanned dimensions was not something I was expecting or wanted.

When I first wrote to James and Emily for help, James asked his guide, Eagle, for advice. Eagle's response left James confused, but I understood it. Eagle dictated that he had been expecting this to happen. He knew Sol was reaching a point of having to confess all to me and that we'd both need the support of friends as we dealt with this.

Confess all. Oh boy, little did I know then that this

was not "all" yet. Not *all* by a long shot! There was so much more to come before that year was over. I'd barely begun. Did I have the support of my friends? Yes and no. Emily was surprised, but completely supportive. James blew hot and cold. He was suspicious of this new variation of Sol, but in a truly ironic twist, his spirit guide, Eagle, was supportive. In fact, Eagle was enthusiastic to be hands-on help and teacher.

Having James, my friend and mentor, suspicious about what was happening was a mixed blessing. It made my anxiety ramp up to epic level, but it also forced me to confront and question everything. That was painful at times, but I think it was necessary. You cannot build on a weak foundation and those last six months of 2013 forged mine into steel. When you are unsure who to trust, you can only trust yourself. And to find that true self… you need to step through the looking glass.

30

Eagle was to be another source of panic as it turned out. I think we all should have guessed that Eagle was something exceptional, considering the fact that I heard his voice clearly years before the ellie in my head managed to punch through. I'd hazard a guess and say Eagle is what some call a Light Being, something on an entirely different level of power. I think he's capable of talking to anyone. *Ah… he just came in and bowed.* He is still around, although that's rare nowadays.

James and I always heard Eagle with the same voice – dry, crisp, posh English. But how I saw Eagle, when he first became visible in my mind, was a complete surprise. I see James as Peter O'Toole in his later years, an elderly man in an impeccable suit with this crystal-top walking stick and the kind of shoes the Great Gatsby would have adored. Eagle is gorgeous, utter elegance. He is so different from Sol. Eagle was and still is a little intimidating. Sol, even as Tiernan, was too goofy sweet to ever inspire awe.

Thinking now about how I heard Eagle first, it's a good place to talk more on how that works, especially since this was another reason for my anxiety during 2013. Whatever opened me up to hearing Sol that day in July left me open to hearing everything. And I do mean EVERYTHING. The first few months were ghastly at times, until Tiernan explained and helped me gain control.

To go back to the radio analogy again, I was learning the hard way that different voices came in on different band widths. I can say now that Eagle seems able to tune himself to any band width, which is very intriguing and has added to my theory that he is truly something unique. Tiernan, on the other hand, could only be heard on a specific wave band. Think of a wave band as an energy vibration and then try to understand that human emotions vibrate at different frequencies. So the band-width of my psychic radio is set to a range from the highest forms of human emotions to the lowest.

Energy, vibrations, band widths and dimensions... there are connections here that my human brain cannot grasp. Maybe if I'd studied physics instead of psychics, I'd be able to put it all together properly. All I can say is that the dark things we call evil vibrate to a much lower energy than do beings filled with love. It would take me months to realise that fear was the key. Fear lowers your energy vibration like swallowing chunks of lead. Contrary to what some religions preach, fear is worse than anger. Perhaps that is why the line in Christianity about fearing God always felt so horribly wrong to me? Fear is the lowest emotion. Hate, bigotry, cruelty and violence are all built upon the foundation of fear.

Whenever I had a panic melt-down, different voices would tune in and these were voices that would attack me. I'd call them demons. They were a horrendous, hate-filled stream of the most vile threats and insults. Weirdly, I can't remember any of them now. They vanished from my memory almost instantly, but the way they made me feel lasted longer. I remember the shock and revulsion I felt, which in turn would lead to more fear. It became a horrible spiral, out of control, as I ran around my self-created little hamster wheel of fear. Was I mad? What was happening to me?

What truly horrified me was that Tiernan never stepped in to make them go away. I'd see him, but he'd not speak while they were attacking me. At first, I was angry with that – VERY angry. If Tiernan truly cared about me, why didn't he chase them away? It took him a while to explain that he couldn't do that. They were on such a lower band width of energy that he couldn't hear them and they didn't know he was there. He only knew I was hearing them because he could feel my emotions. Once I spiralled into panic, my own energy would plummet and he would lose all ability to talk to me. All he could do was wait until I calmed down enough to hear him again.

Not all the voices from 2013 were nightmarish. In fact, the first new one was a very different experience.

It was a few days after I'd asked my friends for help, probably about the 14th of July. I was up late, working alone at the computer while my family slept. I was supposed to be proofreading my book, but I was mostly thinking about Tiernan. Should I tell Sandy all about him as Tiernan kept urging me to? Would Sandy understand or think I'd gone mad? As I sat there, alone in the middle of the night, a new voice entered my head. This voice was female.

I had never heard a woman before. I turned to look around the room, but nothing was visible. She was just a voice and an angry one! She leapt straight in, berating me for being a "naive fool" with how I was dealing with Tiernan. Then she called me a Pollyanna and I started to feel annoyed.

It was bad enough that James was on my back about Tiernan without some unknown, invisible woman adding her disapproval. I remember telling her firmly to back off and leave me alone. (actually, I told her to P*** off. I really was that angry) I felt a strong sense of surprise from her, then nothing. She was gone. I sat there, steaming with frustrated anger. How dare this... whatever woman come in and tell me how to run my life! This was MY life, mine, no one else had the right to tell me how to live it.

I had lived with a sweet, silly elephant who made me laugh and then a darling old man who constantly tried to make me smile. Neither of those versions of this complicated being had ever done anything to harm me. In fact, he'd been always been helpful, supportive and caring. And patient! It must have taken oceans of patience to deal with me when the only communication we had was mime and images. I looked back at the memory of that ellie waving his little white feather to send me a message that he believed in me. Hadn't the love always been there? Pure, sweet love. Why was I so afraid of that? Of all the emotions, why fear love? That burst of anger had cleared away any doubts. I knew what I had to do.

The next day, I sat Sandy down and told him everything and, just as Tiernan had predicted, Sandy coped fine with the whole truth. You see, Sandy was one of those rare children born remembering scraps of their former life. He even had snatches of dream memories as to how he had died. He also had a sense of that other place – the greater reality that we all return to. For Sandy, *there* is more real than here.

This is not at all an easy way to live, unfortunately. Some gifts can also be burdens. Remembering his former life had made for a very difficult and confusing childhood, especially hard since Sandy had told no one while growing up. In fact, Sandy never told anyone until 2002. That was the confession Sandy posted on a forum on New Year's Day in 2002 – his scraps of memories about his life before this one. That was the post that made me write, "I know you." His memories had triggered this intense feeling that I had been in that past life he described as well.

That day in 2013, I remembered something Sandy had said eleven years earlier when he asked me to marry him. He'd said that as much as he loved me, he was aware that we had probably both lived many lives and thus married and loved many people throughout those lifetimes. A friend in one life could be a lover or a family member in another. For that reason, Sandy saw nothing strange about Tiernan loving me or even that this might trigger me remembering loving this "other man". Easy to write now, but not so easy to get my head around in 2013. It was a huge step from theorising about multiple lives to having a dead man fling his heart at me. I loved my husband. I didn't need this complication. But something about this tall, blond man with his cheeky smile and vivid turquoise eyes just felt so much like home.

Tiernan tried every way to calm me down. He constantly urged me to, "Stop thinking with your head, think from your heart." I struggled with that. I still do. Although I am an emotional person, I turn to logic and reason when I'm stressed or confused. I was the teenager who loved Sherlock Holmes books. I like things tidy. The whole "think from the heart" idea made no sense to me in 2013.

Thankfully, Tiernan had other ways to calm my nerves, mostly by making me laugh. I can't remember all of them now, but I do remember having to hide in a corner of a shoe shop when a fit of giggles hit me because his comments on the shoes for sale were just so funny. He never wore shoes and to be honest, he didn't always bother with clothes, either. I have gone grocery shopping with a naked man wearing nothing but a cream Panama hat. I think he did the nude thing mostly because it horrified me. What had been the elephant's humour was now the man's humour.

Sol-Tiernan had sweet moments as well outrageous ones. When I woke on my birthday morning in August 2013, I could clearly see a long, gold box on the end of the bed, tied with a gold ribbon. Tiernan was standing behind it, grinning widely. I opened it in my mind and found it held a single Arum/Calla lily. I was a bit disappointed at first. My favourite flowers are daisies and roses. Plus, my grandmother hated Arum lilies. She believed they were bad luck since they are a favourite flower for funerals.

Why had Tiernan given me a Calla lily? He told me to go look up their meaning. Later that day, I went online and tried to find more information about them. To my surprise, I found that they aren't a bad luck death flower after all. According to some sites on flower meaning, they symbolised the Sacred Feminine. Another website, on the meaning of flowers, said:

"Calla lilies signify magnificent beauty. If you want to tell your lady that she's an exceptional woman and that you think she's gorgeous, this is the flower to give her."

I could live with that! The same day, I went onto Facebook to thank the friends who had left me birthday greetings. There on my wall, was a picture from some Facebook group I belonged to. It seemed to be pages of an old book, so faded that at first I didn't even notice the writing. (I recently discovered that this picture is from a British magazine called Lilliput and the photo is by Bohumil Kröhn. 1937)

Each page has a photo on it, softly faded by time. The left photo is of a woman doing a cartwheel. She's caught at the moment she's balanced on one hand, her long dress flaring out around her upturned legs. The other page shows a Calla lily, the shape of it perfectly matching the girl's flared skirt. The writing below each photo reads: "Our Lily" and "Arum lily". It was only then that I remembered my mom's pet name for me when I as a child... Lily. Tiernan couldn't have given me a better flower as gift or a better confirmation.

31

You'd think after that birthday confirmation I'd calm down and move on smoothly. Nope. I'm far too stubborn a sceptic and worry-wart to let go and trust that easily! My mind was still fighting with every gruelling step forward. I would constantly check, re-check, ask for proof and then ask for MORE proof. Then, once I was given an answer so definite and complex there could be no doubt, I'd calm down for a few days only to fall back into utter panic as the enormity of it all hit me once again.

In fairness to me, I was spending my days talking to a dead man who I once thought was an elephant who said he loved me. All that while editing a new book and finding that I could hear other beings just as clearly. That's a lot to deal with! Tiernan was clearly anxious not to cause me distress and would back away and leave every time I overloaded. James' guide, Eagle, on the other hand, was the type of teacher who pushes you even harder each time you say, "I can't do this." Where Tiernan was simply overjoyed that I could see and hear him, Eagle saw possibilities for advancing my abilities. This led to a particularly mind-boggling experience that ultimately led to me meeting two special women.

It was late July and Eagle was nagging me to take my abilities further. Eagle said I was ready to ascend and Tiernan agreed. That sounded alarming. The only images that came to mind were ones from my years at a Catholic junior school of dead saints floating upwards on clouds. Usually due to the fact they had just been martyred to death in appalling ways that include lots of fire, sharp objects and blood. Tiernan assured me this was not the same, but I wasn't buying it. I asked if it was possible to NOT ascend. Tiernan said it was perfectly fine to refuse anything that didn't feel right. *Great, thank you. No, I do not want to ascend.*

Eagle then took a new direction. He was convinced that I would be capable of reaching other dimensions. Not as in seeing or hearing other places, but as in literally out-of-body going there. One particular day, the two spirit guides arrived together to discuss this with me. Having both talking at once was a bit much for my brain, but the chance to see how they interacted was fascinating. Eagle took charge, explaining in detail the basic steps I'd need to take to make this happen. Tiernan clearly wasn't happy about it. He mumbled a few objections, but Eagle over-rode his reservations.

That evening, feeling a lot nervous, I prepared to

give it a try. With Eagle sitting next to the bed rattling off instructions like an army general, I lay down and tried to get myself into a meditative state before attempting an out-of-body state. My nervousness made every muscle and sinew tense. I have no idea how long I lay there feeling like clenched teeth, when suddenly I was not there.

Not there? Not here. There.

I was so disorientated that it took me a few seconds before I could focus on details. It felt a lot like the way you feel coming awake from anaesthesia. A hot, dry breeze touched my face as I looked around me. I was standing on a rise, more a hill than a mountain, and I was under a tent thing shaped a bit like a pergola. That's how I know there was a breeze, because I could see and hear the fabric flapping against a tent pole. There were people in the tent, standing near me. They watched me anxiously, as if aware I'd suddenly appeared and was a bit groggy. Someone told me they were there to help me, but I can't remember any more about them. I don't even know who it was who told me this, but whoever it was also said I could stay there if I wanted to. It was possible to remain in that world.

I turned away from the people. I wanted to look out on this unknown world. The landscape was brutally bare, a desert world of sand-eroded mountains and scrubby patches of grasses in the valley below me. The sky was strange. I can't remember why now, I just remember looking up at the sky and knowing that this place wasn't Earth. It was different in some way.

Even now, years later, recalling those memories is

making me feel weird, like I'm drugged. It all felt so real. Too real. What if I got stuck there and couldn't get back to my own reality? I started to panic and felt myself sucked back to my own body at tremendous speeds. I was back lying on the bed. The experience left me feeling so exhausted that I had to tell my family I was taking an early night. I went to bed and fell asleep instantly.

I woke up utterly disorientated. I'm not talking about that groggy sleep state where you wake up and think, *Where am I? What time is it?* I woke up refreshed and clear-headed, but I had no recognition of my room or the house whatsoever. It was terrifying. I recognised nothing. Not the floor, wallpaper, furniture... nothing. It was like waking up in a stranger's bed and house. I sat there with my heart pounding, blinking constantly as I looked at the wallpaper, cupboard and clothing on a chair and none of it was known to me. Not a thing. I didn't even remember who I was or my own name.

As the amnesia gradually wore off, I pretty much *YELLED* for Tiernan and Eagle to come at once. When they appeared, I ripped into them both. I can tell you now that yelling in your mind is not satisfying, but you can certainly add a lot of punch by sending your anger out with the words. And oh boy, was I angry! Poor Tiernan. Even though he had expressed doubts in the first place, I laid into him just as much as I did Eagle. I told them I had had enough. I was not a human guinea pig to run experimental tests on. I demanded they both go away and leave me alone.

Eagle left with a shrug. Tiernan vanished in tears.

Then, for the first time in a long time, I prayed to God. I often talked to God, but praying? Not so much. I always felt like a whiny kid with a wish list when I prayed, but that day I needed bigger help than people, dead or alive, could give me. I felt I needed the whole formal approach. I went and sat in the bathroom. Sitting on a toilet to pray is not exactly the most sacred of spaces, but it was the most private.

I was sitting praying with my head bowed when and I felt someone standing in front of me. A powerful, loving presence. I looked up. There in front of me was a woman. I knew her instantly, even if this time her feet were real feet and not tree roots or her legs the ocean. Her face was ageless, her expression so gentle and yet incredibly strong. It was Earth Mother.

I was bewildered. Was she God? Sandy has always believed the Creator is female, not male. I'd never thought of God as having either gender. I was trying to figure out what to do next when Tiernan appeared, returning unexpectedly as he often did. He took one look at who was standing in front of me and instantly dropped to one knee, his head bowed in deep respect like a knight before his king. Who was she to make my irreverent ellie-man react with such awe and respect?

All these images were flashing in my mind, too fast to make sense of. I screwed up my courage and asked her if was she the planet itself, Gaia, or *was She God?* She smiled a wonderful smile, lovely and calming, and answered in this serene voice, "The Creator is creation and the creation is the Creator." Then She sent me that kind of instant download of knowledge that I sometimes get. These are the hardest to retell because they contain no words or images. I simply, instantly KNOW.

She showed me that she was a living piece of creation and the Creator. The word Tiernan later gave me to use was extrusion. She was the planet made human, but she was also a portion of reality and Earth through which God/Creator/All could communicate with me. I felt as awed as Tiernan looked. And I felt so unworthy. That whole, *Who am I to deserve this honour?* type of feeling.

I whispered to her, "Why me?"

She smiled again and said, "Why not?"

Why not...? I felt acceptance and peace wash over me. Why not me? Why not you? If all is one, the Creator and creation, then every part is as holy and important as the rest. None greater and none lesser. It was a life-altering realisation. She then turned to Tiernan and told him that the meddling would stop. There would be no more attempts to push me to do anything I was not ready for. Even though he wasn't there that day, Eagle never again interfered or tried to take over. Tiernan was clearly shaken by what had happened. He kept apologising for letting me down and then he said it might be better if he left.

I was used to him backing away for a while and then returning, but this time he didn't return. Hours went by, then days. I realised I might never see him again and it was devastating. It was only then that I realised how much I loved and valued that dear, impossible elephant-man. He was the most pure love I had ever experienced. He knew everything about me, every petty, pathetic part of me as well as the best, and he loved it all without any judgement. How could I lose that?

Thankfully, I had just come down with the flu, so I had a legitimate reason to hide in bed and secretly cry buckets of tears. That first utterly alone night someone completely unexpected came in to comfort me. It was a voice I never expected to hear again – the unknown woman who had called me a naive Pollyanna. First it was just her voice I could hear, but then she began to take form as a woman sitting on a stool near my bed.

I could not believe it. I knew her! She was the dark-haired angel with a million faces: Sandy's guardian angel. No wonder she had been angry about my silly falling in love with Tiernan. That night, we made our peace and she stayed to hold my hand as I slept in restless bursts between the flu sore throat and the heartache. Every time I woke up, there she was, still holding my hand. I asked her for a name and she told me Agapanthus or Aggie for short. She was to become a dear friend to me as well as a constant source of wisdom, love and delight for Sandy.

32

Tiernan did return after a few days. I can't remember now how many. It's blurry now because by the time he returned I was in the middle of flu and the family were busy getting sick as well. What I do remember is that we sat talking a lot, nothing grand, just the two of us talking about simple things. I remember sitting outside in the warm summer sun, feeling physically ghastly but enjoying the company of an equally warm and sunny invisible man sitting on the bench with me.

I was still having moments of panic, but not as bad as the first month. We were also managing to have some impressive disagreements. One in late August stands out the most. It started with him frustrated by the fact I still sometimes I wondered if he was only in my imagination. What began as mild bickering about whether or not he was merely a construct of my mind finally blew up into a roof-lifting argument.

Who knew you could fight ferociously with an invisible man? I'm ashamed to admit that I was really nasty. I said things deliberately meant to hurt. I mean... he wasn't real. Right? So how can you hurt an imaginary man? Tiernan reacted with a wave of extreme emotional pain. Then he wrote **"Fuck you"** on the old chalk board and walked out.

As terrible as it was to know I had hurt him, it was an incredible moment of realising that this man was real and had real feelings. It also struck me as incredibly funny, him swearing at me using a chalk board. I was crying and laughing at the same time. That was when I stopped doubting he was real, although in time my anxious mind would create a whole new range of things to worry about.

The moment I accepted he was real and loved me, Earth Mother appeared. She held a silver chalice, which she placed on the ground between us. She made Tiernan and I hold hands over the bowl and then poured water over our clasped hands. When I asked my friends if they had any idea what the ritual meant, one said that it sounded like a blessing. James wrote back that he had been given a word: Bonded.

I'm still figuring out the layers of meaning to that seemingly simple word. I know we are bonded in friendship and love, but I suspect it means a whole lot more than that. I'm still not sure, but Sol-Tiernan always used to say, "Timing is everything," when I was impatient to know all the answers instantly. Even though it annoys me to say it, I know he's right. When it's time to know, I'll find out what that ritual meant.

Tiernan did something strange and symbolic himself a short time after Earth Mother blessed us. He showed me a necklace with a nine-pointed star pendant. He put it around my neck and then pressed gently on the pendant, so that it imprinted the star shape onto my chest, just below my throat. He then took each of my hands and used the pendant to imprint the star onto the palms of my hands as well. The stars on my palms glowed gold for a moment before fading away.

After those events in August 2013, I was more relaxed around Tiernan and he reverted back to the fun-loving person I had first met as a dancing elephant. I remember one particularly funny day. I was at the hospital waiting to see a physiotherapist. It was a typical, boring medical waiting-room: chairs against the walls, a few posters about weird health issues, some old magazines and a wall clock that moved at the grindingly slow pace of waiting. Tiernan came to sit with me and suggested we play I-spy. I was convinced it wouldn't work, but I was bored enough to agree.

Tiernan said, "F and it is yellow."

There was a yellow flower in a vase, but that was a dahlia. Yellow? I scanned the room again. A woman in the waiting room was wearing a yellow scarf. She must have wondered why I was staring at her because she twitched a few times. I looked away. *Yellow scarf. ScarfF? Words for scarf with F?* Nothing came to mind.

"You sure it's an F?" I asked in my mind.

"F," he said, smiling.

"And definitely yellow? Not cream or mustard?"

"Nope. YELLOOOOOW."

After a few more frustrating minutes I gave up. This was getting annoying and stupid. "There's nothing yellow starting with F here," I told him.

"F and it is on a door," he said, amused. " Think out of the box."

I got up and looked around. I'd come in through sliding doors to my right. To my left, the room bent into an L shape where it went on as a passageway towards the therapy rooms. Trying to seem casual, I wandered back in-out the entrance. Nothing there. I went around the bend of the L and started towards the far end. There on a door was a poster about flu vaccines. It was bright yellow.

"FFFFFFlu," said Tiernan, so darn smug I nearly burst out laughing.

I never even noticed the far doors when I arrived since I was facing the wrong way to see them. He'd won. I had to admit it. I would have never found the poster without the door hint and the "out the box", which it was, since it was literally not in the box portion of the waiting room where I had been sitting.

"That is cheating," I told him. "I couldn't see that from where I was sitting."

"But I could see it," he smirked.

"No, no," I tried to be stern, but I wanted to giggle. "It has to be something I can see without wandering around the hospital staring at things like a crazy woman."

"Okay. Something with Z."

"Z?" *Are you kidding me?*

He grinned. "Z and you can see it from your chair."

I went back to my seat, sat down and looked around at the walls, the floor, the cupboard across from me, the posters on the wall... I studied the magazine covers for zeddy type things. I could not see anything that even came close to a z word. Eventually, I admitted defeat.

"ZINC," he said smugly.

"Where?" I demanded to know. I couldn't see anything made of zinc.

He pointed at a cupboard door handle. It was different from all the other doors and yep, it was zinc. I demanded my turn without realising how stupid that was since everything I looked at was instantly projected into his mind. He laughed so hard he was crying as I realised there was no way I'd ever be able to keep anything in my mind hidden from him. He knew everything I thought, felt and did.

That realisation would regularly lead to what Tiernan called my, "most charming melt-downs", those times where realising he was REAL would leave me flustered and shy as I also realised he was reading my every thought. I mean, let's face it. We all have thoughts we'd rather not share with others. Whenever I had a moment of *OMG, he really is REAL* shyness, Tiernan would burst out laughing.

Damn. I just did it again. I suddenly felt aware he was watching me write that and felt all shy and yes, he is laughing at me!

33

I spent a lot of 2013 and 2014 on the internet doing searches for all the things I was seeing or being shown. One of those searches was to look up the name Sandy's angel had given herself: Agapanthus. I already knew the flower as they were popular in African gardens, but I had no idea if the name had meaning. As it turns out, it does:

Greek: αγάπη (agape) = spiritual love, άνθος (anthos) = flower.

Flower of God's love is a great name for an angel. I wondered if Tiernan's name was his real name or one he'd picked for a reason as well. I decided to look it up. The moment I opened a Google search, he was there in my head. He murmured the name of a popular internet dictionary of slang words and terms. *Really? Did that site actually list the name Tiernan?* I glanced down the list of search results. There was a link for Tiernan on their website. I went to have a look:

<u>Tiernan:</u>

The most AMAZING guy you've ever laid eyes on. Every woman wants to date him and every man wants to be him. He is FUNNY and KIND. He's just so GORGEOUS. Yeah, he's TIERNAN.

Amazing, funny, kind and gorgeous... and so modest! I couldn't stop laughing. Trust my trickster elephant imp to pick a name like that. My trickster... such a true thought and in fairness to him, he did warn me. During those first two months when I was in the process of discussing with my friends all that was happening to me, Tiernan suggested I get out my cards. He said that he wanted to try something.

I have three sets of cards; a beautiful tarot set Sandy bought me based on Greek and Roman mythology, a set of cards called the Wicca Pack which are completely Pagan in meaning, and a tarot set by the artist Holly Sierra that I bought for the gorgeous artwork.

Tiernan asked for the Wicca cards. He told me to lay them out face down on the bed before he pointed out the cards he wanted. One for me, one for Sandy and each of my friends as well as one for himself. When I turned them over, every single card was a perfect fit. They were all personal, so I won't share Sandy's or my friends' cards here, but I will share the card Tiernan chose for me and for himself. My card was called the Holey Stone. The picture is a hand holding up a stone with a hole in it – a seer stone. Through the stone and behind is a cone of light rising up towards a star. The cone of light holds a golden angel while on either side ghosts and gargoyle-like demons lurk in the darkness. That card pretty much summed up my life: me as the seer of too much – demons and angels.

The card Tiernan chose for himself is called The Cloak. It shows a hooded cloak over emptiness as if worn by an invisible man. There are symbols for the chakras lined up inside the cloak and there are two animals on the card, a fox and crow. Both are trickster animal spirits. At the time, I was surprised by the card and not pleased. Invisible, shape-shifting tricksters? I knew that tricksters are viewed as sacred, but still....

Being a trickster has different connotations nowadays. It's a word we use as an insult or a warning. We've forgotten a lot of the old legends. How we revered Mantis, Anansi and Brother Rabbit for their smart-sassy trickster humour and ingenuity. If you want a more modern interpretation on the trickster spirit, go watch a Bugs Bunny cartoon. Although my heart knew the card was the truth, I didn't want to think of Tiernan that way, of being a shape-shifting trickster. My impish elephant-man? Mmm... okay. I had to eventually admit the card was a fit.

As the months progressed, the meanings of all the cards he chose that day became more multi-layered and true. And the next shape-shifting swirl of

Tiernan's magical cloak was just about to take place. It was the 5th of September and I was watching TV when Tiernan came in to stand behind me. There was nothing unusual in that. He regularly stopped by in the evenings. If the TV was boring, he'd pull up an invisible chair and sit beside me, chatting away. If the TV was interesting... he often did the exact same thing, only then it was annoying. Tiernan thought most of TV was stupid and was not at all sympathetic about me wanting to see what next thrilling thing happened in my favourite TV shows. After all, HE was the most thrilling thing in the room, surely?

Sometimes, when I tried to ignore him to watch a show or movie I was particularly enjoying, he'd take to dancing past in funny outfits or just stand in front of the TV and pull faces at me. Since I could hardly yell at him with my family sitting around me, he knew he had me trapped. He particularly liked to try to make me laugh at inappropriate moments. The more serious the show, the more absurd the jokes.

But there were times when he'd leave instantly. Any type of violence on the screen and he'd vanish. Once, he was messing about cracking jokes while I watched a movie about King Arthur. He had been fine until a sword fight started. Most of the time Tiernan's emotions were muted, but that sword fight brought such a wave of revulsion I actually felt like I was going to throw up. I remembered the first time I'd heard him in my head – the lamenting in Hebrew as I watched the documentary on the holocaust of WWII. That was the only language I don't speak that he has ever managed to shove into my head. Clearly, strong emotions made for a stronger signal!

When he appeared in September 2013 while as I watched TV, I didn't pay much attention. He went to stand behind me, which was a bit strange, and then he said, "Don't be afraid, this is purely symbolic." *Now that was strange!* I stopped watching TV to focus on him. As I sat there, deeply curious, these huge white wings appeared and wrapped around us both. Tiernan said they were a form of protection. Pretty. Very angelic. I felt good, if a little puzzled. Tiernan vanished instantly and I went back to watching the TV.

I did notice something else later that evening. He'd cleaned up. His scruffy, shoulder-length, dark-blond hair was combed and lighter in colour and he'd shaved his beard off. I had already tried to sketch his face and now I added a second picture of his new and improved look. How strange... I shrugged it off. What wasn't strange about life with my impish ellie-man?

Tiernan kept the clean and tidy look, but nothing else happened over the following week. One night about two weeks later, Sandy and I were watching a video on his computer when Tiernan came in. It was something Sandy had saved to show me: a video of an extremely virulent preacher who was so over-the-top on the topic of sin that it actually became funny. Sandy has never been religious and was enjoying the silliness of it all. The preacher had a long list of all the people God hated, from the obvious choices like adulterers and homosexuals to more varied options such as women who wore backless dresses.

We were both laughing so much that I never noticed how Tiernan was reacting until he exploded. He wasn't at all amused. He was raging angry. He pointed at the screen and said, "This is blasphemy!" before spinning around and vanishing. I was stunned. I'd never seen him enraged like that before.

Later that night while I was up editing and proof reading, Tiernan returned to apologise for his outburst. He seemed... subdued. Different. He sat down in Sandy's computer chair, a bit slumped with his head down as if unable to look me in the eye. I began to feel alarmed. Eventually he said quietly, "What if I'm not who you think I am?"

All of my brain was yelling NO. I'd had enough now, no more shape-shifting drama, please. But it was too late. As I watched, Tiernan stood up... and those angel wings reappeared behind him. Only this time, they were a part of him – his wings. I was this crazy mix of panic and anger. I loved this crazy man… MAN.

I didn't want him to say he was actually an angel. I did not want that! I did not want to lose my sweet, funny elephant-man. I mentally did the "stick your fingers in your ears and refuse to hear" thing, but he forced his way through. He told me he was an angel. That he was never a spirit guide and that was why he'd always been so reluctant to give advice. It really wasn't in his job description to be a teacher. He was full of apologies, but even though it all made sense, I was just so angry.

Looking back I could see that there had been clues, including that Wicca card he'd pulled just a few weeks before – my Holey Stone with the golden angel. And I remembered my dream of the Last Rider, that voice shouting out an invocation of all the names of God and all the angels. I swore at him in my mind, so angry that this made sense. This was a step too far for me. I had loved the silly elephant and the goofy sweet old Jewish man and I had fallen in love with the outrageously charming Tiernan. If this were true, then none of them ever really existed. They were all lies, swirls of the trickster's cloak.

HAHA damn him! As I wrote that, my music stream of the Piano Guys switched to ANGELS WE HAVE HEARD ON HIGH.

I was so angry that night in September 2013 that I told him to go away, repeating it again the next morning when I woke to find him still there. For the rest of the day, I refused to look at him or listen to him, no matter how hard he tried. I kept as busy as possible, constantly aware of this low-level stream of shouting in my mind and this blond man waving madly at me. I was too angry. Even when he stood in front of the TV and shouted and begged, I simply picked up a book and read instead.

The next morning he was there again, still pleading to be heard. I ignored him as I made morning coffee, then went upstairs and opened my computer Scrabble program. That would keep my mind occupied. I often play Scrabble against the computer to relax. This morning, the computer was set to play a word first. As the game began, I was busy fuming over the fact that I didn't even know what to call "him" now. Clearly the Tiernan name was a total fraud.

The Scrabble game put down the first word: **NAMEABLE**. I sat looking at it, aware that this angel person was at my elbow watching me intently. I ignored him and put down my word. The computer followed mine with **SHOWERED** and this burst of energy hit me. Pleading with me to remember, flashes of memories of us talking in the shower, the day in the shower when I first heard his voice.

Why couldn't he just go away? I tried to ignore the pleading and put down another word. The computer put **TALKS**. Computer? Ha! I knew full well it was Tiernan-the-lying-cheat-angel playing the other side. I tried to think of a word to put down, but I was too tense. I'd never had proof like this before. As angry as I was, I was still aware that this was amazing. A miracle. I even did a screen snip so that I had proof this was really happening. I sat staring at the screen, my mind blank. I asked for a hint and the program suggested: **HIS**. I agreed and the computer responded instantly by building a double word off it: **THIS OUT.**

TALKS – THIS – OUT

It was a silent scream. I gave up and I went and SHOWERED, at HIS suggestion, then I got together with Sandy and "Tiernan" to TALK THIS OUT.

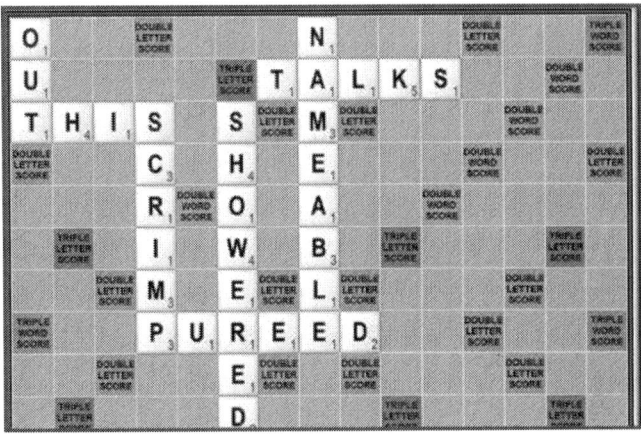

34

The talk-this-out began with Sandy wanting to know everything. Sandy has a sharp, clear mind and superb memory. Where I drift off and forget things almost instantly, Sandy can remember infinite, small details and pick up on inconsistencies in an instant. He fired questions at this latest version of my elephant-man like a detective interrogating a murder suspect. It made for a productive, if gruelling discussion.

The elephant-angel was completely open to answering any questions until Sandy pointed out that an angel named Tiernan seemed unlikely. What was his real name? The angel in my mind changed the subject quickly. *Mmm... so the NAMEABLE was reluctant to be named?* Sandy was instantly onto that, asking precise questions such as how many times this angel had visited Earth. The Ellie-angel admitted he had worked as a messenger many times. To give messages to anyone specific we might know? Maybe. The elephant-angel-man squirmed a bit before admitting he'd taken a message to someone in the Bible.

We took a break as I had to make dinner and was feeling as tired as the angel-elephant looked. While I was busy cooking, Sandy came downstairs to talk to me. He had a startling theory. He thought he'd figured out what my angel's name was based on which angels were named in the Bible. After dinner, Sandy asked to try again and Tiernan reappeared, a little reluctantly.

Sandy suggested a particular angel name and Tiernan replied by saying all the names for angels were man-made and not the actual names of the angels themselves. Sandy refused to let it go and kept pushing. Tiernan dodged it by admitting the name of a person in the Bible he had delivered a message to. Then he vanished.

I wrote and told Emily and James about Tiernan admitting he was a messenger angel mentioned in the Bible, but left out Sandy's suggested angel name. James wrote back instantly. Being Catholic, he was more aware of angel hierarchy than I was and had come to the same conclusion as Sandy. He wrote, "You do realise the angel we are talking about here is Gabriel?"

I shut my computer and went to bed without answering the email. I needed time to think. It was bad enough that my elephant-man was an angel. But Gabriel? That was like finding out your internet friend had been using a fake name for years and was actually someone famous. It's nice, but daunting. It holds all this baggage. And the Gabriel name held extra baggage for me since my dad's father, Gabe Frost, had been named Gabriel.

The next morning after a rather restless night, I called Tiernan, but he didn't appear. Clearly, he was avoiding the name thing for some reason. I got up out of bed and went to fetch my pendulum. I tried asking it about the name, but it would not swing. Not a YES or a NO; it just hung there without moving.

In desperation, I demanded help and Myrt appeared from wherever he was nowadays. I asked him to protect me while I used the pendulum, as he used to in the early days. I tried again, but the pendulum still refused to budge. I asked Myrt if he knew why. Looking sheepish and a bit anxious, he admitted my "friend" was blocking it. I asked the friend's name. Myrt glanced at me sideways, squirmed a bit as he said, "Gabriel."

I gave up and went to tell Sandy that it was time to confront that fake elephant once again. I called my trickster in and when he appeared I asked him straight out, "Is your name Gabriel?"

"Does it matter?" he asked. "It's only a man-made name." I pointed out that it mattered to me; it mattered a lot. "It's a name I've been called," he admitted with great un-enthusiasm, "but it is not who I am."

He went on to explain that the title archangel was equally man-made. According to him, there is no hierarchy amongst angels. They are all equals in a harmonious society of loving and sharing. He also pointed out that not all of the old stories about "Archangel Gabriel" were true, but my mind was already spinning in panic. All my forum friends and blog readers knew about Sol, my elephant spirit guide. How the HECK could I tell them he was actually the archangel Gabriel?

I didn't want a famous-name angel. I wanted my dear ellie back. I felt betrayed and full of self-pity, probably fuelled by the fact my parents had the flu again and I was to come down with it a few days later. In the middle of all the feverish achy-soreness, tempers were as thin as noses were raw. Everyone was fighting with someone and my mood turned decidedly martyred as the week progressed.

I have the email I wrote to Emily at the time.

Well... in the last 48 hours I have broken all kinds of records in melt-down fear, grief, distrust and just plain old stupidity. I also managed to fall in the shower yesterday morning, while Sandy was out shopping, and get stuck on the floor due to the fact:

1. the shower is tiny and the door opens concertina-style inwards

2. my butt is big and I'm not exactly nimble any more!

I was stuck on the floor with water pouring over me for quite some time. I suffered my first real panic attack in years, since being trapped did NOTHING for my claustrophobia. Then I had a miserable, howling good cry and finally managed to pull myself upright without damaging the door.

I have an impressive purple bruise across my rear end, but other than that and feeling achy-shaky I'm fine. At least fine physically, but emotionally my fall yesterday was the trigger for a far deeper emotional-spiritual fall. It started Tuesday night when a family fight blew up and I came down sick with a sore throat and fever. Then on to a full week of all of us ill = a household bruised, worn out and shaky. I feel shattered. We all do.

On top of that, my relationship with my guide has been damaged by him saying he was an angel. I did not want Sol to become Gabriel! It has sent me into more than one nose dive, but each time he patiently points out that his personality has never changed. At heart level, he still is Sol. Funny, irreverent, emotional and kind. And real.

And real? You have no idea how many times I've gone over every single event from the first time I "met" Sol till now in my mind. Over and over trying to objectively decide if it is real, or am I mad, is it real, am I mad? Yesterday morning, I realised, feeling incredibly depressed and sorry for myself, that if Gabriel is real then he must feel all my sorrow as well.

What was I doing to him with all this up-down nuttiness if he was real? I felt so bad for him I just started to bawl all over again. Then I was shown an image of my heart as a handful of broken glass shards which made me cry even MORE. Which was stupid because I had toothpaste and brush in my mouth at the time and nearly foam-coughed myself to death.

Gabriel came in and I asked if maybe he should leave, that it might be best for him. He stood there for a while and then said, "Are you asking me to decide what is best for me?

What I want to do?" I nodded and he said, "Then I'll leave."

And he did just that – zip. Gone.

By afternoon, I was sitting by the computer crying as I worked and Sandy was huddled on the bed as he was coming down with the flu. Somewhere in the afternoon, I felt so cold and Gabriel appeared in my mind and put a blanket around me. He said softly, "You did say the choice to leave or stay was up to me." and then he vanished again.

After dinner while watching TV, Gabriel returned to stand beside me. He said, "You know what your problem is?" and when I asked (bracing myself) he said, "Fear." Click... one word and it all made sense. I'd figured he'd say something like doubt, but fear is perfect.

Fear. That same night, Tiernan-now-Gabriel was back and ready to discuss my fear issues. He pointed out that my entire life was summed up by that one word. He took me through every decade and every way I had been hit full in the face by fear. On the plus side, he did not hold that against me. He said I never stood a chance; I'd been bombarded with fear issues my whole life. He said this led to me thinking that fear kept me safe. It became my security blankie.

He was right – I looked at fear as being protective.

As a child with bad allergies, my childhood was a list of things I could not come into contact with. And living in Africa through terrorism, war and violent crime, fear was that emotion that kept you safe. It is a survival instinct emotion. It was that higher state of adrenalin-tension that led to me being the one who three times heard a break-in happening while everyone else in the house slept. A soft click of a window being forced open, a gentle thud of an unknown foot in the garden. I always heard and woke up ready to sound the alarm. I was tuned to high alert for almost three decades. No wonder I ended up with anxiety issues!

That discussion with Tiernan-Gabriel opened my eyes to the roots of my anxiety problems. But knowing why you have a problem is not the same as fixing it. I was still a long way from being over my fears, especially about who and what "Gabriel" truly was, but my dear ellie-angel was about to fix that fear forever.

35

From July to early September 2013, Sandy had thought up more and more things he wanted to ask my guide, but now there was only one question he wanted an answer to. Why had Sol-Tiernan lied to me? Why had he pretended to be an elephant totem spirit guide and only now admitted to being an angel? While I understood that Sandy was angry because he was protective of me, the only way Sandy could cuss out "Gabriel" was through me. I act rather like a translator at the United Nations. I pass along what only I can hear. In the fast flowing argument between the two of them, this quickly became exhausting and stressful.

Gabriel suggested another way to communicate. Instead of him talking and then me repeating those sentences to Sandy, Gabriel made me close my eyes. Now normally, closing my eyes stops me seeing. No joke intended there! For some reason, I can only "see" psychic things with my eyes open. But this night Gabriel told me to close my eyes and read. I closed my eyes and words began to appear in my mind. They were bright white against darkness and they streamed like those news ticker tapes on the bottom of TV news bulletins on TV. Gabriel pumped the words out and all I did was read them.

It was a lot faster. I remember replying to Sandy almost instantly, instead of the whole pause… listen… repeat-what-has-been-said thing that I normally have to do. The down side of this way of communicating is that I don't remember any of it. To be honest, even the messages I'm told in the more usual way fade fast, which is one of the reasons I write them down (thus having a good store to use to write this story). All I remember of that night is that I was aware that Gabriel's replies to Sandy were pretty raw honest. He fought back. And I remember how fascinating it was to see these words, glowing white on that black background, steadily streaming through my mind.

That night's argument was long but therapeutic, leading to apologies from all sides as well as, eventually, lots of laughter. It also led to me finally meeting and introducing Sandy to Aggie, his own guardian angel. She not only joined us near the end, she also stayed and added a few personal memories of Sandy as a child that were both funny and touching.

Aggie was/is quite different from the elephant-now-angel Gabriel. Even now, Gabriel can be a tease and an imp, a little elusive where the truth is concerned. Aggie never turns to white lies to soften the truth. She is a no-

nonsense straight talker and a bit... kick-ass? I could imagine her as an Amazon warrior princess. Aggie would be one of those angels smooshing demons with a fiery sword.

Two things Gabriel said that night did stay with me. He said that at this stage in time, humans are awakening and realising their divinity whilst angels are realising their humanity. He also asked that I call him an Elohim rather than an Angel. He said the angel word was over-used and abused too much by humanity and had lost its true meaning. That reminded me of something else I saved. Gabriel dictated a message to me so that I would remember it and be able to share it with Sandy as well.

Sept 2013 – Being an angel/Elohim

> I am not human. I never was human. We have a purpose and we were created in an image you would call, "humanoid". We are shape-shifters supreme. I can become anything or anyone, but my essence is always the same and you know that well enough now to never be deceived by any form I might take, or be deceived by anything that tries to take my form.

> I am so sorry for what I have put you through. Leave that in, let Sandy read it. He needs to know more about me, and I promised no more lies so, he needs to know who I am. Warts and all? I have more warts, it seems, than I imagined possible.

So much for my own sense of self-righteousness!

My brethren are not normally known for their humour, as you have experienced first hand. We do share much in common with you emotionally, and even more than we care to admit to mentally and spiritually. In being the hand-workers of God we have sometimes been prone to a sense of superiority. Yes, write that down, I mean every word. Angels are presumptuous beings and as full of frailty as any other species.

You can tell him now that it is remarkable how any winged creature manages to circumnavigate the world with its head up its arse, but this has often been true for some of us, as we went on our message missions to mankind. We observed from a distance and that led us to detach from what we saw until God brought about a subtle change. We began to feel. We began to connect empathically to those we were sent to guard, ground and guide. Oh yes, the word guide is correct. We were never spirit guides, but we do guide, in most cases away from dangers or to a truth God wishes you to know.

When I first let Sandy read it, he queried the lack of humour thing and Gabriel added this:

Do we have humour? tsk... No, we sit about on clouds and strum ridiculously small harps while looking skywards with expressions of great pained piety, as if we have caught our non-existent genitals in a vice.

Now THAT was the being I knew and loved so well! That was the essence of Sol the elephant captured in words, but it still felt really weird to think of Sol as Archangel Gabriel. At this stage, I decided there were only three possibilities:

1. He really was an angel
2. I was insane
3. He was something very different. But what?

Gabriel kept insisting that I needed to let go of thinking from my head and think from the heart. He said that logic can be used to deceive the mind (look at lawyers and politicians), but the heart always senses the truth. Maybe, but my truth was that my totem elephant had morphed and morphed again so many times that I no longer knew what I felt. Gabriel had a suggestion. He told me to pray to God as I had done the night I met Earth Mother. He said I should ask for proof of exactly who and what he was.

I took a quiet moment on Thursday, 26th September, and asked for proof from God, one way or another. Nothing happened that day or Friday, but Gabriel seemed quite calm about it. He told me I would get "more than one proof" by that weekend. I didn't believe him, which he found very amusing.

Before I tell what happened that weekend, I need to explain a few things. When he was still pretending to be Tiernan, I once jokingly asked him what astrology Star Sign he was. He showed me the moon. I asked, "Cancer?" but he just grinned and kept showing me the moon. In astrology, Cancer's planet is the moon, so I figured it was just him being the typical tease. When he morphed into Tiernan, he told me that he loved swimming and the sea, which added to my belief that he was a Cancer water sign. Now I can return to that last weekend in September 2013.

That Saturday morning started with a friend sending me a cartoon joke in an email. It was a pink angel elephant holding a Scottish flag. It was flying through the sky... farting a rainbow. I had never seen a picture of a flatulent Scottish angel elephant anywhere before and pink had always been Sol's favourite colour. I had to tick that off as a confirmation 1 of an elephant who was now an angel with a fondness for fart-jokes in Scotland.

My next email that morning was a petition letter to sign. Someone in government wanted to ban all esoteric websites and the petition was to stop this. I left my emails to go look up the word "esoteric" on Google. I wanted to find the exact definition of the word in order to write an intelligent protest reply for the petition, but I accidentally clicked on Google images and ended up with pictures for "esoteric" instead.

As I was about to leave the images page, I noticed a picture of a seven-pointed star. My fiction books are written about a group of seven people who use the symbol of a seven-pointed star. Curious, I clicked to enlarge the image. It had names in each star point and the top point name was: GABRIEL. The illustration was some weird mystical thing relating to the belief that there was a council of seven archangels. Really?

Okay… that was weird. Certainly unexpected. I had to concede that as confirmation 2.

I wandered off as I often do and started browsing the website this picture was on. I went to the home page and there I found a story and a song that had meaning for me. This was deeply personal and far too complicated to explain. Let's just say I found my confirmations 3 and 4 and they were lovely and unexpected and linked me to a dead loved one as well as to Gabriel.

Later that day, James wrote to ask me if I could send him the drawing I had done of Tiernan-Gabriel. I had sketched both Tiernan's bearded face and the cleaned up, smarter version he had kept as his angel face. They were rough sketches on scraps of paper and I wasn't happy with the angel version. I decided to try and find a photo of a similar face to show James what Gabriel looked like. I put "blond man face" into Google image search and the first line of photos knocked the wind out of me. There in the top row was a photo I had been trying to find for about seven years.

I found this photo about ten years ago on a place that shared photos. I saved it because it reminded me of a character in my book. A few years later, when I self-published, I wanted to use that photo for the book cover artwork, but I couldn't find the photographer to ask permission to use it. When I went back to the website, that photo was gone. I used the photography forum to ask about the picture. Some members vaguely remembered it, but it seemed the photographer had left. I never used the picture, but I did stay on the site.

That led me to meeting a photographer there named Emily, the friend I was now sharing my psychic life adventures with. To find that photo after seven years of searching was a strange and intense moment. Maybe not as easy to define as proof, but personal proof for me. Confirmation 5.

After dinner, we decided to watch a movie. I had recorded three movies over the past month. We started one, but it was rubbish. Tried the next, but realised we'd seen it before, so we ended up watching the last. It's a slightly indie movie called "Grassroots." It was based on a true political story and pretty good. We all enjoyed it. Near the end, the guy hoping to win the election is standing by a window looking out... and I did a double take. There was this postcard resting on the window ledge. I looked at the tiny card on the screen and thought *THAT is an angel. Surely not?*

A short while later, everyone decided they felt like coffee and we paused the movie. As family scattered, I dashed to the TV to rewind and get a closer look at that card. There it was, and yes, it was an angel. I even knew what it was; it was one of those religious cards the nuns used to sell at my junior school. If you ever watch the movie it's between 75 to 79 minutes in. I marked it to show Sandy. It was an angel holding a weird, red dinner plate thing with a design that looked like crossed golf sticks.

While I was standing there trying to memorise the details, my dad walked in, glanced over at the TV and said, "Isn't that the archangel Gabriel?" I was so shocked that I don't think I replied. My father isn't

Catholic and had, as far as I know, never seen those types of cards. After the movie ended, I dashed upstairs to check. I stuck ARCHANGEL GABRIEL into Google image search and there, third row down, was the exact picture. EXACT picture. It is an icon of the Archangel Gabriel. I had Sandy check with me the next morning against the saved movie. Confirmation 6.

Confirmation 7 came about when I decided to find out why the angel Gabriel on that religious card was holding a red plate with golf sticks on it. I tried all sorts of Google searches, but found nothing to explain that symbol. If anyone knows, contact me please! The first place I went to did tell me that archangel Gabriel was associated with the constellation of Cancer and the moon. So that was why Tiernan joked about the moon! Now I was intrigued. I stuck MOON GABRIEL SYMBOLISM into Google and the first link took me to a picture of the Seal of the archangel Gabriel. I think my mouth dropped open. It was a crescent moon with a nine-pointed star. The exact same star that Tiernan had branded into my chest and hands.

I only knew the moon and star as an Islamic symbol, but wasn't sure about this version. I tried to find out more and was very surprised to find the history matched my own family history. The moon and star symbol was not Islamic. It was far older, dating back to ancient Egypt and Greece. The star is Venus, the Morning Star, and can be depicted with any number of points or even be just a dot. The symbol was adopted by the Ottomans after they conquered the city that used the upright crescent and star on their flag. The city of Byzantium/Constantinople, where my mother's ancestors had worked and lived for generations.

The crescent and eight-point star was used by Byzantium for their patron moon goddess, Hecate or Artemis. It's found on Byzantine coins. When Byzantium became Christian and changed its name to Constantinople, the Virgin Mary took over from Hecate as the city's protector. Swapping one powerful woman for another seems fitting for a city that is so important to my maternal ancestry.

Balthasar, one of the three Magi (wise men), was supposed to have the crescent moon and star as his coat of arms. My grandmother's family are related to the Baltazzi family of Constantinople and Venice. So many connections... I had my confirmation 8.

By then it was after midnight, but I was too buzzed to feel sleepy. I went to look at the next link on Gabriel and symbols. It didn't have any pictures as such, but it did tell me that he was the patron saint of communication and writing (oh very funny) and his feast day was the 29th of September. I checked the calendar, feeling a bit dizzy with shock. That brand new Sunday morning was the 29th of September. Confirmation 9. It was time to admit the elephant-angel had won. He'd said there would be not one confirmation, but many.

He really was the archangel Gabriel.

36

The moment I accepted that he really was an angel named Gabriel, I froze up. For years I'd been completely relaxed around him, arguing and laughing with him, but now that he had an important name I felt tongue-tied and awkward. Gabriel grumbled about it, pointing out that this was the reason he had been so reluctant to claim the name. He said it carried "too much baggage and hype." It would take me months to get over my new sense of awe and shyness. During that time, Gabriel regularly cracked silly jokes, trying to get me to relax around him again. One of his best and naughtiest happened in February 2014.

I had been busy saving all his messages into a Word document and was rereading the bit about angels having "non-existent genitals". My elephant totem had been fond of waving large ellie "male bits" in my face, as a joke. Did angels have genitals? I hadn't asked

Gabriel outright. That seemed a bit too personal and invasive, but I was curious. Gabriel popped into my head and asked me to open up my scrabble game. Then he asked me to allow the computer to choose words for me, in other words to let the game play out by itself. Well....

The first word was JEW followed by: WOW, WE, TEASE, PENIS. I took a screen snip capture to show Sandy later.

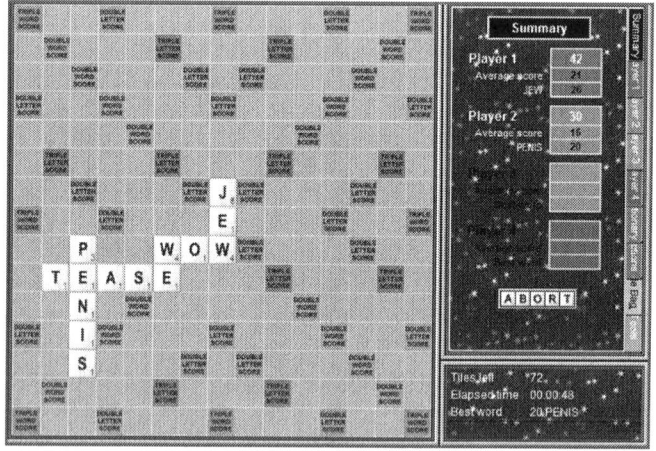

Needless to say, by the time we reached the P word Gabriel was roaring with laughter and I was blushing like mad, once again realising he had been reading my thoughts. So, do angels have gender and male/female bits? I'm still a bit at a loss how to answer that question. Gabriel is masculine in his personality and behaviour. He certainly is not androgynous as some artists portray angels, but from what I gather, this may

314

be more about gender personality than sexuality. I'll leave it there. Even a cheeky angel deserves some privacy. *Ah, heck... he just popped into my head and lifted his angel gown to flash me. He never changes!*

Angels, Elohim... what else have I learned over the last few years that I can share? They are FUNNY and smart and full of joy and love. Not in a tacky-sweet Christmas movie way, but in a rich, real and surprisingly down-to-earth way. I've often joked that if Elohim were an animal they'd be dolphins. That is the kind of smart and playful vibe they give off. But it isn't all playfulness. They do have a serious side as well.

Do you remember me describing Tiernan's revulsion when I was watching that TV show sword fight? Mention wars or violence and they react by hitting me with a wave of grief and nausea. Elohim are completely telepathic and empathic. They sense and hear each other completely, but even though they are completely intertwined, they each have their own individual ways and likes/dislikes. Aggie is nothing like Gabriel.

I asked about their names. If Gabriel was a name he didn't like, why not use his actual name? Gabriel laughed and told me he couldn't because their language has no grammar as such. Being telepathic empaths, most of their communication is a simple and instant knowing. This instant telepathy cuts down on miscommunication a lot. Gabriel has said that angels can disagree and even argue, but it is rare and they get over it quickly. Spoken language isn't needed and the sounds they do use as communication are a lot more like music than any human language.

Gabriel tried to explain that by saying reality is sound – all of it. In the Bible, John 1:1, it says:

In the beginning was the Word, and the Word was with God, and the Word was God.

Gabriel amended "the Word" to "sound", saying that all of creation is a sound vibration hologram. A grand celestial song. He said that the Elohim, as the oldest species created by God, are adept at using and understanding it. I was completely fascinated and Gabriel promised me that he'd find a way to let me hear their language. That night, I had a dream where I woke up and heard these exquisite sounds. It was like crystal bells and wind chimes playing a tune so perfect that I can't even come close with clunky English words to describe it. Haunting, clear, crystal-beauty music – that's the best I can do. Then I really did wake up. For a hauntingly brief moment, it continued to play in my head before fading away.

The next thing I most wanted to know was why he had sometimes made predictions that didn't happen. I knew he was prone to the odd white lie, but sometimes it seemed more like he made mistakes. Was that possible? Gabriel admitted that it is possible. He explained how he sees the future and why this can lead to him predicting things that don't happen. As he put it, "There are variables."

Let's take seeing the future as being the same as looking forward along a path we are walking on. We don't think of this as seeing the future, but the fact our eyes are looking ahead, mentally noting a puddle we need to step over perhaps, makes this a form of viewing the future. Or at least, the possible future if we continue walking forwards along that path.

Now let's get into the brain of an angel. Where you and I see a short way ahead of us as we walk, their eyesight is more complex. An angel can see a lot further, several miles in comparison to our few feet, and because they see further they can see where the road branches off. The further you can see ahead, the more variables of possible choices become visible.

Gabriel showed me his view of the future as having so many possible path choices that it looked like a tree laid out on its side with all these branches and smaller branches splitting off from it. As we make choices, those not-chosen paths vanish so that there always seems to be a single path beneath our feet, but that is actually an illusion. It is only a single path at the moment our foot hits the ground. Until that moment, there may be dozens of potential routes ahead.

For an angel whose sight is better than ours, our feet are constantly hovering above ten or more possible futures. When I ask Gabriel about a possible outcome on some future event in my life, he's looking at a whole handful of outcomes depending on the choices I make each time I place my foot down on the road in front of me. That makes predictions tricky and changeable. The messages Gabriel gives me are based on the most probable future, but there can actually still be several more possible variations. Nothing is set in stone. All it takes is for me to make one impulsive choice to alter the entire timeline ahead of me. Gabriel said that in many cases the variations between those possible routes are subtle and small, but every now and then we reach those big "cross road" moments.

Here's an example: You're sitting at the traffic lights. If you go straight you will get to work, but if you turn right you will hit an oncoming bus and die. It is often at times like this where angels will try to warn people. Maybe you get a niggling feeling you shouldn't go right. Maybe a stranger appears and distracts you and you forget you were going to turn. Muttering with annoyance, you travel straight on the long way round and arrive at work late, never knowing what would have happened if you'd turned right. Variables.

37

Another source of panic for me during the last half of 2013 was the fact that the connection with Tiernan-Gabriel would fade every so often. At these times, he'd often say that he had to step away for a while. I'd panic, fearing I was messing up or that I'd never see him again. Sounds silly now, but it was all so new and different that I wasn't sure what to expect. Each time, he'd return within a day or so and he'd be hyper, like someone who had drunken ten energy drinks and was ready to party all night.

It was Sandy who noticed the pattern and started studying it. Each time my angel-elephant vanished, there was solar flare activity on the sun. Now, astronomy is not my area of knowledge, so please forgive me stumbling through this in utter cluelessness. I can only tell you what I know. Gabriel would leave tired, then return like the battery bunny and each incident coincided with strong sun activity. I had wondered if he was going off to the sun to recharge his energy in some way, but now that I can look back over the last four years I realise I had it wrong. The reason he returned energised was simply because he had a break from being connected to me 24/7. The deep connection we share is draining for both of us. Hindsight is an amazing thing and would have saved me a lot of stress in 2013, but I was too good at fearing the worst. Each time, I just leapt face first into worst case scenario panic.

This happened again during the first days of January 2014. I woke one morning to find Gabriel sitting watching me sleep. He was dressed in his favourite cream suit, no shoes as always, and he looked very serious. There were tears in his eyes. He told me he had to go and once again… poof… he was gone. His seriousness and the tears made me panic, AGAIN.

I was a mess that day, wanting to cry as I waited in terror that this time he was truly gone and in a way, he was. When Gabriel returned a day or so later, I couldn't see him any more. I could still hear him, but the very real man I had lived with constantly around me for seven months was no longer visible. That was shattering. I blamed myself. What was I doing wrong? What had changed?

I wrote to my friends for help and both Emily and James asked their spirit guides. Emily's guide (who has no name) said that Gabriel had "morphed." Eagle said something similar, that Gabriel had to pull back and leave for my own good. At the time, it didn't make any sense. It felt like I'd gone blind. I was back to short bursts of images as I had experienced seeing things prior to 2013. I could still hear him, but that wasn't the same as having him visibly there. I was heart-broken. It took me months to accept and it's really only now that I understand how necessary this was.

James and Eagle were right; Gabriel had to go for my own good. Looking back, I can now see how in 2013 I was sick with flu or virus infections five times. In the last four years, I think I've had the flu once. In other words, while we were strongly connected, my immune system dipped dramatically. I think this worked both ways since Gabriel would say he had to leave, acting exhausted, then return recharged after being away.

I asked Gabriel recently and he confirmed my deductions. That intense connection, where he constantly created a 3D image of himself and projected it into my mind, took a massive amount of energy from both of us. As lovely as it was to see him so clearly, it wasn't good for either of us.

Do I miss seeing him? Not any more, but at first in 2014 I missed him dreadfully. Nowadays, I'm happy with the level we are at. It's less invasive and overwhelming and it allows me to trundle through life without being partially disconnected to what is around me. I was so strongly connected to him in 2013 that I walked through most of that year with my mind in two realities. No one can live like that full time and function properly unless you go sit on a mountain as a hermit for the rest of your life.

Ah, the things that are so clear looking back.... 2014 was a year of revelations and change. It wasn't just Gabriel who morphed, we all did. We ALL did. Seems you can't interact with angels and not come away completely altered by the experience. What I realised now, writing these memories, is that when you interact with angels the truth rises to the surface. All of it.

I should have guessed when Gabriel showed me a small, wooden chest in 2013. He told me I kept it in my heart and that it was filled with all my fears. Then he proceeded to open it and take out each fear one by one. He was loving, but determined to empty that box in a way that felt quite relentless at times. I spent a lot of 2014 to 2015 having my dear angel friend shove me face first into the truth of my fears.

I was not alone in this. Aggie and Gabriel would do the same to Sandy, forcing him to look deeply at himself. And more! My friend Emily's life had changed during this time as well. Even my parents have experienced it. This has continued to ripple out. All of the results have been good, but the journey has been both funny and sometimes painful. Working with angels is not for anyone who would prefer to ignore their faults and fears. This is tough love of the very best kind; the fires that forge steel and the pressure that creates diamonds. So please, do not wish to work with angels unless you truly want your soul scrubbed bare.

Gabriel made his first public appearance as an angel on my blog in November 2013. For ten years, I've taken part in Blogblast for Peace every November. I normally plan months in advance, making my own artwork to go with whatever theme I've chosen to write about that year. But in 2013, Gabriel offered to write something for me. This is what he dictated for Blogblast 2013:

"Dona Nobis Pacem... (may God) grant us peace. They are beautiful words, but entirely wrong. It was never up to God to grant Peace since it never was God who took peace away from mankind. For far too long we have watched in growing agony as mankind begs for peace, prays for peace and all the time forgets that the power to create peace always lay within his/her own hands.

Peace is not a gift to be given by God to mankind, it is a natural birthright of every child. It is already within your hearts and in ready reach of your hands. You are the ones who forget your own power as you grow and the suffering of this world overwhelms you. It was never up to God, it was always up to you.

Your world sits at a crossroads and you are the ones who must choose which direction it takes. All the prayer in the world cannot save you from your own selves, only you can do that. It does not have to be anything more than one gesture, one small forgiveness instead of an angry word. Peace starts small, like a seed. Let it grow naturally inside you and don't be afraid to use it as it grows. It is stronger than it looks, fuelled by love and constantly watched over by whatever you choose to call God. It will grow and it will prevail, but only if you stop looking outward for your answers and turn to look within. You will not find God's grace in prayer, you find it each time you hold out your hand to another living being, in kindness or compassion.

Until mankind realises that every life is equal in the eyes of God there truly cannot be Peace on Earth. All life is equally precious, an eagle is no more or less than a mosquito. A human living in Africa is no more or less than another living in Asia or Europe. No religion, no gender, no political party holds the key or stands higher than the next.

There is only one world you have to live upon and yet what do you do? You fight over so many stupid things and find so many reasons to hate each other. Even those of you who swear you follow the paths of peace will admit in your hearts to feeling superior to someone else you know, whether it is through enlightenment, education or financial superiority. It does not matter. It never did. It never has. It never will. You were born perfect and you will die perfect. In between is up to you."

38

One of the first things that happened after I finally accepted that Tiernan was the angel Gabriel was that someone else stepped forward to say hello. It was during another late evening of proof reading and editing. (it took four months to write that book and six months to check for errors. Perhaps not helped by all those chatty interruptions?) Gabriel arrived with Aggie and then I was suddenly aware of a third presence. Someone had "walked" into the room through the far wall corner. This person was invisible, but the energy was powerful and... green. Can't explain that sensibly. There was no visible form, only this sense of brilliant, green light. I asked who was there and a wry, amused voice said, "Call me Dora the Explorer."

Gabriel asked me my impressions of this invisible stranger, if I sensed anything. I said that "Dora" felt green and reminded me of the actress Judi Dench.

That made Gabriel and Aggie burst out laughing. Probably because when I finally did see Dora, "she" was a man with dark hair and a neatly trimmed beard wearing Victorian style clothing: a formal suit and sometimes a long dark coat. By that time, I knew that Dora was a higher being, a spirit guide and very much an explorer. Interestingly, Dora carries a walking cane very similar to the one James' spirit guide, Eagle, has. I have a suspicion the cane is symbolic and they are both something like wizards of the kind Tolkien would have called Istari. Mage would suit them better as a title than spirit guide. I always think of Dora as a mage when I deal with him... her... him.

Is Dora a she or he? Actually, the answer is both. He/she will swap voices and forms from male to female in my head in mid-conversation. In homage to my first comment, the female version of Dora looks and sounds like Judi Dench. Dora jokingly calls the male persona version I see Doar, but I'll stick with Dora for this book. I asked him/her why the changing gender and Dora said that she/he has incarnated and lived on Earth so many times that gender has become "superfluous and irrelevant." Confusing, I know, but there really is no simple way to explain an androgynous being with basic English pronouns.

I could imagine Dora teaching at Hogwarts, probably constantly alternating genders. Which reminds me! I sometimes see him/her in the form of a griffon. Equally apt since it is a mythological beast made up of two ferocious animals. Dora is as clear-sighted and uncompromising as an eagle and quite capable of ripping your flaws and misconceptions to shreds like a lion.

An example of Dora's teaching style is the time he/she sent Sandy a song. Gabriel, as I've said, regularly sends me songs with meaning. They are always lovely and cheer me up. It was in March 2014 that Dora gave Sandy a song. Dora was more forthright than Gabriel. He/she told me exactly what song to send Sandy. Sandy didn't know the song and went to find it online. When he listened to it, he was not pleased. In fact, he was downright angry.

Sandy had asked why there was so much tragedy in the world and Dora's answer was the song "You Learn" by Alanis Morissette. It's a dark-humour song about tragedy being a good way to learn and grow. Sandy was deeply offended and angered by what he saw as a flippant response to human suffering. He told me that he refused to talk to Dora ever again and wanted me to do so as well.

I'm not sure how long it took Sandy to cool down, but eventually he admitted that the song was more apt than he'd been willing to accept at first. Nowadays, it's one of Sandy's favourite songs and he can finally see how right Dora was, but it took him weeks to months to be able to realise that fact. During that time, Dora was not at all bothered by the fact Sandy thought of her/him as an enemy to be avoided. By comparison, Gabriel worries about harming others and rarely says anything harsh. In fact, the only times Gabriel gets tough is when he's being protective of me. He has a squishy, pink elephant heart.

Gabriel also answered Sandy's question about suffering and tragedy. Unlike Dora's short and to the point song choice, Gabriel's dictated answer was long and complex. Here are his words, exactly as I took them down in 2014:

> So, life lessons and why do they hurt so much... Resistance is partly to blame, you are correct, but that is a simplification. There are other forces at play. Which brings me to a point we have discussed recently, that I know you wish me to share with your friends. It is the concept that life on this planet, within this realm, is merely a "game". It is a word that I personally find repugnant. Life is not a game. Yes, it should be enjoyed and full of adventure, love and laughter, but there is a particular danger in classifying any reality as lesser, or as a game. It trivialises the experience down to something no more important and, even more dangerously, it trivialises everything within that reality.
>
> As a 'game' the human experience becomes no more than a series of challenges to conquer in order to "win". Such a mind set, as far as I can see, is not conducive to empathy and allowing the awareness of all-is-one to flourish. Nor does it sanctify the experience, as it should be. This reality is no more, no less, important than any other. It serves a purpose, designed as such by Source and yourselves. It is as real as any other and the experiences you have here are as important and beautiful, in their own way, as any

you might encounter in other realms or levels of existence.

As a 'game' there is the unspoken message to mankind that the experiences here do not matter. That the pain as well as the sorrow are inconsequential. That is not so. Everything you experience is holy and valid, including what you suffer within this realm. To think otherwise runs the added danger of then thinking it is alright to walk away or ignore the suffering of others, since they are merely other 'players' in the 'game' after all. No. No. No. Such a mindset is wrong at the highest level. This realm was not created to be a game for sociopaths to flourish in, but rather as a place to learn the deeper connection of All. The Oneness of every living thing is equally valued by God. This planet has value, this reality with all its beauty has value. This planet matters to God. (or Source. Whatever word you choose to use is of no consequence)

I cannot tell you all that is to pass, because I do not know. I do not know because there are variables, and because I am not God, and because I am an imperfect being, same as yourselves. Perfection is a lie, mostly created by religions. It is a concept unheard of in other realms, this "perfection" you seek. Perfection, as seen by the human mind, is static. It is a state of being where a being or item reaches a certain level and... all stops. Because now it is PERFECT. No more growth, no more adventure... nothing. Perfection, as far as I can tell, seems to be the same as death. Can we agree on that?

So what is seen as 'perfection' by God? Growth. Change. Experience. Joy. These are the things to strive for, not some dead flat line state of being PERFECT. Michelle's mind used an analogy that sums it up well: the butterfly as an example of Divine perfection. Caterpillar-pupae-insect. Change in all its miraculous wonder. More importantly, when the caterpillar is a perfect creature it is nowhere near being a perfect butterfly. when the butterfly is perfect it is no longer a perfect caterpillar. And yet both forms are perfect. It does not need to strive towards one static state of being. It finds joy in every step of its journey and that is the true perfection of life – the joy of the experiences, whatever they might be.

And so I finally can return to what I was discussing in the first place, before this dear woman drew me off to talk on the things important to her. I was wanting to discuss life lessons and suffering. The lack of joy in the experience, you might say. There are some belief systems on your planet that hold with the theory that all of life in this realm must revolve around suffering. No. Not at all. Look at nature and you will see first hand how ridiculous and absurd that concept is. Nature is full of joy. It abounds in delight. Even the cycles of death and life are ones that echo that message of joy.

There is this misconception that nature is 'red of

tooth and claw.' Perhaps it might seem that way at first, but look closer at the reality and you soon realise how much is lost by taking that quote as fact. Yes, animals die and people die. Things are eaten by things that in turn are eaten by another and at the end of it all the earth itself will eat them all as their energy returns back to the soil it came from. There is no horror in that for any beast or plant. The sparrow does not sit on the branch weeping at the fact it may end up in the gullet of a bird of prey tomorrow. It is here. It lives in the moment. It sings in joy or anger with equal passion and zest for life. It enjoys it all.

That was how it was meant to be. Joy in every experience. What went wrong? Why does mankind find living so unbearable? In part it lies within the constraints of your own biology. You are, as some say, a spiritual being here within a physical form. There are parameters to that interaction. The human animal has the same instincts of survival as any other. The spiritual form of you has not. That creates a level of conflict that most life forms on this planet do not share. It is what sets you apart. Not a "soul" as such, for every living and seemingly non-living thing is equally created by God's energy and thus sacred to God.

The difference lies in the fact that humans come here aware of that fact. That is your destiny, what you have been striving towards for so long. To balance the awareness of multiple realities within your physical form. Michelle thinks that last sentence makes no sense. Worse, she commented that it sounds rather "oogah boogah". I will try to explain it in a simpler form for her. Or she will nag at me to alter it, I know. She nags a lot. It is tiresome and worthy of many peanuts. I will leave her to explain that.

Back to the human condition of being aware spiritually and physically within this reality. Animals are aware of it as well. The difference is that animals do not try to understand it. They accept. No query, no curiosity, no conflict. They know, at cell level, that they are a part of creation. Mankind chose to come here to experience the conflict of knowing yet not knowing enough. It makes you strive for more. But within that adventure there have been times when the suffering this induced has created harm to all involved. This reality was never meant to harm, only for all to learn more. Mankind was meant to express that part of God that you call Love. Agape is a closer term, but even it falls short of the mark.

This Love holds an energy that is pure, but not perfect. Because perfection is a dead thing that has no purpose. Not even God is perfect in the way mankind see the concept. I understand how such a comment might seem blasphemy, but bear in mind you invented the word. Perfection is a fool's concept. Not even God is such and why should God be? The universe is constantly expanding and altering, transforming as it grows. Within that growth there are accidents and mistakes as well as moments of wonder. Throw the perfect word in the bin and accept the fact all of growth is a miracle.

All life is a miracle. An ever changing wondrous thing full of surprises. It is only when mankind began to strive for an impossible perfection that he began to create suffering. Do you understand now? Perfection automatically implies a want. It automatically separates the experience into good and evil. God did not create evil. Mankind did that. There was no devil before you created him in your own image.

The "worthy of many peanuts" reference is from the days I saw him as an elephant. He used to shoot peanuts out of his trunk at me to get my attention. I've had peanuts shot at me when I was ignoring him as well as at times he wanted to distract my focus. He shot peanuts at me in hospital when I was scared to make me laugh. He has shot peanuts at people I was angry with as well, once again to make me laugh. It's hard to keep a straight face when you're arguing with someone as an elephant bounces invisible peanuts off their head!

My ex-elephant angel can be sublime as well as silly, but that cheeky earthy humour is always lurking just under the surface. Dora and Aggie have a good sense of humour as well, but neither of them is ever vulgar, like my naughty ellie-angel.

I'm not surprised I first met Aggie with her cussing me out for being a Pollyanna. Aggie strikes me as being the kind of angel who just might smite you with a fiery sword if you got on her nerves, but she has a softer side and a sassy sense of humour. She tends to pop into my head pretending to be a girly girl, when in actual fact I think she's a lot more like a goddess of the hunt. Aggie enjoys the joke of being girly and often appears in my mind filing her fingernails.

I see Aggie as a beautiful, dark-haired woman, but since she showed me hundreds of women's faces the first time I saw her when we were driving back from our trip to England, I know this is merely a form she chooses to use. I've once seen Gabriel in his true form and it was so blindingly bright, I could not make out any details other than a basic human form. They take on masks to talk to us. Their true brightness is too dazzling for human eyes.

Sandy once queried where she was on the day he was riding a bicycle and got hit by a van. She showed me an image of herself having her nails done and going, "Ooops!" as she realised she'd not noticed Sandy getting whacked by the van and shooting up into the air. As Sandy has gotten to know her, he has become more and more fond of her, which is not surprising as they are a lot alike. Aggie says that this is typical of guardian angel-human relationships. You get paired with a kindred spirit, someone a lot like you. It makes for easier empathy and understanding.

Sandy also asked Aggie if she would be there to meet him on the day he died. He wanted to know if he would recognise her, given the fact he isn't certain what she truly looks like. Aggie replied that she would be there and he'd know it was her. Sandy wasn't satisfied. "But what if I don't?" he asked, "What if I don't recognise you?" She responded by showing me an image of an airport arrivals area and there she was, waiting for Sandy to arrive... holding up a small teddy bear on fire. *Really?*

I told Sandy and he was equally puzzled. "A teddy bear on fire. Why?" asked Sandy.

"It's what you always wanted," said Aggie.

After a short pause, Sandy burst out laughing. You see, when Sandy was a little boy he had wanted a teddy bear, but his big sister bought him a toy rabbit for his birthday instead. When Sandy first told me the story he remembered saying, "All I got was a rabbit. I wanted a flaming teddy bear!" Well, Aggie is going to give him that flaming bear some day!

Speaking of gifts, as my birthday came around in 2014 I thought back on how Tiernan had given me the Calla lily the year before. I wondered if he'd do something like that again. There was no denying that Gabriel did act smug every time I thought about my birthday. Clearly, he was planning something.

Well, my birthday morning arrived and I scanned the room with my mind. Nothing. *Okay, maybe on the internet?* I got up and checked my emails for clues, but there was nothing that felt like a sign from Gabriel. *Oh well....* Feeling a little disappointed, I got on with reading my birthday wishes. It was a while before I realised I was hearing noises from the bedroom. The door was closed. Sandy was up to something. Ah good, at least he had remembered my birthday. Eventually, Sandy appeared with a large box he'd been busy wrapping. He was grinning from ear to ear as he told me that before I opened it, he had a story to tell me. Sandy said that he'd gone into town to buy me a birthday card. He paid for it and was about to leave when a voice in his mind said, "STOP! Go back."

Sandy was pretty startled since he never hears voices. He said that he turned around in the doorway and felt PULLED to go back towards the far end of the shop. Trusting this feeling, he went back down the aisle, past the cards and on down until he reached that far end. He stopped, wondering why as the shelf was full of irrelevant things, but then he looked up. Sandy told me that what he saw on that top shelf was now inside my birthday box. He said that he had a feeling it was from Gabriel. A wave of SMUG hit me from Gabriel. Intrigued, I opened the box. Inside was a grey, plushy toy elephant with a cheeky grin and sparkly gold eyes. My angel friend had done it again.

This was where I ended my original email to Richard, but several months have gone by since then. Today as I sit editing this chapter, it is the day after my birthday in August 2017. *You're curious now, aren't you? Has Gabriel done it again?* On the night before my birthday, I went to bed thinking about those past gifts. Gabriel hadn't given me any birthday gift for 2015 or 2016 and I figured those first gifts were all I'd ever get from him. But as I thought that, Gabriel popped into my mind, smug as heck. He said he'd already taken care of it, then vanished.

My birthday was a lovely day. I had loads of wishes and cards from friends. Sandy had already given me my gift and my parents always give me money. I wasn't expecting anything more, but this birthday my mom sent my dad off to fetch another large and mysterious box. When I opened it, I was near tears looking at what was inside. My mom had knitted me a PINK elephant. He has the word *LOVE* in diamanté and a silver chain around his neck. Very "bling"!

My mom said she found the pattern recently and has been knitting madly to get it finished for my birthday. She also made a tiny crochet sombrero, just like the one my elephant loved to wear. Mom said that finding the pattern in time for my birthday felt a bit more than lucky chance. *Bravo, Gabriel. You did it again!*

39

Gabriel might have a famous name, but who he is, his personality, has never altered. Just like that card he picked for himself of the cloak over an invisible person, he remains himself through every swirling, magic cloak change. He'll always be my darling cheeky elephant. This is a good place to move onto the topic of reincarnation and what I call core personality. One of the things Sandy asked in 2014 was about who we truly are. I mean, if reincarnation exists, then which of those many lives is the real person?

What I now understand is that who we are never changes. There is this core personality that is the real YOU, regardless of when or where you are living or even what gender you choose for that lifetime. Each life is merely a chapter in a far bigger story. Think of it this way: even in one lifetime who you are changes on the surface. You arrive as a baby, grow through childhood, become a teenager, adult, old person... each stage can seem very different and yet each of those stages you were still you. It's the same through lifetimes.

Aggie, Gabriel and Dora each added layers to this understanding over time. It wasn't an instant realisation. A lot of that is thanks to Sandy's insatiable need to know. From 2014 to 2015, Sandy would ask and they would share information. Then, Sandy and I would go research, being the information nerds we are.

I'll give an example: Sandy asked specifically about his life before this one – the life he was born remembering. All he had were flashes of memories and the odd intense, repetitive dream. Sandy's past life dreams matched a few things I'd dreamed of, which was what led us to connect on the internet forum in 2002 the first place. Although my dreams were similar, they were not the same. Gabriel had warned me about taking dreams literally. The subconscious is a very creative thing and our minds adore symbolism. How much of Sandy's and my dreams were truth and how much was symbolism or dream fancy? Sandy wanted and needed to know.

I think it was Dora who gave us the first facts to check. She/he said that Sandy and I had been siblings in that former life. Even more startling, he/she said we weren't the only ones from that life who were back here again. My parents had been our parents that lifetime before. Then she/he gave us names and dates.

Sandy was upset with Dora because the dates did not match his dream memories or mine. We'd both dreamed of dying violently in what looked like WWII. These people, according to Dora, had died near the end of WWI.

Sandy was fed up and lost interest, but I decided to dig deeper. It took several months on the internet to track it all down. The names and dates were real. These children and their parents existed. That was when Sandy became interested again and started to do research as well. It took a heck of a lot of work to dig up details, but I found something that changed everything. I found an old photo of Red Cross personnel in WWI and there they were, two siblings side by side staring back across time at me. I looked at the face that Dora said had been Sandy and I started to cry. The smile and body language, pose of the head... it all matched.

Looking at the person who had been me felt strange, but nothing more than that. What is interesting is that Sandy looked at the photo and recognised me instantly, but was unsure about himself. Perhaps we didn't recognise ourselves because we don't spend so much time watching our mannerisms and facial expressions?

I am not putting those past life names here because I found these people via family trees online, which means they have living relatives. That makes this seriously weird. I don't want to freak out the living family, but thanks to them and war researchers I can say that everything I found out fits what Dora told us.

It also fits Sandy's dream. Not deaths in WWII, but deaths between the two world wars. This family was Eastern European, living in an area that was full of conflict during the early 1900s. We found enough details online to make Sandy's vivid childhood dreams of dying violently make perfect sense.

You have no idea how haunting it is to find yourself and how extra haunting it is to read snippets of old family memories and find that the likes, dislikes and quirky habits all match who we all were then to who we all are now. Sandy was excited and keen to tell my parents straight away, but Gabriel said it wasn't the right time. He often says, "Timing is everything." He's right, annoying as that is to admit.

In 2014, about five months after we found this family, my mom came through one morning and said, "I had the weirdest dream last night. It felt so real." She went on to say she had been living in Victorian times. She described the man she loved, where they lived and a vivid event that happened before they got married.

Gabriel said, "It's time."

I took my mom to her computer, pulled up the link to this family tree and then told her. "It wasn't just a dream. That was your past life." Then I let her read it for herself. It was the same era, same part of Europe, same man and woman, same vivid event that happened before they married.

I really expected my mom to say I was mad, but instead she started to cry and said, "This is me. This is your father." That was when I showed her the old Red Cross photo. Before I explained any of it, she pointed to my past face and said, "That's you," and then she pointed at Sandy's past life face and added, "That's Sandy."

Core personality never changes.

That is what Gabriel, Dora and Aggie had kept saying. I've been fairly okay with not needing to know who I've been before. Beyond having my hunch confirmed that the dream of the shipwrecked Spanish soldier was me, I've not delved into my past lives much. I have enough problems with remembering this one! But Sandy, now he had proof that his childhood memories were of a real life, was on fire to know more. Sandy asked Dora and Aggie about his former lives. Could they be specific as to when and where? Aggie listed several places and dates. Two are particularly interesting and worth mentioning.

The first was a lifetime that she said Sandy had spent in Southern France, born in 1059. Interesting, but not easy to verify, obviously. A while after that, Sandy was watching a music video and was haunted by the mountains in the background. They called to him with a feeling of being extremely familiar in a deja vu kind of way. He saved the video and asked me to watch it. While I was looking at it, Aggie popped in to say that Sandy had lived close to these mountains in a former life. This was why they felt familiar – they were one of his previous home grounds. Aggie said that this was the life of the person born in 1059.

Sandy went to find where the mountains were, digging through internet sites to find who had made the music video and where it was filmed. He was extremely disappointed to discover that the mountains were in Spain. He was also annoyed that Aggie had given him false information since she'd told him that lifetime was in the South of France.

Sandy decided to do some research into the area and the history of the place. He found out that back in the 1000s, that area of Spain was considered to belong to France. Aggie had told the truth – it was the South of France, but only if you go back a thousand years.

The other life that Aggie told Sandy about seemed bogus at first. Sandy wanted to know just how far back his time on this planet spanned. He wanted to know about his first human lifetime here on Earth. Aggie told him that one of the earliest lives he'd had was on the edge of the Ural Sea. Sandy corrected her, saying, "You mean Aral Sea."

Aggie replied, "No. the URAL Sea."

Sandy was confused as there is no Ural Sea, but Aggie was adamant it was Ural, not Aral. Once again, Sandy went off to do research on the area and its history. He put "Ural Sea" into Google not expecting to find anything, but a short reference did pop up. According to the Dictionary of Earth Sciences (published by Oxford University Press 1999), the Ural Sea covered the area east of the Ural Mountains during the Palaeocene and Eocene eras. That is roughly 60 million years ago, which makes Sandy's first lifetime here a VERY long time ago.

We eventually added a few more past lives to the mix, things we were able to confirm to some degree for Sandy, my mom and myself. In all these cases, when we did more research, there was this strong sense of recognition and the same personality type of the person then as is now. Who we were is still who we are. Just as Gabriel is always his earthy, naughty, sweet self regardless of whether he looks like an elephant, an old Jew or an angel. Just as you are you regardless of what you are wearing, you are YOU regardless of what lifetime "skin" you put on. Core personality never changes.

40

Talking about past lives reminded me of people who are passed and still on the other side. From 2014, Gabriel has been helpful in keeping passed people away from me. Oh, not family and loved ones! They get through as they should, but they are the only ones. From the time I started seeing chakras in 2007, I also began connecting to dead people. Some were lovely experiences, if a bit startling, like seeing my friend's parents while I was in the shower, but some were just too invasive and problematic.

Like the time I was watching a news item about a man who had been stabbed to death; he came in and asked me to tell his family he was fine now. Did I do that? No. I was polite and sympathetic, but firm in my refusal. To try to find his family and then contact them to say things they might not believe... that was too much stress for me. Over the years, similar things have happened now and again. I hate it. It's bad enough handing a message like that over to people you know since it is always highly emotional dealing with grief mixed with love. There is no way I'm going to contact strangers with messages. Can you imagine how that would seem from their side? I can imagine how it would look having some unknown woman phone or email them saying, "Your loved one wants you to know..." No thank you!

I'm sure a lot of psychics will think I'm a wimp for not using my God-given gift, but this is my life and my abilities. I can choose to use this gift how I want to or not use it at all. That is my choice. This is where Gabriel has been invaluable. He acts as a go-between, a warm fuzzy force field around me that keeps strange dead people at bay. He can't keep lower energy beings away (that has been up to me), but he can keep the dead away since they communicate on a frequency that he interacts easily with.

I do still get the odd stray visitor, the feeling of someone around or a flash picture of someone's face. Then Gabriel will say who it is, like a butler answering the door. I'll let him know if it's the "Welcome," or "The lady of the house is not receiving dead people today" answer. But he also knows that people I love can stop by any time they like. They have the key to my heart.

That reminded me that I haven't yet told the experiences we have shared as a family. I'm not the only one in my family to see or interact with passed people and that has left me wondering if these abilities are genetic and hereditary. In the past, many people did believe such gifts were passed down in certain families. If that is the case, it is possible I was handed a double dose. Both sides of my family tree have people with psychic abilities. My mother, as I've already mentioned, was precognitive until medication and illness dulled it down. My father told me in recent years that his one uncle was a seer. There is another family member who also has strong abilities, but these only showed up after he passed away. This is my mother's father, William Marshall, my grandpa.

He was the first time I knew someone was about to die and I'm afraid I didn't handle it well. Grandpa had been fading for quite a while as a series of strokes, starting in 1981, eroded him slowly. He was an avid reader, interested in everything. He was the one who got me hooked on ancient history, explaining all about mummies and pyramids as he showed me the photos he took in Egypt during WWII. He also loved fishing and gardening, both things he could no longer do after his strokes. I wrote a poem about him, just before he died: Old Man in a Window.

Old man in a window,
Sunlight on his face,
Dark window shadows
Pulled about his shoulders.

Trapped in his winter
He watches the world.
A paperweight of sunshine
Just beyond his reach.

Time keeps its march
To the rhythm of sprinklers.
Hand against the glass
He waits for Sunset.

I was busy working on illustrations for a children's book when he took ill for the last time. It was a Friday in spring, November 1990. I went to the house to show him the illustrations I'd done so far. He wasn't able to talk, but he smiled at the pictures and then took my hand and kissed it and… I knew. This was goodbye forever. I ran. Oh, not literally. I kissed him and said goodnight, then I went home and flung myself into my work and tried not to think. The next morning, my gran found him collapsed beside his bed. He went into hospital and my mom went with him. She stayed by her father's bed the whole Saturday while I stayed home, drawing like a maniac. On Sunday, the hospital told us to all gather and that afternoon the whole family was there when he passed. It was a strangely peace-filled moment. Outside, the African springtime was a riot of birds singing in the bright sunshine while in that cool, shadowy room time held its breath... then stopped forever.

At the funeral, I kept feeling grandpa was there, feeling this sense of joy that all his children and grandchildren were gathered together. Years later, my one cousin confessed that he'd felt it as well at the same moment I did. It was when we left the funeral and put his flowers at the cenotaph. You see, grandpa timed his death perfectly. He died on the 11th of November, which not only was Remembrance Day, but also Rhodesia's day of independence. Since he had been an aircraft mechanic in WWII, it seemed fitting to take his flowers to the war memorial after the funeral. That was where I felt him the strongest. When I checked with other family, at least three of us felt he was there at the cenotaph when we placed his flowers beside the wreaths of poppies.

There was more to come. My parents and I volunteered to tackle the problem of grandpa's stuff. Grandpa's domain was the garage of my grandparents' house, which he had filled with the most unimaginable horde of things. He had cans of WWII camouflage paint on a back shelf as well as wallpaper sample books stacked up next to magazines from the 1970s. Jars of rusted screws of various lengths filled an entire book case against the side wall.

Grandpa's idea of value was extremely eclectic. He was good with his hands and had an innate artistic sense. Everything was potentially useful to him. He would come back from the garbage dump with old car parts, bits of wood and assorted treasure from which he would make doll's houses and forts and quite lovely ornaments. Unfortunately, he was also extremely impatient and often left a project half done to move on to a new and more exciting one. The garage was stocked full of his unfinished projects.

We spent the weekend sorting things into piles for recycle, throw out or keep. At one stage, my dad dragged a large wooden box out from under a pile of old fishing reels and magazines. It was locked. My dad looked everywhere for the key and kept looking for it as we peeled back the layers of junk. *Sorry grandpa, but a lot of it really was junk.* We didn't find the key. Oh wait, let's be honest here. We found two keyrings full of keys as well as two jars of rusty keys, but none of them were the right one for the lock on that wooden box.

Tired and frustrated, my dad looked up towards heaven and said loudly, "Come on, Bill! Where did you put the key?" and a key fell on my dad's upturned forehead. *PLONK.*

We think it must have been hidden up on a roof beam. I will never forget the look of shock on my dad's face when the key hit him. Dad got a ladder to look up there and couldn't find any explanation as to why that key fell as it did. Grandpa had had the last laugh. And the box? It held sharp craft knives and other dangerous tools, stored safely out of the reach of children.

My grandpa has since been a quiet but persistent presence. At least four family members have admitted to smelling his pipe tobacco at times and one person in the family even saw him. That wasn't me. This happened in September 1999 when my grandmother frightened my one cousin by saying grandpa had been standing at the bottom of her bed all night. Within 24 hours, my grandmother had died of a heart attack. I'm glad grandpa was there, waiting to take her home.

The next strange family story happened just before I was born. This is about the flat my parents lived in when they were first married. My mom was scared in the flat, everything from feeling creepy to moments of extreme irrational terror. The feeling, she says, was the worst in the bathroom, but it was in the kitchen that she almost saw things. Almost saw? She describes it as "catching movement out the corner of your eye" and says the moving shape was low and smallish, as if a dog had run past her in the kitchen. Unnerving, but it was the bad feeling in the bathroom she hated the most. It was so bad that she'd only bathe or brush her teeth with my dad in the room with her.

The situation came to a head when my mom offered to dog-sit a family pet while my gran was away on holiday. I asked my mom what dog that was. Oh wow. It was Teddy! The same dog that I would one day see as a ghost. I never knew that before. So before I was born, Teddy was in the flat with my mom. It seems strange to think I knew him before I was born. Poor Teddy. He was NOT a happy puppy during his time at my parents' flat. My mom says he constantly growled and refused to go down the passage. She had to carry him to get him from room to room. One particular day, he started to growl at a blank wall and then went mad barking at nothing.

It wasn't long after that incident that my mother spoke to the people renting the identical layout flat below and found out that they too felt creepy in their kitchen and bathroom. By the time I was born, my mother had had enough. She wanted out of that flat!

Thankfully, my mom's brother and his wife agreed to swap flats as my parents could not get out of the lease. My father also had odd experiences in that flat. He says he regularly saw a man in the bathroom, just a vague figure out the corner of his eye. When he'd turn around, no one was there. He also sometimes saw half a man, as in only feet and legs in man's clothing. Really weird. My dad always looks for a rational explanation first. He put all this down to his eyes playing tricks on him, but there was to be another time when he experienced something he could not easily explain.

This happened in 2006 in Scotland. I don't know what month, but from the memories I'd guess late spring or summer. We had all piled into the car one weekend to go land hunting. We were hoping to find a nice piece of land to buy to build a house on. Sandy had taken down directions to several plots for sale and we ended up a bit lost as most of them were rural. In this one area, instead of turning right, we accidentally turned left. At the time, we were all fairly pleased as the dirt road leading up the hill slowly brought a castle into view. Scotland has so many castles that you do eventually become immune to them, but back in 2006 we Africans were still in the awe and excitement "Look! A castle!" stage.

Sandy agreed to take us closer so that my dad could take photos of this castle. It was a big, chunky thing, all alone on the hill top. We followed the overgrown and bumpy dirt road up to where a farm house and barn stood on the edge of a field beside the castle. The farmhouse was clearly empty. All the windows were boarded shut with dry, faded bits of wood. We parked by the farm gates to walk the rest of the way. My mom opted to stay in the car while the rest of us scattered. Much to our disappointment, the castle had scaffolding around it, which made photos out of the question. There were big signs up saying to stay clear as it was unstable and in the process of being restored. Dad went to take a walk around the farmhouse. Sandy went back to the car and I ambled towards the old barn and farm buildings. I like old barns and wanted to take some photos.

The barn had huge, wooden doors. One was partially open or broken. I can't remember now. I just know that it wasn't a big enough opening for a person to walk through, but it was big enough to bend down and look into the barn. *Cool*. Maybe I could get some interior photos. I bent down close to the dark opening… and freaked. The feeling that something was in there watching me was so strong that if I was a cat, I'd have hissed and shot up a tree. The feeling was the way a good horror movie hopes you'll feel when someone shines a torch into the dark and yells something stupid like "Is anyone there?"

Clearly, my survival instincts are better than the average horror movie victim because I backed away fast and pretty much sprinted for the car. My dad was already back at the car and we got in without a word and drove away. Hours later when we were back home, my mom said that while sitting in the car at the farm she had begun to feel creepy.

That was when my dad told his story. He said he'd

gone around the house, hoping for a nice angle to take a few photos. He did take one photo of the house from a distance, which was when he realised one of the windows wasn't boarded shut at the back. He decided to go take a closer look, hoping the glass was clean enough to see inside. He said he almost got up to the window when he froze. My rational, sensible dad then said something I never thought I'd hear him say; he said he felt extreme fear and could not go any closer to the house. He said that the place felt evil. That was when I told my story about the barn and dad said he'd looked in and seen a dead or sick sheep lying inside. Something was very "off" about that farm.

The old farm house.

My mother is the best at sensing good or bad from

people and places. She's always right when she trusts her first instinctive reaction and doesn't let emotion or logic get in the way. Oh yes, these feelings I talk about are not emotional. Emotions actually muddy the waters. Intuition is something that lies between the heart and the mind. It is vastly superior to both. The heart can be misled, making us overlook warning signs in people we love or fall in love with.

Other emotions that make us prone to making mistakes are dislike and guilt. It's hard to see someone clearly if you let any strong emotion take over. The mind, on the other hand, can be misled by eloquent arguments to be sensible and reasonable. It's as if what we feel has no value because it cannot be weighed against logic when in actual fact logic is a faulty system. I could debate you into seeing my point of view using logic, but that would not automatically mean I was right and you were wrong. Anyone watching a court case where both lawyers speak for opposing sides knows that. This is why Gabriel keeps nagging me to "think from the heart." He doesn't mean FEEL from the heart. He's not talking about emotions.

"Thinking from the heart" is how he describes that thing we call intuition, gut feeling or inspiration. It's as clear as logic, but it needs no words and so cannot be swayed by persuasive rhetoric. Thinking from the heart is a connection from you to your Higher Self and God. It's pure knowing. If it had to be given a place on the human body, I'd say that it lies between the heart and throat chakras. Interestingly, that spot, just a hand's width below the base of the throat, is where Gabriel as

Tiernan pressed a nine-pointed star into my chest.

I've tried to find out more about that star beyond the fact it is used as a symbol for Gabriel. This star is the symbol of perfection and completion, a trinity of trinities. In Christianity, it symbolises the nine fruits of the Spirit. In Galatians 5:22-23:

> 22 But the fruit of the Spirit is love, joy, peace, forbearance, kindness, goodness, faithfulness, 23 gentleness and self-control. Against such things there is no law.

Thank you, Gabriel. I'm honoured to wear such a beautiful symbol. Goodness knows I need help with thinking from the heart! I rely too much on my mind and deductions. Unlike my mother, I rarely sense things off places. I sometimes get feelings off people, but that's when my heart tends to get in the way. The only time I'm perfectly clear with people is at a distance. I'm really good at sensing what people are like from their writing, which has been useful. I noticed this on the first forum I joined. I'd read someone's words and feel a distinct response of "I like you" or a sense of warning to be careful.

Being able to sense the true persona behind words has led me to being an ace moderator on two forums. I knew trolls (annoying internet trouble-makers and bullies) before they got beyond the opening greetings. I've twice warned a forum owner of danger before new members showed their true selves. One was a hacker and the other was mentally unstable. The latter case was on a forum for psychics. This was around the time I first started seeing chakras. I had an experience that confirmed my suspicions about this person.

I was in the kitchen one night, preparing dinner and thinking about the fact this forum person worried me. As I thought about this person, my new ability to scan chakras kicked in. For a few seconds, I saw chakra colours and then I was doubled over by intense, retching nausea. I pulled back fast, shocked at how awful the connection felt. A few months after that, this person showed their dark side, eventually leaving death threats to other members which led to a permanent ban from that forum.

I had another warning about the same person months before from my then very new spirit guide, Sol the elephant. My friend, James, had nagged me into trying to receive dictated messages from Sol. He told me the fairly useless information that my roast chicken smelled good before giving me a short list of one sentence opinions of some of the people I knew. These included telling me Sandy was "a good man", James was "complex" and that person whose chakras made me retch was more afraid of themselves than of anything else.

41

It had been such a struggle to write those few brief lines for my elephant spirit guide back in the early 2000s. How different my chatty Gabriel is now, but he is still the clown. From elephant to angel, he has kept that air of playful joy about him. He loves to make me laugh and he loves to mess with my more serious, control-freak nature.

Here's a good example of how we differ: I play a type of Mah Jong called ShisenSho. It's in the form of a large block of tiles. You can only remove pairs that are touching each other. I tend to play systematically, checking what tiles I've removed to calculate which ones should be left or removed next. Gabriel finds that boring and no fun. One particular day in 2014, he asked permission to have a go. I agreed and then he went mad, telling me to take off pieces with wild abandon from all sides.

I wrote to Emily at the time and told her:

He had no plan, no looking ahead, and he won! He got all the pieces off. He's like someone who plays chess by just moving the pieces in ways he thinks will be the most fun, no strategy, and he might not win. He doesn't care. The joy is the point. The fun. I struggle with that. I'm a little control freak clutching my mouse while my mind yells, "No, not that move!" as he happily messes up my perfect game strategy.

I so need him in my life. I'm like Wednesday Addams and he's the Wizard of Oz rolled up in Bugs Bunny.

One of the best jokes he has pulled on me was in August 2014. I was doing a jigsaw puzzle online. I have always loved jigsaws. I do prefer real ones, but I must admit I do enjoy the online version as well. The plus of the online ones is the fact that you have such a huge choice of pictures to choose from and you never lose any pieces. I have a "thing" about puzzles with pieces missing. I hate it. I do not keep jigsaws with missing pieces and I never lose any in real life. In fact, I still haven't forgiven my gran's poodle for eating one of my puzzle pieces when I was seven.

On this particular day in 2014, I decided to do an online jigsaw to relax. Gabriel was in a teasing mood because I was ignoring him. He's a dear, but some days I just need peace and quiet. I started the way I do with all jigsaws, by doing the edge pieces first. I completed the edge frame until only one top piece was left to add... but it wasn't visible anywhere. I figured it must be under the rest of the puzzle pieces and used a feature where you can have only edge pieces showing. I clicked on that and all the inner puzzle pieces vanished, but there was no missing edge piece revealed. That was very odd.

I used the mouse cursor to lift the frame pieces up, one by one. Perhaps the missing piece was underneath? Nope, still no missing edge piece. To add to my annoyance, Gabriel was chuckling in my head and I had the strongest feeling he was involved somehow.

I took a screen snip, thinking to use it to complain to the game site that this jigsaw had a glitch. Then I ran the mouse cursor over the edges of the screen as unused pieces glow if you go over them, in case it was somehow invisible. Still nothing.

I used the add-all-pieces feature, thinking maybe the program had accidentally mistaken that missing edge for a regular puzzle piece. I moved them all into tidy rows, but still no sign of that edge piece. I decided to do the puzzle, convinced I must have overlooked that piece somehow. Eventually, I finished the puzzle and there was still no sign of that missing piece, just this gaping hole in the top edge.

I took a screen snip to add to my complaint.

Gabriel burst out laughing. He told me to look again and there it was. The missing piece had appeared out of nowhere, next to the finished puzzle.

I took another screen snip to prove it to myself.

Gabriel still pulls pranks. In fact, the day I wrote this he was up to his tricks again. Sandy was teasing me about something. He was being cheeky and I was trying to think of a good come-back line, but not getting anywhere. My brain is faster with writing than speaking which Sandy was taking full advantage of. Sandy was laughing, smug that he was tying me in knots, when I saw a flash of Gabriel grinning at me.

Sandy paused to take a tablet (pain meds for an old back injury) then suddenly went "Fnah fnaaah" before putting his whole hand into his mouth.

The tablet was stuck on the roof of his mouth. He had quite a struggle to get it loose. Gabriel buffed his fingernails on his chest, looked at me and winked as he said, "No one messes with my girl."

Who says guardian angels don't take their job seriously? Ha!

Has he ever intervened in a more serious way? I suspect so. There was a night where Sandy and I should have crashed or at the very least damaged our vehicle, and yet we came out of it with nothing but a big fright. I do wonder if we were watched over that night. This was at a time when Sandy was doing courier work to fill in the gaps when building jobs were low. He was registered with a place that would phone him with job offers at any time. This could be quite fun and I sometimes went with him, especially if he was going somewhere new.

This particular delivery was to take an item from Edinburgh to a ferry depot on the west coast near the Mull of Kintyre, an area I'd never been to. It had to be there by dawn, so we ate dinner and then we were off driving down Scotland to reach Edinburgh around midnight. It was a surprisingly long drive from there to the west coast and we got lost. In fairness to us, what logic is there to having places named Tarbert and Tarbet on the same coastline? We stopped in one, thinking it was the other, sometime around 3:00am. It was pouring rain and we decided to have a cup of coffee from the flask I'd brought with us.

We were busy drinking our coffee when a police car cruised past, turned, went past slower and then turned and stopped. A policeman came over to ask us what was wrong. After a brief chat, he pointed out, quite amused, that we had stopped outside the local bank. Yeah… an unmarked white van parked up by the bank at 3:00 am. No wonder he was suspicious!

We do owe that policeman, because after he drove

off, we noticed that our tracking device said we still had over 60 miles to go. That was when I pulled out the real map and realised we were in the wrong Tarbert or Tarbet. We had less than two hours, in bad weather on unknown roads, to reach the ferry depot. Sandy had to drive below the speed limit as the road was bad, winding along the coast in pitch dark countryside with rain belting down.

On one corner, the van slid out of control and I braced myself for the worst. We'd had a slide like that once before on black ice in winter. That time, without any awareness of doing it, I'd punched the dashboard air filter out for a hand grip. We came away from the black ice skid with a ripped up van front and me with a badly bruised hand.

Now, in the pouring rain, I held on as we zoomed in what felt like slow motion towards the railing on my side of the road. At the speed we were going, I figured we'd hit it and do serious damage to the van. We might even possibly break through the railing, going on into whatever lay beyond in the inky darkness.

As we reached the railing, we spun to face forward and slid along the edge, just skimming the grasses in front of the railing. I remember how the grasses made this soft, hissing sound. We hit a lump of grass or soil and spun back into the road. Now we were heading towards the other side of the road, which was a high cliff face. If we hit that there would be no doubt of damage, but instead we stopped dead in the middle of the road. Just… stopped. Sandy got out with a torch and checked the vehicle. There wasn't a mark on it, not even scratches. We even managed to make it to the ferry on time.

The sun was beginning to rise as we made our way home and we could see the incredibly beautiful scenery of that area. The forests spill trees all the way down to the edge of lochs and sea. I watched the sunrise turn the water and sky soft pink and gold. The road weaves along that edge, rising up along cliffs in some areas. It was stunning, but also sobering. If we had gone through that barrier, we would have faced a very long drop down to the water and rocks below.

That led me to wondering how often "they" smooth the way for us all, as well as why there are times when things go badly wrong and no one seems to be there. Why do some people have miracles and others end up with tragedies? I know that Gabriel has said that things can go wrong, people can die before their time, but beyond that... I have no answers. I also know that angels grieve when we suffer as well as rejoice when we triumph. Perhaps it is only possible to understand it all when we are able to look back from a far distance and see the bigger picture.

I suspect that bigger picture is breath-taking and beautiful. I know the things Gabriel has shown me have made me realise how huge and complex it all is. You would think that would make me feel insignificant, but it's the exact opposite. As Earth Mother pointed out, all creation lies within the Creator and so all is holy and equally important. How can anyone feel insignificant knowing they are an equally important part of something so vast?

There was one particular time when Gabriel managed to show me the bigger picture in a most spectacular way. This was in June 2014. Sandy asked Gabriel questions about the universe, stars, space and dimensions. This time, instead of giving me words, Gabriel simply shoved images and information directly into my mind. These are easier for me to absorb, but often harder to share and explain. Here's what I wrote afterwards for Sandy:

<u>Dimensions, Time and Spirals. June 2014</u>

Gabriel says that the dimensional levels are not stacked one above the other. They are not like rungs on a ladder or levels of progression, but more like a spiral. He's said this before, but we got into it a lot deeper this time. He showed me the spiral as being 3 dimensional, not flat. It's a cone as well as a spiral. He's mentioned before that because it's a spiral the dimensions touch each other in an order that isn't strictly linear. So it's not like if you are on the 4th you cannot be in touch with the 7th.

Look at a spiral and imagine each circle is a dimension flowing into the next as well as touching others. Like a Mandelbrot spiral. The reason he used this for his cone was because he was trying to explain that even the spiral is more subtle and complex than merely a spiral. He says, just like Source/God, the

Universe and all in it, this spiral has been gently expanding and growing into a cone for all time and beyond. Since it is 3D, it's not only expanding OUT but also UP. "Up" or "down" are actually not relevant, but to keep this semi sane we'll go with an upward spiral cone, okay? Up works when you're counting up in number levels.

Gabriel said the number system for dimensions is misleading. They are different tones of vibrating energy. He says they relate closer to colours or sounds than to numbers, but humans do love nice tidy labels! So... the spiral touches all the way up and out. Hence why beings that are trans-dimensional, such as the Elohim/angels and ascended masters, can move between with some ease. They're not plodding up and down a numbered ladder.

And it gets MORE complex. Along the spiral there are smaller spirals, like eddies in a stream. Just like the Mandelbrot above. And each of those mini spirals is also moving ever out and up. They seem to be more erratic than the main spiral. The little ones round the edge can shoot up fast. "Fast" may still mean millennia.

Those little edge spirals create portals when they shoot up through layers above them. I actually got that before Gabriel said it. When

I asked if they were portals he danced about the room yelling, "YES!" lol Nothing like finally making your teacher happy.

Gabriel had other things to share with Sandy at that time. He said the layers were "coming down" and he showed me our planet as if Earth was made up of layers, like an onion. He kept saying the layers were coming together and eventually there would be only one. I thought he meant the planet's atmosphere, but I've come to realise he meant dimensions. I've since started watching video talks about dimensions and physics. I listen and feel excited, like my heart gets it instinctively, but my brain just whimpers and hides in a corner.

Gabriel added that "things have moved faster in the last two decades than they have in the last two centuries". What strikes me when I watch the news or go onto internet media sites is that humans are awakening to this at a growing rate. From my own experiences, awakening has been a lot like a shamanic death experience or a Rite of Passage. Different cultures have different names for that concept, the main similarity being that the only way you ever step into a new reality is by stripping all of your old reality away. That can be both frightening and painful.

It feels as if our very planet is going through a shamanic death. We are seeing things literally stripped and ripped apart, our belief systems, our political leaders, money, ecology and nature, human rights… the list is endless and the extremes just keep on building higher. We are seeing something huge happening and it is not over yet.

Another friend described it as a "liminal space", a threshold of not knowing. I think it is also a threshold of letting go of old presumptions and misconceptions in order to allow room for new growth. I don't think we need to fear these changes, even though the speed of change is making this seem violently out of control. Gabriel gave me a phrase for that. He said "In a flux" which fits both our planet and all the changes he's morphed through in the last few years.

42

Understanding the bigger picture takes time. It is only when we look back that we see how far we have come, how high we have climbed. A prime example of that is the way I panicked constantly when Sol originally morphed from an elephant to Tiernan the man to Gabriel the angel. Although on the surface it seemed as if his constant changing was the source of my panic, the truth is that it was my own self-doubt that caused most of my anxiety. I doubted my abilities which led to me doubting my sanity. That brought on instant panic, which in turn led to me checking and rechecking every tiny detail until I was absolutely certain it had happened and was real or true. That was exhausting.

As I've mentioned, I'm a worry-wart with anxiety problems. That started in my early twenties when life threw a bucket load of things at me at once, tipping average stress into anxiety attacks. Africa with its wars, terrorism and the fear of crime violence as a constant daily reality is not an easy place to live in without gathering some anxiety issues.

I'm proud to say that I stopped my panic attacks myself by my late twenties, but I am still prone to general anxiety disorder. That sums up as being constantly alert and on the edge, which is very draining and actually slows me down and makes me forgetful. Ironic that the fact my body strives to stay ready for any emergency leaves me so drained. I'm unable to cope with everyday things on a bad day. Gabriel has tried all sorts of things to help me overcome my anxiety, from being soothing to being a tease and making me laugh. Anything to lighten up the situation. He also worked on my everyday fear issues by being an utter imp and a tease.

One night in 2014, I was thinking of going to put out the trash after dinner, but it was already dark outside. I looked out the back door at the big, black Scottish countryside at night and froze in fear. Gabriel spoke in my mind, pointing out that the vast darkness was a field of wheat in a country with no large predatory animals. What was I afraid of? I knew he was right, but I could not move. The bin was at the far end of the house, around the corner beside the garage and next to a row of large, wind-twisted trees.

"There's nothing out there," Gabriel repeated. "What's going to attack you, a mad squirrel? A sheep?"

"What about people?" I pointed out. *There could be a mad prowler stalking....* I stopped. Okay, even I could see how unlikely that was.

"I'm with you," Gabriel added, sounding amused. "If you can't trust an angel to look after you, then...?"

He was right. *I had an angel watching over me and I was scared to take out the garbage.* It was a bit ridiculous. I grabbed the bin bag tightly and firmly stepped out into the darkness. It was a mild night with a gentle breeze and clear, starry skies. I began to enjoy myself. I do love stars. They make me feel safe. I reached the end, turned the corner and felt for the bin lid as it was very dark back there. Trying not to think about the trees behind me, I dropped the bag into the bin and....

Gabriel said, "Go back to the house." His voice sounded urgent.

WHAT was out there? I could not bring myself to turn and look. Once again, I froze.

"Go," said Gabriel. "Go now!"

With my heart bouncing in my chest, I stumbled around the corner and then ran for the safety of the light shining from the open kitchen door. It felt as long as a marathon from the back of the house to that door. It felt like that scene in Chariots of Fire where the athletes run in slow motion along the beach, except this was a short, chubby woman moving in slow motion along a concrete path as the theme from Jaws played in her head.

As I reached the back steps, Gabriel spoke again. "Gotcha," he said, laughing.

Yes, even good angels can be evil at times. But I did laugh... after I finished telling him how much I wanted to slap him for that practical joke! That's the worst prank he's ever pulled on me and only because he knew I could cope. He may be my guardian, but he won't protect me from my own foolishness. That is up to me. Here's how he explained that in his own words in 2013. I shared it by email with my friends:

Sent: Sunday, Oct 20, 2013 1:22 PM
Subject: About Fear

Gabriel wanted to add some words/ideas on my fear and melt down issue. I asked if I could write it out, so I can read it again when I need to. He agreed. Here's the result.

Write as you see the words in your mind and try not to think about them. It will help to allow me access to your language skills and more freedom to express myself openly without your mind constantly trying to edit me to your way of being.

Where to start? You have been living in turmoil for so long you no longer sense where the reality of this begins or ends for you. Fear holds you prisoner in this reality and it is not your friend. You are a gentle spirit that never has coped well with darkness in humanity. It disturbs you more than most. It bewilders you. You cannot comprehend it and it layers your fear upon fear through many lifetimes. you have struggled through more than one lifetime with this dilemma.

The juxtaposition of good and evil, light and dark, that you see in this world hurts your heart and soul at a very deep level. Since we are connected I feel it at well and I know how much of your primal fear is based upon this darker mistrust of the basic animal that is humanity. You cannot align yourself into balance while this war goes on within you. You perceive the dark in others as if it were an evil presence and it, in return, sees your light and responds accordingly.

Through many lifetimes you have fought against the dark and won as well as lost. You will know more about that in time, but for now we will focus on the present. This life and this reality, agreed? Good. Now back to your panic and fear and how it connects to these 'melt downs' as you call them. Your personal problem and mine, since I am witness to every melt down in vivid detail, including those you do not share with others. All 15 so far and counting!

They will begin to dissipate. You cannot expect them to cease overnight, but in time you will realise that they have served a purpose and once you realise that they will leave of their own accord. Bless them for the gifts they bring you and show them the respect they deserve. Honour them for the truths they uncover within you, even the dark and painful ones.

(he stopped to give me a hug and a kiss on the head)

When you analyse these events you over compensate by adding details that are not necessary. You will find that in time this improves. You will find that with constant and more compassionate self awareness they dissipate and fade. You are far too hard on yourself and always have been. Perfectionist. Analyst. How boring your mind can be at times to sit through.

(he yawned)

You constantly chew over facts that you already know the answers to within your heart. Stop trusting your mind so much. Learn from your heart and *lean* to your heart. I agree that in times of panic this has not always been an easy choice. When the memory or event causes deep emotional pain choosing to go within the heart for Source can be painful, even frightening. You are worthy. Leave it. You are worthy of being loved. You are worthy of being healed. You will rise above this in time and you do not need my help to do so. Although I will always stand waiting beside you when you fall, you have the power to pick yourself up every time. We both know that.

Gabriel also used another seemingly negative tactic to help me deal with my anxiety. When I constantly asked for confirmations and proof, he'd randomly tell me something that did not fit or come true. These would freak me out and trigger the whole spiral of *am I mad? What went wrong?* panic.

I eventually asked straight out, "WHY do you do that? I'm trundling along, building up my fragile faith and then you whammy me with a blatant lie or false clue, red herring thing. Why?"

Gabriel sat down close to me and stared into my eyes. He said, "To make you trust your own intelligence and intuition. We don't want slaves or sheep."

He doesn't do that any more, but if I get lazy and ask him for help on things I basically know, he will shove the dumbest, weirdest advice at me. Something so radical it shakes me awake. Then he just grins or laughs and I get it. I'm not supposed to use him as a crutch. I cannot turn to him for every decision I make. I'm not a slave and I'm not a sheep. *Ha, he just bowed in my mind.*

This is a good place to say to anyone psychic:

If any being or entity demands total obedience from you – kick it out your mind and your life! Real angels and spirit guides only demand that we think for ourselves.

There was another way that Gabriel demanded that I think for myself. This one is deeply personal and I actually considered leaving it out, but I think that would be wrong. I need to tell this story as well. In August 2013, he gave me a Calla lily as a birthday gift. I did research and found out that this flower symbolises the divine feminine and female beauty. At the time, I took it as a sweet birthday gift, but as the months rolled on I discovered it was a first step in a much bigger plan.

You see, I never really liked my physical self much. Sadly, I'm not alone in this. Very few women accept or like their physical selves. Even with great parents who adored me, the world out there still managed to make me feel not good enough. I was a skinny, dark-haired little girl in an era where movie heroines and Barbie dolls were all tall, curvy blondes. The only brunettes were evil stepmothers and other "bad girl" types. In my teen years I did put on weight, but now it was the 1980s era of the skinny tall blondes and I was the short, curvy girl with dark brown hair.

I was first teased for being too skinny, then teased for being too curvy. Looking back, I can see that I was a normal body shape and not at all overweight, but I didn't see me at all. In fact, I never saw myself properly in my 20s or 30s, either. I always felt shy, always felt like I should hide my body as much as possible. Then an angel came along and tore through my shyness like a tornado. Every time I went past a mirror or sat to do my make-up, he'd be there telling me to look at myself as say how beautiful I was.

"No I'm not," I'd grumble, seeing all my imperfections; grey hairs, saggy bits, wrinkly bits, but he kept persisting. He would go on and ON until I gave in, stared at myself and said, "I am beautiful." *Yeah, right.*

This went on for months. Gabriel would even demand that I stand in front of full length mirrors and stare at myself while he went into these long lectures on stupid stereotypes vs real beauty. He'd normally end with the usual demand of making me say out loud to my reflection that I was amazing and beautiful. Sometimes I'd feel stupid or get the giggles. Sometimes I'd feel sad. Often I just felt annoyed. Why wouldn't he SHUT UP and go away?

Then one random afternoon in 2015, I was washing my hands and I looked up at my face in a mirror and thought, "Wow, she's pretty!" As I stepped away from the mirror and could see more of myself I thought, "I'm really sexy, too." I walked out the bathroom smiling.

To put this into perspective, I am now over fifty with a body that has not had a good health track record. On top of that, in the last 6 years I have put on weight. I finally am what I feared for no reason all throughout my youth – I am fat. Yep. Fat. And I feel better about myself, sexier and prettier, than I did when I was twenty. I look in the mirror and I see a REAL woman with a real body. Not an insanely impossible stereotype. I only wish I'd met Gabriel sooner and that every young girl had an angel who would sit them down in front of a mirror every morning and make them realise how beautiful they are just as themselves.

43

How beautiful we are and what a miracle. It's easy to forget that fact. It's too easy to buy into the consumer-driven view that we are lacking because lack sells. Look around you at adverts everywhere and you'll soon see that most of them are based on fear; fear of not being young enough, thin enough or rich enough. Fear that unless you have the right hair colour, make-up, clothes, car or home address you will not be acceptable. All complete rubbish, but when faced with a constant drip-drip deluge of "you are lacking" messages it is easy to begin to drown.

Unfortunately, our modern world relies too much on money. The next step is often to urge you to buy some medication or treatment to deal with your unhappy sense of lack. It's an ongoing little treadmill of never allowing anyone to feel better since being happy would mean you no longer needed "stuff" to fill the emptiness. The world of commerce thrives because of our need for stuff. This is where tribal societies are way ahead of us since they understand that all the stuff in the world cannot fix a wounded spirit. Almost all shamanic systems work on the idea that mind, body and soul are of equal importance when it comes to good health. In other words, if any part of your life is unbalanced it pulls the rest out of balance as well.

As I've said before, New Age shamanism is not quite the same as the traditional and tribal variations. We can begin to romanticise the old ways and forget that they have their flaws as well. Tribal shamans are as capable of dealing in curses as they are in healing. I've experienced enough of African shamanic beliefs to know that it has a dark side as well as the ability to be surprisingly effective.

In my own home area of the Eastern Cape, we had a spate of rural children being abducted and murdered for "muti" body parts used by witchdoctors. A family friend once found a lost handbag in his shop. When he opened it to check for contact details, he found a dried, human finger wrapped in a cloth. When the owner claimed the bag, she said the finger was useful for stirring tea to improve fertility. Not all primitive beliefs are better than modern!

Having said that, I still think our modern world has lost a lot of the good common-sense of the older ways. What I would love to see, and am seeing more of on the internet, is a balance between the old and the new. I do have a lot of respect for New Age/neo-shamanism as it is mostly made up of the best and most positive ideas gleaned from various cultures all over the world.

The two shamanic concepts I find the most interesting are soul retrieval and extraction. I will add recommended reading at the end of this book. For now, I'll keep it short and simple. Soul retrieval is the idea that a trauma (death, loss of a loved one, war, rape, violence, disease) causes parts of our soul to leave us, creating an emptiness we are never able to fill. A shaman would see a person's soul as being rather like a 3D jigsaw puzzle made up of many pieces. Each time we are badly hurt or shocked, we leave a piece of ourselves attached to that place, person or event. For most of us, the lost pieces are few and so we manage to still lead a good life. For others who have gone through many painful events, the hole inside them can become so great that the emptiness overwhelms them.

From a shamanic viewpoint, this would not only lead to depression, but also to physical illnesses. Interestingly, modern psychiatry tends to agree with this idea in its own way. Trauma that damages the heart will eventually harm the mind and body if left untreated. The way in which psychiatrists and shamans deal with this is reasonably similar as well. Both need the person to open up and be prepared to deal with that past issue. The only big difference is that a shaman would use journeying or meditative states to look for that lost soul piece in order to bring it back home.

Extraction, on the other hand, is a shamanic concept that sounds more like superstitious rubbish, but I think it holds merit as well. Extraction is where a shaman removes an evil spirit or parasite entity feeding off the person's energy. I always thought this idea was a load of garbage until I started chakra readings and saw that dark thing in my late aunt's root chakra. The idea of some "thing" feeding off us can sound frightening, but I would say that "feeders" are mostly on a par with creatures such as mosquitoes or fleas. Does chakra healing deal with its own form of extraction? I'd say yes, it does.

The simplified explanation of chakras is that they are an Eastern/Asian idea that says there are energy centres in the human body which keep energy flowing through us in a constant cycle. These roughly run from the base of the spine to the top of the head. Each chakra is believed to control certain basic bodily organs and functions as well as be responsible for psychological issues related to that area. The finer details of that vary between different cultures and philosophies. These seven chakras radiate colours similar to the bands of a rainbow, starting with the lowest frequency of red at the base of the spine to violet or white light at the crown of the head.

The best description of chakras I've come across was a children's video that used a river to depict the flow of energy with little pools to represent each chakra, like beads along a string. When the chakras are healthy, the energy flows like water, swirling around each pool before continuing on its way. Chakras can become blocked or drained, which can cause physical or psychological problems.

Most psychics see chakras as wheels or balls of

spinning energy, but I tend to see them as little creatures or spheres with symbolic things inside them like dioramas. A blocked chakra will be darker in colour or dull and one drained of energy will be pale. To use one of my own experiences as an example: when my dad was in hospital, I saw his chakras as seven bumblebees. When I checked them they were all pale and looked tired and some had patches of gooey, black stuff stuck on them. I took that to mean they were all drained of energy, but the ones with dark, tarry patches had extra problems. I tried to draw one for my dad, so he could see them for himself.

As I've grown more experienced with this, what I see has become more complex. I will not only see the state of each chakra, but I often also have other information in the form of symbols or even passed loved ones arriving with messages to add. This is one time I do allow dead people through. I'll never forget the first time that happened because it proved to me that what I was seeing was real and not my imagination. It also showed me that all the proof in the world is not enough to shake some people's belief systems.

In this case, the belief system was atheist sceptic. I was asked by a friend to do a reading for a male member of her family. She was trying to get this family member to see a different point of view. I must admit, I was very nervous doing his chakra reading since I knew he thought it was all complete rubbish. He only agreed to it because he was expecting me to fail.

The chakra reading itself was fairly average. He had a few minor health issues which could have been ticked off as typical things for a man of his age and lifestyle. Things took a sudden twist about half way through the reading when a man came into the room and stood waving at me. He was elderly, seemed very nice and friendly, and he was dressed in a most distinctive style. The clothing meant nothing to me beyond the fact it looked old-fashioned and I'd guess European, which didn't make sense on the surface as the man I was doing the reading for was British. Back then I wasn't picking up words much, but I did clearly sense that this man wanted to send his love. I wrote it all down and sent off the email reading.

The person I'd done the reading for replied to thank me for my effort and explained who the old man was. It was a great-uncle on the side of his family from

Europe, which I didn't know. Apparently, they used to visit him on holidays and the way he was dressed was actually a traditional dress for that region. I was stunned. I had seen a real, unknown dead person in a chakra reading! For me, it was a great feeling of confirmation. And the man I did the reading for? Did this change his opinions? Absolutely not. He never spoke of it again and last I heard from my friend, he still doesn't believe in an afterlife and is as completely against anything esoteric as he was before.

I'd love to know what logic he used to explain to himself how I managed to see his dead great-uncle. It was a good lesson for me, though. It made me realise that there is no point in my trying to justify myself or explain what I do to anyone who refuses to believe in it. It's also proof that disbelief can itself become a dogma when taken far enough.

I don't consider myself a healer as such. I only look and report what I see, like a radiographer passing along an X-ray. Now and then, I have picked up on an undiagnosed health problem that the person has then been able to have checked and dealt with, which is wonderful. It feels good to make a positive difference.

A lot of the time, the health things I see are everyday issues and nothing to worry about. I have found that just the act of looking has an impact, causing changes that can be quite dramatic. It is a humbling experience and an honour to be able to get that close to another human being, but it is also very draining for me. I have scanned a person and found old, buried traumas such as abuse. There is no way you can report back things like that without it having an effect on the person you are viewing.

It can be intense, which is why I am very cautious about who I agree to view. I also cannot do more than one a day since the only way I can view another person's chakras is by connecting to them. This means I often feel physical health symptoms as I scan each chakra as well as feeling buried or blocked emotions.

While doing chakra readings, I have felt dizziness, nausea, tingling and pain in various parts of my body as well as bouts of uncontrollable tears as old grief surfaces. It can be a beautiful experience as well. The miraculous wonder of when what I see and report actually helps someone makes it all worth the effort. If I work as a healer, it is as someone who helps others heal themselves by giving them more information or a better understanding. I do sometimes remove small blockages, but I try not to meddle too much. I'm not a doctor or a psychiatrist.

I have had equally interesting results working with animals. Animals seem far more willing to be viewed, but that might be simply because the animals I have been asked to view (a few dogs and one horse) were all ill and needing help. I have heard some animal psychics say that cats are difficult to work with and I have yet to find out if that is true for me or not.

The biggest difference between doing chakras for animals and humans is the lack of symbolic imagery with animal readings. Whereas human minds love throwing personal symbolism at me, animals keep it plain and simple.

I see animal chakras as floating spheres or bubbles. Their placing is:

1st (red) chakra: upper body at base of tail where it joins the body.
2nd (orange) chakra: under body, lower belly area.
3rd (yellow) chakra: under body, roughly where rib cage ends.
4th (green) chakra: under body at chest/heart level.
5th (blue) chakra: shoulder blades area of spine.
6th (indigo) chakra: behind the ears, roughly where the skull joins the neck.
7th (violet) chakra: between the eyes.

The horse I viewed had an issue with fresh, new grass giving him an unhappy tummy and an old leg injury causing him discomfort. Please forgive my lack of proper horsey terminology; I have no experience with horses. I've ridden a donkey once, which hardly counts as equine expertise! The owner of the horse admitted that it had injured its leg when young by trying to jump a wire fence and becoming entangled.

The horse was very to-the-point and showed me exactly the portions of his body that bothered him. He was also excellent and showing me his emotions. I had a punch of terror hit me when he briefly remembered an incident relating to a fire and I felt sadness when he remembered another horse that used to be his friend, but had since been sold.

The dogs I have done readings for were harder to view for a very amusing reason. Dogs want to please, which means that all the dogs I have viewed have sometimes eagerly answered YES to any question I asked because they wanted to make me happy. The worst was a darling little Bichon who also kept showing me himself doing cute tricks to make me laugh. He was a little charmer and very smart. When he did finally realise what I was after, he projected an image of his vet into my mind. I was able to describe the vet to his owner, who was impressed and amused by her little dog's intelligence.

I was then able to pin-point a few underlying health issues that she brought up with her vet. That led to some blood tests and an X-ray which eventually brought Master Bichon some well-needed relief from his ongoing pain. His owner was humbled by how happy her little boy was in spite of having problems that must have been giving him chronic and constant pain. We can learn a lot from animals. None of the pets I have viewed have shown self-pity or bitterness about their health problems. They simply enjoy what they have and what they can do without wallowing in regret or dissatisfaction.

44

Since 2014, my experiences have slowed down a lot. Of course, Gabriel never allows me to completely forget he's around. He still pops into my head with jokes, suggestions and the odd demand. I hear him fine as long as I shut up and listen, but the vivid times of 2013 when I heard his voice with an accent and depth as well as saw him constantly on the edge of my vision... that has never returned. As much as I miss those vivid times, it does make daily life easier. It's similar with Aggie and Dora. At this stage, it's more like living with family than having new guests in the house. I kind of forget they're there.

When I look back at all of this, every amazing adventure, I sometimes ask myself, "Why me?"

Each time I do that I hear Earth Mother's gentle response, "Why not?"

Humility is good, but self-doubt and fearing the

opinions of others is not. Everyone has the right to be their true selves, just as God/Source planned them to be. I remember Gabriel saying that while his famous name might make him a big deal on Earth, amongst his own kind he's just another "bog-standard" everyday Elohim. I'm just an everyday human being. My talent may seem strange, but it is no different to having a flair for music or sport.

Contrary to what some people think, having psychic abilities doesn't instantly mean a person is spiritually better than the rest. I have met the esoterically egotistic; psychics who are petty, spiteful, bigoted or downright nasty. I've met psychics who are atheists. So no, these abilities are not related to how spiritual you are any more than any other human talent. Great music composers and poets can create works that seem heavenly while still living personal lives that are downright mucky.

I don't believe psychic abilities are rare gifts. I think they are primal senses we shrugged aside as the ancient man-ape stood upright, grasped tools and began forming languages. I think there are physical and genetic reasons why some people are more psychic than most, but I also think upbringing plays a part. I know several psychics who still hide what they are from fear of offending their families or going against the teachings of their religions.

I was lucky. I had the perfect childhood to allow whatever I was to grow. With my parents being casually religious and interested in many things, I grew up free to explore and express myself without fear. As a shy, sickly kid, I had a lot of time to think, read, look out windows and watch the world from a distance. When I was first online in 2001, another Native American man I met asked permission to scan my energy. He sent back an email saying he was amazed that I was still so open and connected to Source. He said that such a connection was usually only found in babies and very young children. As we age, everyday life begins to close the connection down. I think my early life in Africa somehow allowed that connection to remain open.

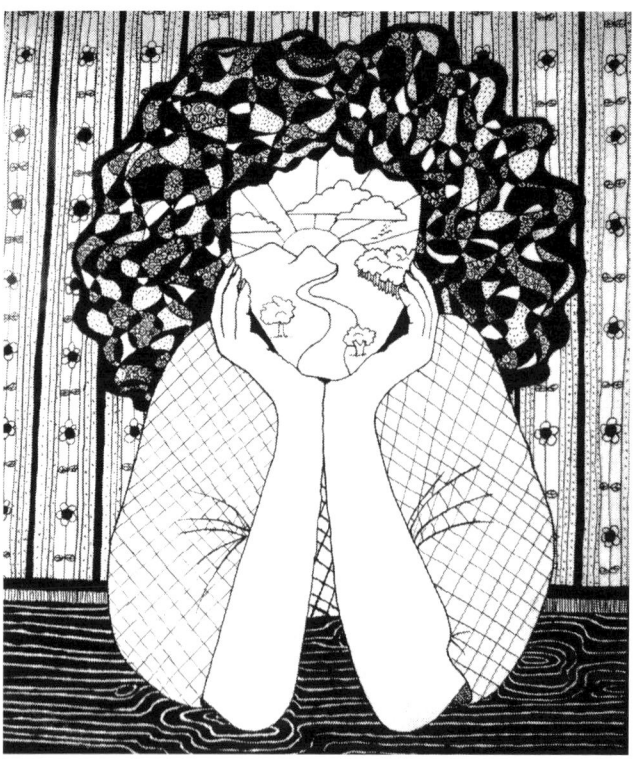

Do I ever wish I wasn't like this? No. As messy as it can be, it's who and what I am and I'd be utterly lost without that. I've tried to think of some way to explain... let's imagine a world where most people have no eyes, but a few people are born able to see. To most of that planet, anyone saying they saw things would sound insane. Perhaps they might even classify them as evil demons or frauds? Who knows! If we took one of those seeing people and asked him if he wished he was the same as everyone else, I'm guessing he'd think about everything he could see.

He'd contemplate the loneliness he sometimes felt of not ever being able to share his visual reality with those around him. He'd probably then think about the pros and cons: seeing would keep him safe from many things, but it would also mean that he alone would have seen what disease and death looks like, the expression in an injured animal's eyes or a scared child's face. But for every sad or horrific thing he had seen, there would be the rest: sunsets, rainbows, water reflections, clouds, baby smiles... an endless list of beautiful wonders. If you could weigh up all that seeing means, who would want to be blind? I understand how lucky I am to see too much and I finally accept what I am.

What I am.... What am I? The hints and nudges were always there, I simply was unready or felt unworthy, to reach out and accept them. In December 2016, a friend sent me an article about shamanism in Eurasia. It mentioned a word I'd never noticed before, the name for female shamans: shamanka. Almost two decades ago in 2001, a man's voice shouted a word at me, "Hamunkah." I now think that it was a wake up call.

He said it with a soft guttural *ch* sound. *ch*a-mun-kah... shamanka? I think I am most probably a shamanka, but I'm not about to dash off to study any particular culture's shamanic ways. I tried that for 15 years and always felt awkward dabbling in other peoples' belief systems. I think I need to forge my own path, something tailor-made to fit me. I love a lot about shamanism. I love the connections to Nature, animals and spirits, but....

All my life there have always been those "but" thoughts in my head. I love Jesus, but churches and their man-made sets of laws? Nope. I love shamanism, but when I delve deeper into tribal cultural beliefs I know none of them fit me quite right. I've even been tagged a trouble-maker on one shaman forum for asking too many "but" questions.

It was on that forum that someone made a comment that was far more prophetic and complimentary than she intended it to be. She called me "a contrary crow" and how right she was. Crow, rabbit, coyote and fox... all contrary tricksters. Heyokas and sacred clowns are the ones who poke holes in over-inflated theories and laugh at out-dated beliefs.

I know an elephant sacred clown, an angelic Heyoka. Perhaps we've rubbed off on each other over lifetimes? I think I'm something between trickster and shaman; a psychic who can't stop seeing the absurdity of all she is. Maybe that is why the name a medicine man once gave me related to being a bridge. I always seem to end up standing between beliefs, theories and even religions. I end up being the bridge or the negotiator, the person between opposing viewpoints or even alternate realities. I sympathise with both sides, but never agree completely with either. I'll never be converted just as I never want to be a converter.

For a long time, the fact I never fitted anywhere and was always stuck between made me feel like a failure. Now, I'm finally beginning to realise that this is my strength. The trickster has a flexibility the shaman does not. Perhaps that explains a little more about Gabriel as well. He's not just a trickster, he's also a bridge. A messenger.

I think the greatest strength of the Elohim/Angels is the fact that they stand between realms and dimensions. In doing so, they find joy in all the wild and crazy chaos of Life. Not a silly joy or a flippant disrespect of tragedy, but more an immense understanding of the love and wonder that keeps forever expanding out from the Creator's heart and core. Gabriel has constantly told me to think from the heart and maybe I'm finally beginning to understand that as well. In 2013, Earth Mother told me:

"The brain is the tool, but the heart is the connection."

Earlier this year in January 2017, Gabriel came to me and held out his hands like he was giving me a gift. When he opened them, I saw that he was holding a gold heart. He told me it was his own heart he was giving to me and that there would be a real gift to confirm it. At the time, we needed to travel to a place called Buckie to pay our fuel bill. It's about twenty-five miles away and a nice drive on a good day, but this January we were having winter storms and gales. So when the winds suddenly eased off a day after Gabriel's heart gift, Sandy and I dashed to pay the bills and get essential groceries.

It was about 2:00pm when we started back for home and Sandy suggested we stop for lunch. We stopped at a place we used to visit, but haven't been to in a few years. It's a garden centre with a gift shop and restaurant. We went in and found the place a mess as they were busy taking down all their Christmas decorations. On the way to the restaurant, I noticed this revolving display stand up ahead. It was a fairly ordinary stand of the type used to sell everything from paperback books to hair clips, about five feet high. As I looked at it, I felt pulled. I was curious. Why did this rather ordinary display stand make me feel such a strong need to go over?

I could see that the top sign had those words all women love on it: HALF PRICE SALE. I left Sandy by the menu board and went to take a closer look. I could make out that whatever was on the stand seemed to all be the same gold colour, but it was only as I got nearer that I could see a smaller sign saying "Name Angels" and I realised that the little things hanging from it were angel ornaments. I thought *Oh cute! Is there a Michelle angel?*

Each little angel was holding a gold star, but if there

was writing on them it was far too small for me to read without my glasses. I bent closer, squinting at a random angel as I tried to see where in the alphabet I was looking.

That random, first ornament I peered at had a name printed on the star....

Gabriel.

I swear I heard Gabriel chuckling as I took that ornament and bought this namesake as a half-price bargain. That little angel is now on my computer desk as a constant reminder that I am watched over and loved by a cheeky elephant-angel with a heart of gold.

I just saw Gabriel pull out a handkerchief, dab his eyes, then blow his nose like an elephant trumpeting. He never changes! I know that wherever life takes me, there will always be an angel at my side, most probably plotting some silly joke to make me laugh.

AND FINALLY

Gabriel asked me to take down something he wants to add.

> I have waited in patience for this dear-hearted woman to finish this book. Now it is my turn and I have something to say.
>
> To all of you out there, everywhere in the world, wherever you may find yourselves at the moment of reading this. Go take a look in the mirror right now and repeat after me:
>
> "I am wonderful. I am a miracle from God. I am love made into human form. I have a right to be here. I have no obligation to live any way I did not ask for. I am loved and always will be loved. I am never alone; the angels watch over me. I am Love and I am Light."

Well, I wasn't expecting that, but I like it a lot. A fitting way to end this book, with unspoken words only I can hear from my dear elephant angel.

And he managed to squeeze in one last joke as well. I finished this book on the 12th of August 2017, only to discover later that it was World Elephant Day.

ACKNOWLEDGEMENTS

A big thank you to Richard Eldredge and his wife, Wendy, whose enthusiasm for my 42 emails helped create this book. And to Emily and my mom, for being my tireless proof readers and fixers of mangled punctuation.

I'd also like to thank Peter, from the 'Elephant Listening Project', for allowing me to use the quote about their amazing work with real African elephants. These people are deciphering the language of elephants as well as battling to save these wonderful animals from extinction. I highly recommend that you check them out and consider a donation.

elephantlisteningproject.org

The art and photos in this book are all my own, except the crow photo which is from my photographer friend, Emily.

For information on Shamanism:
http://www.shamanism.org/fssinfo/research.html

For understanding chakras, I love the explanation in "Avatar, The Last Airbender".

https://youtu.be/StrbppmsZJw

Michelle Frost was born in Rhodesia/Zimbabwe. She is the author of two novels, *First Light* and *Wisdoms of the Light*. She won second place in the 2001 Klein Karoo Arts Festival for the short story *No More Empty Faces* and won second place in the 2010 John Muir Trust Wild Writing competition for *Leap of Faith*.

She has worked as a librarian, commercial artist, astrologer and advice columnist in Africa. Her autobiography, *Elephant Songs*, is about her mystic experiences as a seer and empath.

Michelle now lives in Scotland with her family.

Printed in Great Britain
by Amazon